HENRY GEORGE
and
EUROPE

HENRY GEORGE and EUROPE

The Far-reaching Impact and Effect of the Ideas of the American Social Philosopher

By

Michael Silagi

Translated from the German by

Susan N. Faulkner

Volume IV of the George Studies Program

Edited, with an Introduction, by

Will and Dorothy Burnham Lissner

ROBERT SCHALKENBACH FOUNDATION

NEW YORK

HENRY GEORGE AND EUROPE

Published by the
Robert Schalkenbach Foundation
149 Madison Avenue, Suite 601
New York, NY 10016-6713

Library of Congress Cataloging-in-Publication Data

Henry George and Europe: The Far-reaching Impact and Effect of the Ideas of the American Social Philosopher.
By Michael Silagi. Translated by Susan N. Faulkner. Edited, with an introduction, by Will and Dorothy Burnham Lissner. 173 pp. Includes index.
ISBN 0-911312-91-9
1. George, Henry, 1839-1897. 2. Philosophers, United States — Biography. I. Silagi, Michael, 1948 --. II. Lissner, Will. III. Lissner, Dorothy Burnham

The Robert Schalkenbach Foundation funds research in the economic, political and social philosophy of Henry George, as well as publication of books and other materials by Henry George and by others on related topics. The foundation does not engage in partisan politics; it affords its collaborators and beneficiaries the widest freedom consistent with the equal freedom of all its associates.

A catalogue of books, pamphlets and papers published and/or distributed by the foundation is available upon request.

Printed in the United States of America
by John S. Swift Company of New Jersey, Inc.

Contents

Author's Preface

THE VOLUME here presented is the translation of a study in German accepted as a doctoral thesis by the Department of Philosophy of the University of Munich and published by Etana Buchverlag, Munich, in 1973.

This is what I said in the German preface about the scope of the study:

"The subject-matter of this work is the effect of the ideas of the American Henry George (1839-1897) on Europe in the last decades of the 19th and the early part of the 20th century. One might expect that the teachings of Henry George mainly affected the technicalities of landownership reform. But in actual fact, George primarily was not an economist but only a practical, albeit most significant, corollary of his fundamental concepts. His effect turned out dominantly ideological. It was his social philosophy that influenced so many Europeans, not necessarily in the direction of his concrete proposals, but rather as spur and inspiration (so that in Great Britain, he became—involuntarily —animator of the Fabian movement).

"The effect of George's philosophy proved significant in the United Kingdom, in imperial Germany, in the Kingdom of Hungary, and in Denmark. Each case was utterly different, yet always exemplary.

"In Great Britain and Ireland, the impact of George's ideas manifested itself in the arena of inter-party struggles. In the German Empire, they influenced Berlin's colonial policies on the one hand; on the other hand, they became the ferment for the rise of a huge non-party, chiefly petit-bourgeois, mass movement. In Hungary, where—up to 1918—conditions similar to those of the era of Enlightened Despotism prevailed in many areas of political life, it was a lone individual, a respected member of the intelligentsia, who tried single-handedly, and with astonishing initial success, to radically alter the parameters of the Hungarian world through George's social philosophy. In Denmark, the reception of Henry George's teaching was somewhat heteroclite insofar as it was neither politicians nor academics who appeared as conveyors of Georgist thinking, but rather the broad social stratum of small landholders, who discovered in George's writing the appropriate tools for an up-to-date articulation of their needs."

In my thesis, I concentrated on the four paradigmatic case studies. (Thus, the treatment of my subject in the present book has been limited on the whole to the period before 1920; I went beyond 1920 only in a few cases to furnish some biographical data or to show the aftermath of a movement.) But Henry

George's influence could be studied elsewhere in Europe too, e.g. in the Netherlands, Norway, Spain—and I hope that one day Georgism in other countries will be investigated as well.

In the preface to the German original of 1973, I thanked several active participants or close observers of the events dealt with in my book for information and advice: V.H. Blundell, London; Robert Major, New York; Aladár Sós, Budapest; Dr. Viggo Starcke, Lyngby; and Dr. Sun Fo, Taipei. The personal recollections of these contemporary witnesses were of inestimable value for my work. Since the publication of my German book, most of them, alas, have passed away. This English translation of my study is dedicated to them and their memory.

The undertaking of an American version of my book could hardly have ever been brought to fruition had I not been fortunate enough to have Dr. Will and Dorothy Lissner look after and promote the publication with supreme competence. The help and encouragement I have received from them throughout was enormous. I trust that this acknowledgment will be taken as an expression not only of indebtedness but also of heartfelt gratitude.

M.S.

Göttingen, Germany
1994

Editors' Foreword

THE SUBJECT of this book by a European legal scholar and American historian is the far-reaching effect that the thought of an American social philosopher, Henry George—an economist of the English classical school of Adam Smith, David Ricardo and John Stuart Mill—had on European social thinking at the end of the 19th century and the first decades of the 20th.

The scholar who produced it after an historical investigation as noted for its methods and procedures as for his findings, Michael Silagi, a senior research fellow in the Institute of International Law of the University of Göttingen, Germany, has set, as the reader will see, a new standard for accuracy and comprehensiveness in such studies.

A German publisher made the German book available to scholars abroad under the title *Henry George und Europa.* That it is now available to English-reading scholars and serious readers is due to a number of individuals whom we acknowledge with heartfelt thanks.

First, to Robert Schalkenbach, the New York master printer, who funded a foundation to provide an agency to which followers of Henry George could contribute by benefaction and bequest to finance and publicize scholarship in George's contributions to economic science, social and political science and social philosophy.

And to Francis Neilson, Anglo-American essayist and journalist, and his wife, Helen Swift Neilson, the novelist and publisher, who established the Francis Neilson Fund associated with the Robert Schalkenbach Foundation.

Third, to the late Violetta Peterson Graham, executive secretary of the foundation, and her successor, Dr. Oscar B. Johannsen, executive director, who initiated the project, and coached it to completion.

Next, to Dr. Susan N. Faulkner, who translated the book from the German with complete dedication to faithfulness. And the late Dr. Gabriel Kerekes of Columbia and New York Universities in New York, foundation vice president, who recruited her.

For the first presentation of the translation to English-reading students we owe a debt to the collaborators in the *American Journal of Economics and Sociology.* To assist scholars, the published sections are presented here without change.

For the funding of the project we are indebted to the late Dr. Lancaster M. Greene, then the foundation's president; his successors, Dr. C. Lowell Harriss, emeritus professor of economics at Columbia University, and Dr. Nicolaus Tideman, professor of economics at Virginia Polytechnic Institute; the members who have served on the foundation's executive committee, Dr. Mary M. Cleveland, Clifford Cobb, the late William P., Davidson, the late Roy A. Foulke, Jr. , Dr. Mason Gaffney, Albert Hartheimer, Dr. Jerome F. Heavey, Dr. Johannsen, the late Thomas A. Larkin, Richard Noyes and Francis K. Peddle; and the other directors.

And the foundation's staff members over the years: Dr. Johannsen, retired executive director; Susan Klingelhoefer, former executive assistant; Pat Aller, M.A., retired assistant director; the late Frances Soriero, retired assistant director; J. Ted Gwartney, executive director; Mark A. Sullivan executive assistant; Nan Braman; and Sonny Rivera.

Research and fact checking were facilitated by librarians and archivists of the public and university libraries in the Tampa, St. Petersburg and Clearwater area in Florida, the library of the Maine Maritime Academy in Castine, the Henry George Collection of the New York Public Library and the research library of the Henry George School of Social Science in New York.

We should add, however, that none of those named above should be held responsible for any opinions or statements of fact in the introduction which are solely those of the editors.

For the index we are indebted to Ms. Aller and Lindrith Davies, program director of the Henry George Institute. We also thank Ms. Klingelhoefer and, after her, Mr. Sullivan for seeing the book through the typesetting, printing, production, promotion, and distribution phases of publication.

This book is one of a series produced in the Henry George Studies Program of the Robert Schalkenbach Foundation. The program is one of many constantly carried on by the foundation, sometimes aided by grants from other foundations, large and small, but mostly funded by contributions and bequests. All have one aim: to publish or publicize George's contributions to the social sciences or social philosophy, thereby winning adherents for the ethical democracy he crusaded for as a means of winning the economic and social justice which assures equal individual freedom.

W.L.
D.B.L.

Introduction

GEORGE AND DEMOCRACY IN EUROPE

By Will and Dorothy Burnham Lissner

LEADING PROFESSIONAL PHILOSOPHERS in Henry George's lifetime, after his death and even now, nearly a hundred years later, equate his social philosophy with that of less than a dozen other thinkers, among them such giants as Plato and More.[1]

Yet, after the first World War, George's social philosophy became all but forgotten in the United States, his homeland.[2] There the movement he had founded had emphasized, over his objection, his utopia, his fiscal panacea—the "Single Tax".[3] The Single Tax Movement died in the early Twenties,[4] and only the smaller Georgist movement survived.[5]

However, in Great Britain and some other countries abroad George's social philosophy was not so readily abandoned,[6] although historians, except in Great Britain had little knowledge of the fact.[7]

That situation ended when a German scholar, Michael Silagi, then at the University of Munich, took on the gargantuan task of researching George's impact and influence in Europe during the last two decades of the 19th century and the first two of the 20th. He reported his findings in a book, *Henry George und Europa*, which immediately became a resource for scholars.[8]

This present book is an English translation of the German work by the specialist in belles-lettres, Dr. Susan N. Faulkner, formerly of the faculty of Hunter College of the City University of New York. The translation, edited by Will and Dorothy Burnham Lissner, was published serially in the *American Journal of Economics and Sociology*, and for the convenience of scholars, is reproduced here exactly as it appeared there.

The translation and its editing have been overseen by the author, who is multilingual.[9]

Silagi took a Ph.D. in American history after earning a doctorate in jurisprudence, a fact which explains the insightfulness of his investigation. He is presently a senior research fellow in the Institute of International Law of the University of Göttingen.

Dr. Silagi has not only gone over the British ground to set out with precision the nature of George's impact and influence but he undertook the same painstaking approach with respect to three other major countries, Germany, Hungary (much neglected because of the difficulty English speaking people experience with its language) and Denmark.

We would note that George's influence on British thought was shown at some length in the second book of the Robert Schalkenbach Foundation's George Studies Program, *George and Democracy in the British Isles*.[10] That book reprints research reports by Elwood P. Lawrence, Peter d'Alton Jones and other historians and social scientists.[11]

Dr. Silagi's research shows that what George brought to England, Scotland, Wales and Ireland was not only his English and Franco-American social philosophy based on the contemporary European understanding of "natural law" but his own original contributions to moral philosophy and natural theology.[12] Three principles underlie George's whole social system: Freedom, Rationality and Personal Moral Responsibility.[13]

Another aspect of George's originality was the application of these principles to human behavior in everyday life, as Silagi indicates.[14]

Widely held in England, in spite of the efforts of Christian social reformers, was the idea that poverty was the temporal punishment due to sin.[15] Devout Christians who were better off than most found that rationalization very comforting. It was also their way of rationalizing the fact that some suffered sickness and disabilities despite the dogma that their Creator is good and merciful—a position that persisted until 19th century freethinkers pointed out that handicapped or otherwise suffering children were innocent and sinless, according to ancient teaching, until they received 'the use of reason' at the age of seven.

As Silagi points out, George argued before his British audiences (and his ideas spread to other European countries through his writings) that poverty is the result of economic and social arrangements made by men and hence can be changed by men to the advantage of the majority.[16] Economics, social and political science could be used, after the example of the Good Samaritan, to relieve the unfortunate and to advance the common welfare[17], as religion was then being used to justify the exploitation carried out by the ruling classes. Just as the advance of science and particularly of the medical sciences can be used by people to ameliorate the lot even of the crippled and suffering child.

George's contributions to theodicy, the subdiscipline of theology concerned with defending the attributes of the divinity, and to apologetics, the defense of the faith, went further, as Silagi observes. George did not follow Comte and Marx in blaming society for all its ills. He believed that certain behaviors that were generally deplored could result from economic, social, historical and environmental circumstances also.[18]

The second of the seven "deadly sins," Covetousness, was to a significant extent, George argued, the result of fear of poverty, which afflicted the rich as well as the poor. Envy was aroused by the maldistribution of wealth and income, tolerated by society. Sloth resulted from the life of leisure than many of the rich enjoyed and sought to preserve for themselves and which the lower classes aspired to. But most of all, wealth gave the rich power (and, as Lord Acton held, power corrupts) leading to the first of the "cardinal sins," Pride.[19]

To a considerable extent poverty was caused by monopoly and oligopoly, particularly that of land and natural resources, in George's view. This was brought about in several ways.

Oligopoly enabled the monopolists to exact tribute in the form of higher prices from the general public which heightened the cost of living while providing the monopolists with unearned income.[20]

Monopoly burdened the poor and middle classes with taxes.[21]

Monopoly was responsible for irrational economic decisions, which also raised the cost of living and hampered economic development.[22]

Monopoly kept free, open and fair competition in a free market from regulating the economy and thus helped to produce business cycle slumps and to prolong them.[23]

Monopoly's curb on economic development made jobseekers more numerous than jobs, so competition for jobs kept wages low and working conditions deplorable. Men and women had to chase jobs; only in wartime did jobs chase them.[24]

These are some of the ideas George brought to Europe, Silagi notes.

Natural monopolies were the only monopolies considered during the 19th century: the railroads, the postal service, the telegraph, the highways and so on.[25] At the end of the century when industrial competitors conspired to control the market for goods and service, George and other critics observed that another type of monopoly was being created—"trusts," oligopolies, monopolies by the few or the many—such as the oil monopoly, the coal monopoly and the steel monopoly. The same development occurred in Britain and on the continent.

George inveighed against the "trust" in Europe as he did in the United States. His was one of many voices that helped produce anti-trust legislation.[26]

History has guidance for leaders and members of social movements. One is the lesson for which Silagi presents a host of evidence. George was able to win advocates for his economic reforms by presenting them within the context of his social philosophy—ethical republican democracy.[27]

Silagi's work reminds us of the adage that those who ignore the lessons of history are condemned to repeat its mistakes. Reformers have now learned that economic and social advances are dependent upon monetary stability.

In Germany George's followers achieved a plank in the Weimer Constitution calling for land reform but it came to nothing. The runaway postwar inflation made the issues of land reform and tax reform moot.

Even at that, however, George's economic insights were used to overcome the inflation. The government put a mortgage on every piece of land in the country to give a solid base to the mark and reduced the excess purchasing power by instituting a draconian universal sales tax.[28]

In Hungary land value taxation was also introduced just before the runaway inflation made the mandated tax meaningless. There, working in different periods, two single individuals had gained wide support for George's ideas. One was the sociologist, Robert Braun. Later, his work engaged the commitment of a leading physician and statistician, Julius Pikler. Dr. Pikler waged a one-man campaign to convince municipal officials and legislators of the need for property tax reform.

Even if the German and Hungarian Georgists had campaigned for money of stable value through an equitable monetary system controlled by the people's representatives in government rather than the banking industry, inflation would not have been avoided. Much greater reforms would have been needed to change the course of history—the full social philosophy developed by George and his followers on the basis of their predecessors in the 17th and 18th centuries—such reforms as:

A complete change in the structure of taxation.
A rational system of public and corporate finance
Total defeat and elimination of the politics of monopolistic capitalism and imperialism.

Certainly the work of a lifetime, not to be achieved in a matter of months.

Every good investigation opens the way for further research. Certainly Silagi's does. He himself was sorely tempted to pursue George's influence throughout the British Empire, particularly in Australia and New Zealand, where thriving Georgist movements have existed since George's visit to the region. But he decided time demanded that he limit his scope and that his four case studies exemplified his method and provided the data he needed to evaluate George's influence in Europe.

He hopes that the rest of the field will attract present day researchers.

In Spain, many middle class and working class intellectuals became active Georgists. They were joined by leaders from the anarchist and social democratic movements. The anarchists promoted a translation of *Progress and Poverty* before Professor Baldomero Argente produced the Beltrán translation.[29] And when the social democrats came to power at the end of the Franco period, one of the first things their government did was publish and promote a translation of that classic, with a lengthy history of the Georgist movement in Spain included.

In Italy, Achille Loria, social scientist and land reformer, prepared the way for the Georgist activist, Fisk Warren, who won many adherents in several enclaves.[30]

In France, a number of intellectuals became Georgists and their periodical, *Terre et Liberté*, spread the social philosophy in the French Union.

Norway and Sweden learned about George's system through the efforts of a Norwegian publisher.

The Netherlands produced a vigorous movement which was known abroad through its periodical *Rech en Vriheid* and the papers presented by its delegates to international meetings.

Czarist and ex-Czarist Russia were the best example of how the vicissitudes of history and the efforts of reactionaries thwarted and delayed progress in human social advance. George's writings won a following in the Social Revolutionary party (the 'Essaires') and the Social Democrats (the 'Mensheviks'); Alexander Kerensky and the intellectuals; and the peasants and Christian Democrats through George's ardent follower, the great novelist, Leo Tolstoy.

In the real Russian Revolution, the Kerensky administration came to power and built its program around land and tax reform. The peasants, especially in the Ukraine, formed their own cooperatives, originating three types that met their needs.

Russia, however, was thrown into chaos almost immediately by Czarist troops aided by the great empires abroad and by the forces of violent revolutionaries at home. The terrorist, Leon Trotsky, aided by disaffected and defeated soldiers, staged the Bolshevik coup that brought V.I. Lenin to power.

Lenin and his troops overwhelmed the sailors at the Kronstadt Naval Base, who were anarchists and sympathetic to the democratic regime. Soldiers brandishing bayonets carried out Lenin's and Trotsky's order to abolish the Duma and the Kerensky administration.

At the command of Joseph Stalin, Lenin's successor, soldiers, directed by the secret police, suppressed the peasants' cooperatives, murdered their political leaders and herded farmers into State-controlled collective and State-administered farms—killing more than six million peasants in the process.[31]

The impact that George had through the whole of Europe and in Africa, especially South Africa, was not duplicated in the vast spaces of Asia, it must be admitted. But it was felt in such places as Japan and China. Professor Yoshisaburo Yamasaki, who spent a year at Columbia University in New York doing research on George's system, brought the American's ideas to many Japanese intellectual circles. As did Dr. Sun Yat-sen and his followers, including Chiang Kai-Shek, in China.[32] The work of the Chinese and Japanese scholars attracted attention in Hong Kong and Singapore.[33]

Silagi's investigation of George's impressive impact on European thought illustrates what a single individual can accomplish who hones his or her talents to achieve the professional standards of the time.

George first went to Europe out of sympathy for the struggling Irish people. But, as Silagi notes, he was also determined to prove that his vision of a free society was universally applicable. He hoped to do so by launching a world-wide movement, one not solely confined to his homeland.[34]

Dr. Silagi's investigation proves that George's impact on modern European thought is in many ways far greater than had previously been recognized.

He was a disturber of Europe's social conscience, as he was that of the United States.

He was a catalyst for social reform, there, as well as in his homeland.[35]

He brought to a focus the Anglo-Franco-Germanic-American movement for democracy, the last to develop it in a line of American thinkers of the 18th and 19th centuries. To that movement's ideology he contributed a needed moral basis.[36]

He helped to make Europe aware that poverty (failure to reap the full reward for labor, enterprise and investment) was the result of social institutions which enabled some of the rich to get richer while the poor got poorer—institutions which could be changed.

He pointed out that the great scientific and technological advances of the 18th and 19th centuries (and the greater ones of the 20th which could be foreseen) distributed wealth and income to some who did not earn it and thus deprived the many of their advantages.[37]

He helped people realize that their monetary and banking systems could be reformed and brought under public control, to produce more stability in their media of exchange and standard of value, for the benefit of all, not merely the wealthy.[38]

In particular, as will become apparent from reading Dr. Silagi's remarkable case studies and analyses, the idea of freedom, and the rule of rationality and personal moral responsibility, governed George's approach to European problems. He was anxious to make the people he reached see that they could reform their culture and their society and that real social progress was up to them. He stressed that the perfect society was a fellowship of free men and women, cooperating fully under conditions of equal freedom which only they could establish and maintain, not one created by any divinity, any prophet or any dictator.

Equal freedom was not total freedom, according to George; the freedom of each was limited by the equal freedom of others; the freedom of the individual had to be harmonized with the freedom of the majority. As economy and society have become more complex, so must government, George reasoned, so must its bureaucracy, ever a threat to human freedom and progressive social change.[39]

Was George's effort at a one-man economic, social, political and cultural crusade in Europe a success or failure? He might have called it a failure—he'd hoped that Europe would lead the way in land reform and tax reform.

But it took years for early capitalism to develop out of the feudal manorial system, and for industrial capitalism to grow out of master and journeyman workshop capitalism, and for advanced industrial capitalism to evolve from industrial capitalism. Vestiges of each stage still survive and in the less developed countries so markedly as to hinder their economic and social progress.

If scientific/technological change takes so much historical time to evolve, surely it is not too much to expect that it will take comparable historical time to achieve George's real goal of fundamental change in the basic institutions of the economy and to create a society of individuals governing their conduct on the principles of freedom, rationality and personal moral responsibility.

From Michael Silagi's studies there seems little doubt that Henry George's social philosophy made an indelible, compelling and lasting impression on European thought.

Notes

1. John Dewey evaluated George in several essays. Perhaps his best known judgment is: "It would require less than the fingers of two hands to enumerate those who, from Plato down, rank with George among the world's social philosophers." From the introduction to H.G. Brown, ed., *Significant Paragraphs from Henry George's "Progress and Poverty"* (New York: Robert Schalkenbach Foundation, n.d.). As quoted by S.B. Cord, *Henry George: Dreamer or Realist?* (Philadelphia: University of Pennsylvania Press, 1965), p. 133. See also G.R. Geiger, *The Philosophy of Henry George* (New York: Macmillan, 1933,) p. 562. The other philosopher of world renown in the 20th century, Bertrand Russell (Lord Russell), identified with the English socialists (the reformers, not the Marxists; he considered Marx "unscientific") but he had "high" respect for George (personal communication). In discussing the political and ideological divisions of his time, he classed George among the Liberals, implying his own membership in the group. The other two "camps," as he called them, were the Marxian socialists and the Fascists, whom he criticized harshly, as might be expected. See his *A History of Western Philosophy* (New York: Simon and Schuster, 1945), pp. 788-790. Typical of other philosophers' accounting is Maurice M. Kaunitz, the ethicist: George "was the outstanding social philosopher of the past century," *A Popular History of Philosophy* (Cleveland: World, 1941), pp. 374-377.

2. G.R. Geiger, "The Forgotten Man: Henry George," *Antioch Review*, Vol. 1, No. 3 (September, 1941), reprinted in *George and the Scholars* (New York: Robert Schalkenbach Foundation, 1991), pp. 87*ff*; s. Bruchey, "The Twice Forgotten Man," *American Journal of Economics and Sociology*, Vol. 31, No. 2 (April, 1972; reprinted in *George and the Scholars, op. cit.*, pp. 104*ff.*

3. Actually the term, "single tax," is a misnomer, as George maintained. As the theory of land value taxation suggests, each type of land use in the hierarchy of uses requires a different fiscal procedure. Professor John R. Commons devised a bill for the Wisconsin Legislature applying the "single tax" to agricultural land. It differed significantly from what it would have been to reform the urban property tax. See also D.B. Ibach (U.S. Soil Conversation Service), "Tax Leverage for Efficient Land Exploitation," *American Journal of Economics and Sociology*, Vol. 1, No. 1 (October 1941), pp. 13*ff*; and on the timberland severance tax see Lawrance W. Rathbun (National Resources Planning Board), "Forestry as a Profitable Form of Farm Land Use," *ibid.*, pp. 455*ff.*

4. Perhaps its last gasp was in 1924 in New York when a handful of the more zealous attempted to run a candidate for President under the banner of a "party," the Common Wealth Land Party.

5. Several important institutions of George's movement survived, like Joseph Dana Miller's magazine, *Land and Freedom*, in New York; the Women's Henry George Society in Chicago, and the several single tax colonies in Delaware, Alabama, New Jersey and New York, as well as the United Committee for Land Value Taxation and Free Trade and John Paul's magazine, *Land and Liberty* in London and their counterparts in Australia and New Zealand.

6. In England the term "single tax" was rarely used and the Georgist movement, which has been a vigorous one all through the 20th century, is just as active today, with a strong international influence through the leading journal of the Georgist movement, *Land and Liberty*, edited by the Oxford and London economist, Fred Harrison.

7. One of the exceptions to the exception is Sir Eric Roll, author of one of the more widely read histories, *A History of Economic Thought*, (New York: Prentice Hall, 1942): "George's writings have ceased to command much attention", *loc.cit.*, p. 464. *Cp.* with the evaluation of another intellectual historian, Mark Blaug, *The History of Economic Thought* (London: Cambridge University Press).

8. A collaborator located it in the library of the Catholic University of America, Washington, D.C.

9. Personal communications between the author and the editors. Any errors remaining are the responsibility of the editors alone.

10. New York: Robert Schalkenbach Foundation, 1992.

11. Besides a study of George's influence in Ireland by several social scientists, the work contains Professor Bernard Newton's analysis of George's impact on British economists and on the British democratic socialists.

12. Charles Albro Barker considers George's contributions to moral philosophy his most original and enduring legacy to future generations. See his *Henry George* (New York: Oxford University Press, 1955, now reprinted by the Robert Schalkenbach Foundation), Chap. 20, pp. 620*ff*, especially p. 621.

13. George considered freedom—equal freedom—the most important of the three. Teilhac believed he brought to economic thought an emphasis on rationality that laid the basis for a genuine science of economics in the next century; Ragnar Frisch and Irving Fisher developed econometrics (an integration of economic theory—economic history and economic philosophy—together with mathematics and statistics) simultaneously in the first decade of the 20th century. Barker and John R. Thomas argued that George's great achievement was in communicating the idea of personal moral responsibility for the state of affairs. Ernest Teilhac, *Pioneers of American Economic Thought in the Nineteenth Century*, trans. by E.A.J. Johnson (New York: Macmillan, 1936), Chap. 3, "The Social Economics of Henry George," pp. 114*ff*, especially p. 174; John R. Thomas, *Alternative America* (Cambridge, MA: Harvard University Press, 1983), pp. 345*ff*.

14. George was one of the more practical philosophers (as was Plato!). Joseph A. Schumpeter was the first to point this out: "he was careful to frame his 'remedy' in such a manner as to cause the minimum injury to the efficiency of the private enterprise economy." See his *History of Economic Analysis*, ed. by Elizabeth Boody Schumpeter (New York: Oxford University Press, 1954), p. 825, quoted by R.V. Andelson, *Critics of Henry George* (Teaneck, NJ: Fairleigh Dickinson University Press, 1979), p. 16.

15. R.H. Tawney points out that "Matthew Arnold observed that 'in England inequality is almost a religion.'" See, in his *Equality* (New York: Harcourt Brace, 1931) his Chap. 2, pp. 12*ff*, especially p. 12. See also Paul Needham, *The Printer and the Pardoner* (Washington, D.C.: Library of Congress, 1986), p. 29; also the article "Indulgence" in the *Columbia Encyclopedia*, William Bridgwater and Seymour Kurtz, eds. (New York: Columbia University Press, 1968), p. 1020.

16. George's idea is now widely accepted, even when its practical implications are ignored. For example: the English philosopher L. Susan Stebbing: "It lies within our power, if we so desire, to make the familiar world we inhabit, more worthy of habitation by beings who aspire to be rational and are capable of love." *Philosophy and the Physicists* (New York: Dover, 1958), p. 286.

17. "To remove want and the fear of want, to give to all classes leisure, and comfort and independence, the decencies and refinements of life, the opportunities of mental and moral development, would be like turning water into a desert." George, *Progress and Poverty* (New York: Schalkenbach, 1979), p. 470.

18. "The Creator showers upon us his gifts -- more than enough for all. But like swine scrambling for food, we tread them in the mire -- tread them in the mire, while we tear and rend each other!" George, *op. cit.*, p. 550.

19. "As social development goes on inequality tends to establish itself. . . . The unequal distribution of the power and wealth gained by the integration of men in society tends to check, and finally to counterbalance, the force by which improvements are made and society advances . . . . [T]he masses . . . are compelled to expend their mental powers in merely maintaining existence. On the other side, mental power is expended in keeping up and intensifying the system of inequality, in ostentation, luxury, and warfare." George, *op. cit.*, pp. 518-519.

20. George equated the monopolist's exaction with a tax, a tax which the consumer of the monopolist's product or service cannot avoid. In his view, the government, in supporting absolute private property in land or in industrial production, gives the power to tax to the monopolist. See Geiger, *op.cit.*, pp. 275*ff.*

21. That is, monopoly created a privileged class, the beneficiaries of it and they, by using the power of their activists, get the enactment of a tax structure which falls proportionately more heavily on the poor and middle class.

22. Tax avoidance (or, sometimes, evasion) leads corporate managers or investors to make decisions not in the best interest of consumers, or investors or producers. Its importance can be gauged by the number of people making a living as tax lawyers and tax advisers, as well as those administering and enforcing the tax laws. All must be paid by the consumer out of prices or taxes.

23. See Geiger, *op.cit.*, pp. 260-261; 272-274.

24. See Geiger, *op.cit.*, pp. 275-280. The English Georgists emphasized the critical role that labor played in the economy. They said, 'Labor has only to fold its arms; then what can government, or factory managers, or owners do?' History provides the only answer: Violence waged against the producers by the military or the police controlled by the ruling class.

25. Economists during George's time considered these services "natural" for several reasons. They required governmental power (the right of eminent domain) to acquire the land they needed for road beds, wire networks, etc. They called for vast investments to cover capital needs. And it made no sense to duplicate capital investments to achieve competition. In our day other considerations apply. All transport modes are so vital to the economy they have to be provided by the government or regulated by the government. This approach was aided in gaining public acceptance by the criminal actions of railroad magnates, the failure and the final disappearance of the telegraph companies and the rapacious charges and poor maintenance of the private toll roads before federal, state and local governments took them over. The same experiences occurred in water supply and garbage removal.

26. In Europe as in North and South America industrialization produced an array of industrial regulations.

27. We use the term "republican democracy" because it was the one employed by Paine, Jefferson, Madison, Mason etc. to designate the democratic theory they espoused. In the United States it covers progressives in the Republican party as well as the Democratic. In England it would be misleading; it would be unacceptable to ethical democrats who find a constitutional monarchy preferable and would include advocates of a republican form of government who have other allegiances.

28. According to professor Gerhard Colm, who was an adviser to the Weimar government as well as to the (F.D.) Roosevelt and Truman administrations. Use of the sales tax (if universal, and preferably as a value added tax) to mop up excess purchasing power is an obvious device -- the very aspects that make it scientifically and morally objectionable as a normal tax device are what is needed when the monetary system gets out of rational control.

29. Baldomero Argente, "A Classic American Guide to Democratic Triumph and Lasting Peace," trans. by Joseph M. Sinnott, *American Journal of Economics and Sociology*, Vol. 1, No. 2 (January, 1942), pp. 201*ff*

30. Paul Meadows, "Achille Loria: Agrarian Determinist," *ibid.*, Vol. 9, No. 1 (October, 1949), pp. 145*ff.*

31. Will Lissner, "Land Socialization in Soviet Agriculture, 1917-1949," *ibid.*, Vol. 9, No. 1 (October, 1949), pp. 145*ff.*

32. *Cf.* Yoshisaburo Yamasaki, "The Influence of Henry George's Ideas on Modern Japan," *American Journal of Economics and Sociology*, Vol. 21, No. 2 (April, 1962), pp. 189*ff.* See also Will Lissner, "Nationalist China's Land Reform in Formosa (Taiwan)," *ibid.*, Vol. 21, No. 3 (April, 1953), p. 300.

33. Both Hong Kong (soon to be returned to China) and Singapore (now an independent republic) addressed the land question. In the former the colony retained title to the land, leasing it for residences and business; in the latter George's precursor, Sir Stamford Raffles, prepared the way.

34. The movement still is worldwide but small; the losses have been heavy. In Germany, for example, whereas Damaschke headed 100,000 activists, it survived the Nazi era only in the person of Ludwig Erhard, the Christian Democrat and second chancellor.

35. In the U.S. George was the chief inspiration of the Progressive Era, which won partial land value taxation through the capital gains tax along with many legislative programs and devices to maintain free, open and fair competition. Similar laws and regulations were adopted abroad. There, as well as in the U.S., the other social critics must also be credited for these progressive advances.

36. The reference is to the worldwide movement for greater democracy after the second world wear, symbolized by the heroic demonstration by Chinese students in Beijing's Tinannenmen Square.

37. Various issues of *Science* in the 90s have recalled the advances in science and technology in the 19th and 20th centuries and those in the last quarter of the 20th century. It is evident from the lists that the pace of scientific and technological change has accelerated in recent times. Many believe that a wholly new era is on the horizon. For example, physicists are discovering a wholly new source of energy, much greater than the vast source of atomic fission and fusion, in their atom-splitting experiments.

38. George indicates this in his brief sketches of his ideas on money, credit and banking in his posthumous *The Science of Political Economy*, which he did not live to finish. But great contributions in this area have been made by economists of the next generation, some of whom he influenced, e.g., Lord Keynes, Irving Fisher, Harry Gunnison Brown, Milton Friedman, Morris Copeland and Joseph Schumpeter.

39. Professor C. Lowell Harriss has pointed out that the proliferation of bureaucracy in government, the economy and perhaps even politics and society is needed to assure stability, even though it inhibits innovation and change; and willingness to change and innovate are needed for progress. The challenge of our time, he holds, is to achieve a harmonious balance of these influences.

1

Henry George and Europe:

The Far-Reaching Effect of the Ideas of the American Social Philosopher at the Turn of the Century

By MICHAEL SILAGI*

(*Translated by* SUSAN N. FAULKNER)

ABSTRACT. The progressive democratic *social philosophy* of a *19th century* American *economist, Henry George,* has had a far-reaching effect on some *European* intellectual and political leaders. Not all adopted his practical proposal, the *single land value tax* as a substitute for other *taxes.* But the *British Liberal party,* a section of the *British Labor party* and *Danish smallholders* did. George's ideas were absorbed into the long-standing European *land reform* tradition and he became the initiator and theoretical founder of the modern movement there, as *Heinrich Erman,* the German legal scholar, held. It is a mistake to say that the *French Physiocrats* anticipated George; their *produit net* was a tax on output, not highest potential use and was aimed to achieve *stability,* not *development.* Europeans see George and Georgism the same as Americans but in a different context, that of *natural rights.*

I

Introduction

AN AMERICAN ECONOMIST'S IDEAS had a far-reaching effect on European intellectual and political leaders as the 19th century waned and the 20th dawned. He was

* [Michael Silagi, Ph.D., J.S.D., is a senior research fellow, the Institute of International Law, University of Göttingen, Nikolausberger Weg 9c, D-3400 Göttingen, Federal Republic of Germany (West Germany).] The present work is based on my Ph.D. dissertation presented to the Faculty of Philosophy of the University of Munich. I am grateful for valuable help and for personal recollections of inestimable value to the following: Mr. V. H. Blundell, London; Mrs. Julia Major, New York; Mr. Robert Major, New York; Certified Architect Aladár Sós, Budapest; Minister of State Dr. Viggo Starcke, Lunby, Denmark; Dr. Sun Fo, President of the Examination-Yuan, Taipei, Taiwan, Republic of China. I thank the following organizations for data and source material: the German Service Office, Berlin; the Henry George School of Social Science, New York; the New York Public Library, Manuscript Division and its Henry George Collection and the United Committee for the Taxation of Land Values, London. A scholarship grant from the German "Studienstiftung" enabled me to undertake archival studies in the United States which greatly enriched my work. And a grant from the Robert Schalkenbach Foundation funded the translation by Dr. Susan N. Faulkner, formerly of the City University of New York, whom I thank for painstaking work.

American Journal of Economics and Sociology, Vol. 45, No. 2 (April, 1986).

Henry George (1839–1897), a journalist who had mastered the teachings of the English classical school of political economy. He became known as a land reformer and one might have expected that his influence would be felt in the controversies at that time over modernization of landownership. In fact, however, the influence turned out to be primarily ideological.

George's main concrete proposal—the public collection of the economic rent of land and all natural resources to be used to finance government and public services in lieu of taxes on labor and capital—was only the practical, though decisive, outgrowth of his ideas. But he regarded this conclusion to his investigation of the causes of such economic ills as poverty, unemployment and underemployment as fundamental to the system of ideas he developed.

George became known in Europe not as an economist—the classical school with which he identified was already well known from the work of Scottish and English members and from its French precursors—but as a social thinker. His concern was the philosophy of society and it was as social philosopher that he influenced many Europeans. Not all were swayed in the direction of his practical proposal. In Great Britain, for example, he was a spur and a catalyst to the movement for the formation of a parliamentary labor party, as well as the unwilling pioneer of Fabianism. But it was the middle class Liberal party that, as a party, sought to achieve his land reform.

However, George's influence on Europe is to be seen not only in the United Kingdom but in the Wilhelmian German Empire, the old Hungarian Kingdom, and Denmark, with each case being utterly different from the others, yet always prototypical.

In Great Britain and Ireland the Georgian influence was manifested in the field of domestic political struggles.

In the German Empire it was brought to bear on colonial politics; in part it became a moving force of a supra-partisan, chiefly petty bourgeois, mass movement.

In Hungary conditions existed in many areas of political life, even up to 1918, almost like those of the era of Enlightened Despotism; there it was a single man, one risen to the upper classes, who tried—initially with surprising success—to move the Hungarian world in the direction of progressive reform by employing the message of Henry George.

In Denmark the acceptance of George's teachings was unusual too. There it was not party politicians, city folk or the intelligentsia that conveyed Georgist thinking to the general public, it was the broad class of smallholders who found in George's system of ideas the articulation of their needs.

Like so many other optimistic movements of the 19th century, whose originators hoped to win over all mankind to their doctrines whether by logical argument or by emotional appeal, Georgism, too, lost its powerful dynamic after World War I. Thus, by its very nature, the subject has called for limiting the present work, in the main, to the time prior to 1920. This limitation has been exceeded only where the concluding portion of a biography and the gradual dissolution of a movement made a time extension necessary.

II

Henry George—the Man and His Doctrines

THE UNDERSTANDING of George and his ideas in Europe is very similar, basically, to that in the United States. For European scholars, like the American, have read and been influenced by George's leading biographers and principal expositors—George Jr., de Mille, Post, Nock, Geiger, Neilson, Teilhac, Lawrence, Barker, Rose, Cord, Oser, Andelson and Thomas.[1]

But the Americans have a limited tradition of land reform. It goes back to colonial times, true; that is, to the 17th and 18th centuries. We Europeans assimilate George into a tradition that extends back to the beginnings of civilization itself, into a history dramatized by peasant wars, rebellion against the exactions of a universal church and even popular revolutions, as Franz Oppenheimer showed in his *History of Land Reform.*

To some English-speaking readers, the details of George's life and of his social philosophy are very familiar. But I recount them to show how similar, and yet, in a way, how different, is the way Europeans understand them.

At the end of 1879, a treatise of several hundred pages appeared in San Francisco and, shortly thereafter, in New York. It sought an answer to the question of why, despite ever-increasing technical progress, hunger and poverty was as great a threat or actuality as ever for many people. At its center stood the thesis that the root cause of this continuing poverty was private ownership of land and all natural resources. This was held to be unjust, since land, water, mineral deposits and other sources of raw materials and energy were gifts of nature, created without aid of mankind, and freely given to people.

The single individual could lay exclusive claim only to the products of human labor. All people, however, had an equal right to land and natural resources. The book proposed, for the assertion by everyone of his or her equal right to the bounty of nature, that land values be transferred from private property to common property by means of a tax absorbing its annualized economic rent. At the same time, all other taxes on labor and capital were to be abolished; the yield of the land value tax could provide all the revenues needed to cover government expenditures at that time.

The book became known by the terse title of *Progress and Poverty* but its author was more explicit: "Progress and Poverty: An Inquiry into the Cause of Industrial Depressions and of Increase of Want with Increase of Wealth . . . The Remedy." It first appeared in an edition of only 500 copies, published by the author himself and set by him and his friends. Trade editions thereafter turned it into a bestseller, and not only in America. It was to have an immense effect in many parts of the world. The German economist Franz Oppenheimer, in 1902, spoke of its "unmatched success, which in fact elevates it to a kind of Bible of our time."[2]

The author, Henry George, was the initiator[3] and, according to Professor Heinrich Erman,[4] the legal scholar, the theoretical founder of the modern efforts to achieve land reform.

In examining the doctrines denoted by the words "land reform," one finds that they are manifold and not always compatible with each other. Common to most land reform teachings are these convictions: first, that the existent socioeconomic order is inadequate; second, that one of the principal causes of this inadequacy is a false relationship between people and the soil, people and landownership; and third, that a better socioeconomic order can be founded through the establishment of a correct relationship between mankind and land.[5]

Of critics of the prevalent conditions of landownership there has never been a lack. Benedict Friedlander, German land reformer and social democrat,[6] speaks of "objections by numerous authors in almost every epoch against the ownership of land."[7] But it was only recently that modern criticism developed into action, that greater understanding led to real efforts toward land reform, and that proposals for a new system of land ownership were being advanced which offered promise of a decisive improvement in socioeconomic conditions.

The criticism, of course, extends back to ancient times. In the 25th chapter of the third book of *Exodus,* Moses is represented as presenting a complete program for a just system of land tenure.[8] During the early years of the Christian era various systems prevailed in Europe and on the other continents, and history records peasant wars and wars of conquest that had their origins in disputes over land and access to land.

Since the 18th century there have been more than a few of literary polemicists advocating land reform. Thus, the Englishman Thomas Spence (1750–1814) demanded the socialization of the land without compensation to those who claimed ownership of it and its leasing to the highest bidder at a rental fee to be determined anew every seven years.[9] The Scotsman William Ogilvie (1736–1819) did not recommend the expropriation of present landowners, but urged a shift of all taxes to the land.[10] His compatriot, Patrick Edward Dove (1814–

1873) took the same position at first, but in 1850, Dove proposed, a decade before George, the elimination of land rent through taxation.[11] But, unlike George, Dove did not base his proposal upon the principles of political economy.[12]

Yet, as Friedlander stated in 1901, all these authors "who have been torn out of the past and, as it were, unearthed only recently, thanks to the Georgian formulations" remained voices in the wilderness; they left no impact on history.[13]

The first historically significant land reform movement in recent times was that of the *Économistes*—a French term designating writers who specialized in political economy—or Physiocrats in 18th century France. The best known representative of this school of political economics, François Quesnay (1695–1774), the son of a peasant who became a physician, drew an important inference from his observation of social conditions in the time of Louis XV. He thought that, in actuality, only agriculture was productive because agricultural land alone produced a surplus yield which he called "produit net." Manufacture, commerce and labor, he held, were "sterile." Therefore, he reasoned, the State should encourage agriculture above all and free it from the fetters of the old mercantilist order, government regulation. The State Treasury's need for revenue would have to be met by a tax to be applied upon the source of wealth, the land. Thus the physiocratic system proposed a new tax, a tax on the yield of the land, with all other taxation abolished.[14]

The physiocratic theories are, for the most part, abstruse and highly intellectualized. The *Économistes* were so happy with the seeming nicety of the geometric construction that they did not worry about the fact that it did not correspond in the slightest to reality. Mark Blaug comments, in his history of theories of political economy, that their theorizing reached "conclusions which struck observers even at the time as slightly absurd."[15] But this overlooks their positive accomplishment.

The ideas of these men, as the German historian Franz Schnabel puts it, "destroyed, if only theoretically for the present—through the liberation of the land and the abolition of serfdom and of the guilds—the entire social order handed down over a thousand years."[16] Nevertheless they had one enormous historical effect: their negative demands, those directed at the dissolution of the old ties, were in fact met by the Executory Decree issued by the Constituent Assembly on August 4, 1789. According to Schnabel, "it was through these laws that the Middle Ages finally came to an end, and that a new society was founded, first in France and then throughout Europe."[17]

With this accomplishment, however, the history-making force of the Physiocrats' ideas was spent. The new society made no effort to realize the positive proposals of the Physiocrats as well. While their writings were not without a certain influence on Adam Smith and later on Karl Marx,[18] posterity came to look upon their doctrines as a somewhat charming and not infertile aberration.

The widespread notion, by the way, is incorrect that the Physiocrats had proposed the same remedy for the social ills with their *impôt unique,* as Henry George was to do later, though their goals differed. Thus we read in the George biography by Charles Albro Barker of the "famous similarities"[19] between the doctrines of the Physiocrats and of the American social thinker, without, however, further elaboration. Stephen Cord, in his book about George, believes that it is a matter of the "same conclusions,"[20] and Vernon Louis Parrington even speaks of "identical conclusions."[21] But in reality, the *impôt unique* of the physiocrats was a tax on the land yield (*produit net*), in other words, on work performed, on the land's output, on the product of the land in its present use. That is why the German writer and land reformer Bernard Eulenstein said that the land yield tax of the Physiocrats resembled Henry George's land value tax as much as "an egg a plum."[22] But even when *produit net* and land value (*i.e.* the potential land rent) might be seen as similar quantities, the two taxes are actually not comparable: the physiocrats wanted to remove by taxation only a part of the *produit net,* George the whole land rent. Because of this difference in levels, Emile Rivaud calls the *impôt unique* "a measure of social conservation,"[23] George's Single Tax, on the other hand, "a revolutionary means."[24] The "famous similarities" of which Barker speaks are, in fact, limited to what Rivaud calls the "destructive consequence,"[25] namely the abolition of all other taxation.

As far as the more recent land reform movements are concerned, the Physiocrats were indeed their precursors, but not their ancestors. The ancestor, the father of the new land reform campaigns, is the American Henry George.

III

George's Life

HENRY GEORGE was born on September 2, 1839, in Philadelphia.[26] His father, Richard, was a customs official and from time to time bookseller and publisher for the Episcopal Church. As the second of ten children, Henry George was raised in quite modest circumstances. Although in his childhood his parents gave him spiritual instruction, he was not provided with a formal higher education.[27] He attended school only until his 14th year. In 1855, George went as cabin boy to Australia and India, and fifteen months later, back again in Philadelphia, he began a printer's apprenticeship.

At the age of eighteen, in 1857, he moved to California, where he first became a gold miner, then was active, except for short interruptions, until 1880 as printer, journalist, and author. It was in newly settled California that he followed attentively a development which, in his opinion, passed within a few years through all those stages for which the American East Coast and Midwest and the nations of the Old World had required decades, if not centuries: In the beginning the freedom and wealth of the pioneers, then the influx of ever greater masses of people into the still free land, followed by the seizure of the land by an unscrupulous minority (in California these were partly speculators, partly the large railroad companies), and finally the poverty of the masses along with the enrichment of the few. As several historians have put it, George witnessed the telescoping of history.

Henry George began to seek the causes of these defects. He writes that in 1869, while horseback riding, he had a sudden insight akin to an "illumination"[28]: These evils persisted because a selfish minority monopolized the riches of nature, especially the land, despite the equal natural right of all men to the earth.

In 1871, George published his first program, *Our Land and Land Policy,*[29] and in 1879 he completed *Progress and Poverty,* his most successful work. It was the latter book which, as Parrington reports, "for thousands of Americans removed economic theory from the academic closet and set it in the thick of political conflict."[30]

In the following year George returned to the East Coast, where he settled in New York. From then on he lived and worked exclusively for his ideas, which he sought to popularize in a series of books and essays, in meetings throughout America and overseas, and as a candidate, though always unsuccessful, for political offices in the city and the state of New York. In 1886 he ran for mayor of New York City, the next year for secretary of state of New York State, and in 1897 again for mayor. During the last campaign, however, on October 29, 1897, he died of a stroke. Several hundred thousand New Yorkers paid him the last honors.[31]

IV

George's Social Philosophy

WHAT MADE Henry George's program special? What were the fundamental ideas on the strength of which this program became so popular that George as "Third Party" candidate in the New York mayoral elections of 1886 received more votes than the Republican candidate, Theodore Roosevelt?[32]

For the answer to these questions we shall present George's theories somewhat differently than is commonly done (*i.e.* by George R. Geiger and Charles A.

Barker) in considering the structure of *Progress and Poverty.* For in this work George presents his ideas in a way which will serve propagandistic ends—he wants to impress, persuade, and win for himself, not only the general public but also the professional economists.

That is why he places at the beginning a discussion of those theories of political economy which he designates as dominant, then continues with Ricardo's Law of Rent, and finally derives the rest from these principles. In fact, he himself learned of the theories of political economy as well as of Ricardo's Law only after he had already worked out the basic insights and programmatic ideas for himself.[33]

At the beginning was his unbiased, detached view of his American environment. "He was a free-lance . . . , thinking as if he were the first man who ever thought,"[34] according to Parrington's apt formulation, and according to George's own description of how he came up against the question of why hunger and misery remained undiminished in the midst of increasing wealth:

> When, after growing up here [*i.e.* in California], I went across the continent . . . and in the streets of New York for the first time realized the contrasts of wealth and want that are to be found in a great city; saw those sights that to the man who comes from the West, affright and appall, the problem grew upon me. I said to myself there must be some reason for this; there must be some remedy for this, and I will not rest until I have found the one and discovered the other.[35]

In the course of the search for causes and of the discovery of the solution for his problem, George based his reasoning, as we shall show in detail, on foundations inherited from the doctrine of natural right of the European Enlightenment and further developed in America during the 18th century. George was not necessarily conscious of this relationship; he described his perception of the root cause as a sort of illumination:

> Absorbed in my own thoughts, I had driven the horse into the hills until he panted. Stopping for breath, I asked a passing teamster, for want of something better to say, what land was worth there. He pointed to some cows grazing off so far that they looked like mice and said: "I don't know exactly, but there is a man over there who will sell some land for a thousand dollars an acre." Like a flash it came upon me that there was the reason of advancing poverty with advancing wealth. With the growth of population, land grows in value, and the men who work it must pay more for the privilege. I turned back, amidst quiet thought, to the perception that then came to me and has been with me ever since.[36]

It was George's chief aim to eliminate those causes which, despite material progress, had led to persistent, even growing, want and misery for many people. "This association of poverty with progress is the great enigma of our times . . . , the riddle which . . . not to answer is to be destroyed."[37] For George was convinced that this situation was incompatible with natural rights, *i.e.* with the to him synonymous will of God. In other words, either the persistence of poverty was in harmony with the will of God and the laws of nature, or man was evading, through ignorance and a religious belief corrupted by egotism, the rights of nature.[38] If poverty is not destined for us by God, then it represents a crime for which society must be held responsible.

> If poverty is appointed by the power which is above us all, then it is no crime; but if poverty is unnecessary, then it is a crime for which society is responsible.[39]

George could not believe that God could have willed a condition where, even in the most advanced countries, a large part of the population must suffer want. There were, indeed, clergymen who wanted to make us believe that this was part of the creative scheme—as if the Almighty and All-Knowing had blundered at the creation of the world, like an architect who builds a theater in which only one-tenth of the spectators can hear and see.[40]

But that was out of the question: only when all possibilities for production were exhausted, when nature given to man by God had been used up to the limits of its capacity and still could not produce enough for everyone—only then could one call poverty natural and justified. But, in fact, everywhere one could see land lying fallow, unemployed labor forces, unused capital—in short, there existed a waste of productive power which, George was firmly convinced, only had to be fully utilized to produce enough, yes more than enough, for all.[41]

But certainly it was not a lack of goods that was responsible for want. George made this observation even in America: Here, material progress and an immense growth of the production of goods did not only leave poverty untouched, but actually increased it.

> Material progress does not merely fail to relieve poverty—it actually produces it. . . . It is in the older and richer sections of the Union that pauperism and distress among the working classes are becoming most painfully apparent.[42]

But although it was becoming particularly evident in America that the fault for persistent misery did not lie in an inability to produce enough goods for the entire population, George found that this was true as well of the rest of the world. In *Progress and Poverty,* he argued in great detail against the doctrine, which he called "current,"[43] that nothing could be done about poverty, since production could never increase rapidly enough to keep pace with population's tendency to multiply. Book II of *Progress and Poverty* is given over to this thesis, known as the Malthusian doctrine, and to its refutation. George examines the causes of recurring famine in a few countries (India, China, and Ireland) and shows that, in each instance, it is neither overpopulation nor reaching the limits of natural productivity which leads to misery and poverty.

Thus, for example, the Irish people, using practically the same agricultural methods throughout, suffered the same hunger when they numbered two million, namely at the beginning of the 18th century, as at the time of the great famine in the middle of the 19th century, when their number had multiplied four times, to eight million.[44] Yet, at the same time, Ireland's agriculture was producing for more than merely the domestic market. At the very time when the population had reached its greatest number, Ireland was still exporting food products. The American author gives an impressive description of this fact: "Even during the famine, grain and meat and butter and cheese were carted for exportation along roads lined with the starving and past trenches into which the dead were piled."[45]

This showed that it was not the parsimony of nature, that it was not God the Creator who was to be held responsible for poverty—he who still thought so was either blind or blasphemous.[46] For God, in fact, has showered His gifts upon man, more than sufficient for all:

> Though it may take the language of prayer, it is blasphemy that attributes to the inscrutable decrees of Providence the suffering and brutishness that come of poverty; that turns with folded hands to the All-Father and lays on Him the responsibility for the want and crime of our great cities. We degrade the Everlasting. We slander the Just One. A merciful man would crush with his foot such an ulcerous anthill! It is not the Almighty, but we who are responsible for the vice and misery that fester amid our civilization. The Creator showers upon us His gifts—more than enough for all.[47]

The poverty in the world, in other words, is not divinely ordained, but an evil caused by man. He could, if he wished, abolish need and poverty: "Human will is the great factor, and . . . taking men in the aggregate, their condition is as they make it."[48] Of this Henry George, the American social philosopher of the second half of the 19th century, is convinced. Indeed, he is filled with the same confidence that the German historian Fritz Valjavec described as the "predominant trait of the Enlightenment."[49] "It lies within man to overcome difficulties. He can master them because the nature of things enables him to do so."[50] For George, as for the men of the Enlightenment, "evil is not a metaphysical power, but an unfortunate aberration, a flaring up of human weaknesses. It is not God who tests man through Satan; rather man tests himself."[51]

What is required is to understand the all-embracing law of nature and to act in accordance with it; then there would be no more poverty. That there is such an absolute right is self-evident: It is after all the law of the Creator which He has imprinted upon nature, and which unfolds itself through nature.[52] George does not see social progress directed either by a special destiny or by a merciless fate, but rather by this law which is both unalterable and well-disposed toward man.[53]

For George, progress is a function of social arrangements. ("The advances in which civilization consists are . . . secured . . . in the constitution of society."[54] Genuine progress can be made only when social institutions are in accord with the laws of nature. The author of *Progress and Poverty* denies, on the other hand, any biological advance of man, be it of the individual or whole races: "There is nothing whatsoever to show any essential race improvement. Human progress is not the improvement of human nature."[55] The engine of each human forward movement is, more correctly, the natural law.[56]

Notes

1. Henry George, Jr., *The Life of Henry George* (1900), (New York, 1960); Anna George de Mille, *Henry George, Citizen of the World* (Chapel Hill, N.C.: 1950); Louis F. Post, *The Prophet of San Francisco* (1904) (New York, 1930); Albert Jay Nock, *Henry George, An Essay* (1931), (New York, 1939); George Raymond Geiger, *The Philosophy of Henry George* (New York, 1933); Francis Neilson, "The Gospel of Justice" in *The Cultural Tradition and Other Essays* (New York, 1957) and his *From Ur to Nazareth* (New York, 1959); Elwood P. Lawrence, *Henry George in the British Isles* (East Lansing, MI, 1957); Ernest Teilhac (trans. by E. A. J. Johnson), *Pioneers of American Economic Thought in the 19th Century* (New York, 1936); Charles Albro Barker, *Henry George* (New York, 1955); Steven B. Cord, *Henry George: Dreamer or Realist?* (1965) (New York, 1984); Edward J. Rose, *Henry George* (New York, 1968); Robert V. Andelson, ed., *Critics of Henry George* (Teaneck, N.J., 1979); Jacob Oser, *Henry George* (New York, 1979); John L. Thomas, *Alternative America* (Cambridge, MA, 1983).

2. Franz Oppenheimer, "Henry George und sein Werk," *Neu Freie Presse,* No. 13641, (Vienna, 1902), p. 10.

3. Charles Albro Barker, *Henry George* (New York, 1955), p. 312 ff.

4. Heinrich Erman, *Die Bodenreform in der Reichsverfassung* (Berlin, 1930), p. 7.

5. Compare: Adolf Damaschke, *Die Bodenreform,* 19th ed. (Jena, 1922), *passim,* and Heinrich Niehuus, *Geschichte der englischen Bodenreformtheorien* (Leipzig, 1910), *passim.*

6. On Friedlaender see Adolf Damaschke, *Aus meinem Leben* (Leipzig, 1924), pp. 329 *ff.*

7. Benedict Friedlaender, *Die vier Hauptrichtungen der modernen sozialen Bewegung,* 2nd part, (Berlin, 1901), p. 145.

8. On land reform movements in general: Damaschke, *Die Bodenreform, passim,* and Samuel Milliken, "Forerunners of Henry George," *Single Tax Year Book* (New York, 1917), pp. 306 *ff;* on England: Niehuus, *op. cit.,* passim; on the Bible: Frederick Verinder, *My Neighbour's Landmark,* memorial ed. (London, 1950), *passim,* and Adolf Damaschke, *Bibel und Bodenreform* (Berlin, 1929), *passim.*

9. On Spence see H. R. Tedder, "Spence, Thomas," *Dictionary of National Biography (DNB),* Volume 53 (London, 1898), pp. 338*ff.,* and also Niehuus, *op. cit.,* pp. 17*ff.,* and J. Morrison Davidson, *Concerning Four Precursors of Henry George and the Single Tax,* (London, 1899), pp. 25*ff.*

10. On Ogilvie, see J. R. MacDonald, "Ogilvie, William," *DNB,* Volume 42 (London, 1895), p. 211; and also Niehuus, *op. cit.,* pp. 31*ff.,* and Davidson, *op. cit.,* pp. 1*ff.*

11. On Dove, see "Dove, Patrick Edward," *DNB,* Volume 15 (London, 1888), pp. 379ff.; and also Niehuus, *op. cit.,* pp. 111*ff.* and Davidson, *op. cit.,* pp. 379*ff.*

12. On the comparison between Dove's and George's doctrines, Niehuus, *op. cit.,* writes: "His

excluding from consideration the difference in land quality and the law of diminishing land yield precluded him [*i.e.* Dove] from penetrating more deeply into the highly complicated problem of land rent. It remained for George, because of his attention to these points and to the teachings of classical economics, to erect a closed system," p. 123.

13. Friedlaender, *op. cit.*, p. 145. Also see Henry George, *The Science of Political Economy* (New York, 1968), pp. 185 *ff.*

14. Mark Blaug, *Economic Theory in Retrospect*, rev. ed. (Homewood, 1968), pp. 25 *ff.*; G. Weulersse, "The Physiocrats," in "Economics," *Encyclopaedia of the Social Sciences*, Vol. V (New York, 1953), pp. 348–51.

15. Blaug, *op.cit.*, p. 26.

16. Franz Schnabel, "Das 18. Jahrhundert in Europa," *Propyläen-Weltgeschichte*, Vol. VI (Berlin, 1931), p. 234.

17. Schnabel, *Deutsche Geschichte*, Vol. I., 5th ed. (Freiburg, 1959), pp. 116 *ff.*

18. Blaug, *op. cit.*, p. 30.

19. Barker, *loc. cit.*

20. Stephen Cord, *Henry George: Dreamer or Realist?* (Philadelphia, 1965), (New York, 1985) p. 125.

21. Vernon Louis Parrington, "The Beginnings of Critical Realism in America," *Main Currents in American Thought*, Vol. III (New York, 1958), p. 126.

22. Bernhard Eulenstein, *Henry George's 'Single Tax'-Nur eine einzige Steuer!* (Berlin, 1894), p. 11.

23. Emile Rivaud, *Henry George et la Physiocratie* (Paris, 1907), p. 80.

24. *Loc. cit.*

25. *Op. cit.*, p. 92.

26. On what follows cp. Barker, *op. cit.*, *passim*; Henry George Jr., *The Life of Henry George* (New York, 1900), *passim*, and Edward J. Rose, *Henry George* (New York, 1968), *passim.*

27. To this George R. Geiger writes in *The Philosophy of Henry George* (New York, 1933): "George's schooling seems almost nonexistent," p. 20.

28. Henry George, *The Science of Political Economy*, p. 163.

29. George, *Our Land and Land Policy* (New York, 1904).

30. Parrington, *op. cit.*, p. 126.

31. Rose, *op. cit.*, p. 151.

32. George received 68,110 votes, Roosevelt only 60,435. But it was the Democrat Abraham S. Hewitt who was elected with 90,552 votes (Rose, *op. cit.*, p. 122).

33. Niehuus is mistaken here when he asserts that the "point of departure" for George had been Ricardo's Law of Rent theory (*op. cit.*, p. 7). Already George's [auto]-biography shows this view to be erroneous.

34. Parrington, *op. cit.*, p. 126.

35. Henry George, "Justice the Object-Taxation the Means," *Our Land and Land Policy-Speeches, Lectures and Miscellaneous Writings* (New York, 1904), p. 300.

36. Quoted in George Jr., *op. cit.*, p. 210.

37. Henry George, *Progress and Poverty*, (1879) (New York, 1898), p. 10.

38. "Either it is in accordance with the will of God, either it is the result of natural law, or it is because of our ignorance and selfischness of our faith that we evade the natural law." in "Justice the Object-Taxation the Means," *op. cit.*, p. 302.

39. Henry George, "The Crime of Poverty," *Our Land and Land Policy*, p. 190.

40. Henry George, *Social Problems* (New York, 1898), p. 72.

41. "If there is not wealth sufficient to go around, giving everyone abundance, is it because we have reached the limit of the production of wealth? Is our land all in use? is our labor all employed? Is our capital all utilized? On the contrary, in whatever direction we look we see the most stupendous waste of productive forces–of productive forces so potent that were they permitted to play freely the production of wealth would be more than sufficient for all," *op. cit.*, p. 73.

42. *Progress and Poverty*, p. 9.

43. *E.g.*, *Ibid.*, p. 17.

44. *Ibid.*, p. 126.

45. *Ibid.*, p. 125.

46. "Yet who can look about him without seeing that to whatever cause poverty may be due, it is not due to the niggardliness of nature," *Social Problems*, p. 73.

47. *Progress and Poverty*, p. 546.

48. *Ibid.*, p. 558.

49. Fritz, Valjavec, *Geschichte der abendländischen Aufklärung* (Vienna, 1961), p. 102.

50. *Loc. cit.*

51. *Ibid.*, p. 103.

52. "There are some facts so obvious as to be beyond the necessity of argument. And one of these facts is that there are rights between man and man which existed before the formation of government, and which continue to exist in spite of the abuse of government; that there is a higher law—to wit, the law of the Creator, impressed upon and revealed through nature." *Social Problems*, p. 92.

53. *Progress and Poverty*, pp. 557 *ff.*

54. *Ibid.*, p. 560.

55. *Loc. cit.*

56. About the significance for Henry George of the Enlightenment's natural rights, Parrington, *op. cit.*, states: "The foundations on which [he rests] is the eighteenth-century conception of natural law, all-comprehensive, beneficent, free, enshrined in the common heart of humanity, and conducting to the ultimate of social justice" (p. 132).

2

Henry George and Europe:

As Social Philosopher, He Was Seen as Synthesizing Jefferson, the Enlightenment and Mother Earth

By MICHAEL SILAGI

Translated by SUSAN N. FAULKNER

ABSTRACT. In the eyes of European scholars, publicists and politicians who studied *Henry George's* work, he, as a *social philosopher,* had adopted the position of the *natural law* philosophers of the 18th century. The latter inspired the Declaration of Independence, the U.S. Constitution and its Bill of Rights, as well as the political philosophy of *Jeffersonian democracy,* the ethos of the 18th and 19th century *pioneer settlers.* George rejected *Social Darwinism.* He saw natural law as the only true and reliable basis for a just social order. Like *Karl Marx* he mastered *Ricardian economics;* unlike Marx, George made two factors the basis of his system, *labor* and *land.* George saw that each person had a *natural right*—and a natural imperative for *survival*—to apply his or her *productive capacity* to the *earth*—as *living space* and as *storehouse* of *nutrients* and *raw materials.* The *person-land relationship,* he discovered, lay at the basis of human *culture.* And so the land's *rent,* now monopolized by the few, had to be appropriated to meet the needs of *society,* most efficiently and justly by a *land value tax.*

I

George as a Natural Law Philosopher

IN HENRY GEORGE'S CONCEPT of natural law, we encounter the principle typical of the world view of the Enlightenment, especially in the America of the 18th century.[1] In contrast to the Social Darwinists of his time, George rejected the doctrine of the survival of the fittest; he interpreted the law of nature not as a law compelling the termination of individual and social development, but, on the contrary, through adaptation, offering a chance for progress.[2]

While George did not want to decide whether there are higher values in the area of morality than justice, he thought that natural law should be the foundation of any ethical hierarchy: "That justice is the highest quality in the moral hierarchy

* [Michael Silagi, J.S.D., Ph.D., is a Senior Research Fellow at the Institute of International Law, University of Göttingen, Nikolausberger Weg 9c, 3400 Göttingen, West Germany.]

American Journal of Economics and Sociology, Vol. 45, No. 3 (July, 1986).

I do not say; but that it is the first. That which is above justice must be based on justice, and include justice, and be reached through justice."[3] George, a Puritan here, does not see even love of one's neighbor unconditionally as virtuous. That also must be built on justice: "Charity must be built on justice. It cannot supersede justice."[4]

It is for this reason that Henry George sees natural law as the only true and reliable basis for a proper social order. Ills in the socio-political sphere imply a transgression against, and ignorance of, natural human rights as surely as the poor functioning of a machine leads to the conclusion that the mechanic has disregarded the laws of mechanics in its construction.[5] Thus, prevalent poverty must be a symptom of an error in the foundation of the existing social order. As already discussed, there is no lack of productive capacities, since, after all, those available are not even wholly utilized. Yet, in fact, the actual production is quite sufficient for everyone. Therefore, George seeks a remedy that would eliminate the causes of industrial crises and poverty in the midst of wealth.

George also searches for the mechanisms which lead to the unjust distribution of wealth, unjust because it brings about poverty and misery.[6]

He designates as "wealth" all that which results when products of nature are grown, mined or developed, refined, transported, combined, separated, or changed in any other way by human labor in order to satisfy human needs.[7] Hence, wealth is matter which is mined with human exertion so that it stores up the wish-fulfilling power of labor as does coal the sun's energy.[8] George counts as wealth only "value from production,"[9] *i.e.* values produced by human exertion. Labor is one factor of production indispensable for the manufacture of goods; the other one is land, which for him means not only real estate, but in actuality the entire natural, still undeveloped environment of human beings. The unimproved, "naked" land belongs for this American philosopher not to "wealth," not to goods. It is, rather, the second prior condition indispensable, next to human exertion, for the production of wealth.[10]

To these two primary elements, George adds the derivative factor of production, capital; in this manner, he takes over the classical tripartite form of factors of production. He views that part of wealth as capital which is not used directly for the satisfaction of human needs, but rather for the production of more wealth. It is for him only a secondary factor, which serves to increase the productive capacity of labor. George defines the concepts "wealth" and "capital" as follows:

> Wealth, in short, is labor, which is raised to a higher or second power, by being stored in concrete forms which give it a certain measure of permanence, and thus permit of its utilization to satisfy desires in other times or other places. Capital is stored up labor in the production of fresh wealth or of larger direct satisfaction of desire.[11]

For George, capital played only a subordinate, though useful role. It was for him, as Geiger puts it, "a product and not a fundamental determiner of man's energies"[12]—quite a different conception from that of his older contemporary, Karl Marx, who placed capital in the center of his chief work. This assessment of capital by George can be explained by his non-historical, typically American,[13] thought processes: George abstracted from the conditions of production prevalent in his time; he proceeded from the observation that historical development, especially technical advances, had brought about no fundamental changes in the relationship to each other of the factors of production.

He saw the vast accumulations of capital in his century as basically not different from the stone hewn by primitive man: both were forms of capital, for both served the worker as a tool, thereby increasing his productivity. George was convinced that the economic laws which had been valid for the economic life of the most primitive society retained their validity through all times, and that even the most complicated processes within the economy of the modern State should be reducible to these simple laws.[14]

There could be no doubt for him, furthermore, concerning the just distribution of wealth. The point of departure, as he saw it, was man's claim, based on natural law, to life and freedom. This freedom includes two rights which, if secured, would lead to a harmonic economic order—the right to work and the right to a due reward for labor.

The right to work, in George's opinion, did not carry with it the duty of the State to find jobs or satisfy the worker's right to employment. Rather, everyone had the natural right to apply his productive capacity to the inexhaustible storehouse with which God had supplied mankind. "The natural right which each man has, is . . . that of employing himself—that of applying his own labor to the inexhaustible storehouse which the Creator has, in the land, provided for all men."[15] This "storehouse" is the passive factor of production, land, on which the capacity to work, as already discussed, necessarily depends. Only when man has access to this factor can he realize his right to work.

Each individual should be able to deal freely in all goods which are produced and which can be increased by human labor. That is why disposition over the natural environment—air, water, sunlight, and in general soil and land, *i.e.* the space on earth everyone needs to exist—should not be left in the hands of a few. These vital pre-conditions for labor cannot be made subject to exclusive rights of private ownership, for they are not products of human labor, but on the contrary gifts from God, not multipliable or reducible like wealth, and available only to a limited extent.[16]

In contrast to the value of the products of labor, that of land depends, in the final analysis, on supply and demand. That amount which the landowner can ask for letting his land to another (land rent) is determined by the amount of demand for this relatively and ultimately inelastic factor of production—land. As long as land of equal value is obtainable without cost, the landowner cannot realize any land rent. But as soon as only that land is freely available, which, with the same expenditure of labor and capital, gives a smaller yield, whether due to lower quality of soil or unfavorable location or whatever, the surplus yield of the better land will flow to the landowner in the form of rent. In other words, according to George, who here adopts Ricardo's Law of Rent,[17] neither workers nor capitalists can receive more wages or interest than that derived from the poorest land—the marginal land—on which labor is performed. Whatever is produced above that minimum represents the land rent.[18]

II

George's Fiscal Approach to Societal Reform

IT FOLLOWS from the foregoing argument that land rent is a function of land value. But this value is not produced by the landowner, but by the community. For through the increase of population and through social advance, there is a growth of demand for land so that this relatively inelastic factor of production—land—constantly increases in value. But this is not a "value from production," as in the case of goods produced by labor; the value of land indicates, rather, that a landowner has the power to appropriate a part of the produced wealth as land rent. Consequently, land value is "value from obligation."[19]

Henry George graphically describes this process in *Progress and Poverty.*[20] He gives the example of a settler who once occupied a piece of worthless, free land on the Pacific Coast, fell asleep and, similar to Rip van Winkel,[21] woke up after many years. In the meantime, San Francisco had expanded so far that his parcel of land was now located in the business section of the city and was worth millions.

From his thesis that land is God's gift to all, and that its value increases and grows, not through individual effort, but through community progress, George draws the conclusion that land rent should go, not to individuals, but to the community. Similarly, all men are on this earth through God's mercy, and they have, therefore, the same right to those gifts which nature offers impartially to all.[22]

According to George's doctrine, the corollary to this right to work is the right to a due reward for labor: everyone has full claim to the entire fruits of his exertions, to a just wage. For just as man belongs to himself, his work must also belong to him whenever it takes palpable form.[23] Thus, the only just foundation for private ownership is man's claim to the fruits of his labor, because only labor produces wealth—from the natural material which the Creator has made available—and only labor is rewarded by nature with wealth.[24] In contrast to Marx, George does not deduce from this formulation a rejection of income from capital. As George sees it, the capitalist is also entitled to a share of the product (interest), for capital is stored-up labor, and within the right to a reward for labor is included as well the right to the fruits of one's labor.[25]

Yet, in none of the social systems showing material progress does George find a realization of these two corollaries of the natural right to life and liberty. In his opinion, this disregard of the principles of natural rights derived from natural law, is the true source of social ills.

The basic evil of the prevalent economic order is the appropriation of the land rent by private persons.[26] This appropriation represents a violation of the right of the community to the land values it has produced. Furthermore, this appropriation brings about, in two ways, an infringement of the rights of productive man to the fruits of his labor, as George sees it.

Since the State does not rely upon land rent for its necessary expenditures, it must cover its budget through other revenues, namely the customary taxes and duties. George rejects, on the basis of natural rights, all taxes not imposed on land rent ("save, of course, where the motive of the tax is public safety, health or morals"[27]). Such taxes, after all, are aimed at labor and capital; in other words, that is taken from the individual which belongs to him by natural right, a portion of his work products. At the same time, such taxes are fines on diligence and thrift. For these reasons, George is convinced that they are unjust; he writes:

> All these taxes violate the moral law. They take by force what belongs to the individual alone; they give to the unscrupulous an advantage over the scrupulous; they have the effect . . . to increase the price of what some have to sell and others must buy . . . ; they fine industry and thrift, and enrich some by empoverishing others.[28]

In addition, private ownership of land values bestows upon the owners a monopoly over this inelastic property. In this way, to the natural factors of increased value (growth of population and progress) another factor is now added: land speculation. In the expectation of ever-growing increases of land value, the owners hold back their land from optimal usage, or even withdraw it entirely from use; fallow acreage in the centers of large cities certainly attests to such practices. By this means, an artificial scarcity of supply is created in the market. Since the entire land is not utilized to its maximum, the workers are forced to switch over to less productive or unfavorably situated land than that which should be available to them under just conditions; or they may be obliged to pay a higher land rent, which already anticipates the owner's hoped-for increase in value. Thereby, the landowner's income, in itself a violation of natural right, rises even further, while the worker's share of the goods produced sinks even more. The outcome is want and misery.[29]

From this premise George draws the conclusion that the existing system should be changed in such a way as to make land speculation impossible, and to ensure that a just share of the goods they produce goes to the workers. This would require establishing the equal right of all to the land values produced by the community. But in George's view, to accomplish this purpose it is neither requisite nor expedient to confiscate the land.[30] Taking away, through a tax on land value, the rent obtainable in each instance for the benefit of the community not only fully satisfies the demands of justice, but creates a practical and incorruptible tool for carrying out such demands: "It is not necessary to confiscate land; it is only necessary to confiscate rent."[31]

It is unimportant who the factual owner of the land is. Hence, there would be no formal change in the ownership conditions following a Georgian reform—only that "special gain" would be taken from the landowner which he had hitherto received by means of private monopoly. Such a land value tax could not be shifted—this, by the way, is recognized not only by George[32]—since such a tax would cause a rise in supply on the real estate market and thereby lower the price of land. A tax imposed on the value of all land would, after all, affect also those parcels of land which previously had been withheld from use, either in part or wholly, due to speculative expectation of a further advance in the price of land. In this way, the owner would find himself obliged either to use his land completely or to sell it, because his property would be taxed high whether it was used or lying fallow. After the land value tax has been introduced, the land rent would tend to become commensurate to that land value seen by George as natural, and would no longer receive a speculative addition.[33]

The land value tax would actually affect him who is assessed for it, the landowner, and until now the unauthorized usufructuary of the land rent. It is a practical tax, the amount of which can be determined readily—any appraisal can estimate the value of land—and it cannot be evaded, for land cannot be hidden.[34]

George believes, as already mentioned, that all other taxes are contrary to natural law. He proposes the abolition of all taxes and duties with the exception of one tax, the "Single Tax,"[35] which should be levied against the unimproved value of the land alone. He has no doubt that such a tax would be sufficient to cover all official expenditures.[36]

Furthermore, George rejects any compensation for landowners: Since the land belongs by right to the community, it would be as absurd to let these owners continue to have the rent as it would be to compensate them for its future withdrawal. For the original appropriation of the land by its first owner was not the only transgression against the rights of the community. Private land-ownership signifies, in effect, a continual robbery of its property committed against the community. Should one indeed draw the conclusion from the fact that the community has been robbed throughout all these years that the robber has acquired the right to continue his depredations? Surely not, answers George:

> It is not merely a robbery in the past; it is a robbery in the present—a robbery that deprives of their birthright the infants that are now coming into the world! Why should we hesitate about making short work of such a system? Because I was robbed yesterday, and the day before, and the day before that, is it any reason that I should suffer myself to be robbed today and tomorrow? any reason that I should conclude that the robber has acquired a vested right to rob me? If the land belongs to the people, why continue to permit land owners to take the rent, or compensate them in any manner for the loss of rent?[37]

What are Henry George's hopes for the introduction of the Single Tax? In his work *Social Problems* he explains his proposal as follows:

> To appropriate ground-rent to public uses by means of taxation . . . would enormously increase the production of wealth by the removal of restrictions and by adding to the incentives to production. . . . It would at the same time make the distribution of wealth more equal. That great part of this fund which is now taken by the owners of land, not as a return for anything by which they add to the production, but because they have appropriated as their own the natural means and opportunities of production, and which as material progress goes on, and the value of land rises, is constantly becoming larger and larger, would be virtually divided among all, by being utilized for common purposes."[38]

The introduction of the Single Tax would mean the end of unemployment, an increase in wages, and the disappearance of poverty and, with it, of pauperization and crime. The abolition of all taxes except the land value tax would substantially simplify the administrative apparatus[39] as well. Finally, such a measure would elevate public morals:

> We should get rid of the fraud and false swearing, of the bribery and subordination which now attend the collection of so much of our public revenues. We should get rid of the demoralization that proceeds from laws which prohibit actions in themselves harmless, punish men for crimes which the moral sense does not condemn, and offer a constant premium to evasion.[40]

III

The Intellectual Foundation of George's System

Henry George's theory, here described, makes clear that he thought in terms of natural rights. His two most significant premises are, first, that an absolute right exists, and second, that its clauses must be observed unconditionally by humanity; their disregard, on the contrary, will inevitably lead to want and misery. He counts among the most important clauses of this absolute right the equal claim of all, given people by nature, to the soil, to the gifts of nature. It was his principal aim to make his ideas ultimately prevail.

George's system is not a curriculum of economic instruction, his prescription for the elimination of poverty not merely a tax reform. In his works, George took the classical theories of political economy into consideration and accepted in the main Ricardo's Law of Rent. On the other hand, in *Progress and Poverty* as well as in other writings, he refuted at length the theories of economics designated by him as prevalent. In doing so, he made a contribution to this discipline which Franz Oppenheimer, in the already cited article, describes as "one of the most marvellous and brilliant systems developed since the origination of the science of economics."[41] Similarly, it led the American historian, Parrington, to call George "our most creative economist."[42]

For George himself, however, Ricardo's writings, as well as politico-economic theory on the whole, had only a serviceable function. They were for him solely the building blocks for a theoretical foundation of his Single Tax doctrine.

Basically, George saw in the social question a religious problem,[43] since even the political and social sciences could teach nothing which was not already contained in the simple truths of religion:

> Political economy and social science cannot teach any lessons that are not embraced in the simple truths that were taught to poor fishermen and Jewish peasants by One who eighteen hundred years ago was crucified—the simple truths which, beneath the warpings of selfishness and the distortions of superstition, seem to underlie every religion that has ever striven to formulate the spiritual yearnings of man.[44]

The laws of economics and ethics are here identical in character.[45] If one wishes to solve economic problems, one must recognize the will of the Creator. For God, who created man and who gave him the capacity for higher civilized development, must have foreseen that with social progress would come the growth of the State's financial needs. Therefore, God also must have provided a way to cover these expenditures.[46] But this way, as George—here following entirely deistic teaching—sees it, is not disclosed to man either by revelation or by Holy Scripture. It is, rather, human reason alone which can fathom this means foreordained by God, and the intellect says that God has assigned the land values to cover the needs of the community.

The introduction of the land value tax is, thus, not a fiscal measure, but an adaptation of the most important social arrangements to natural law. So George believes, as set forth in his book *Social Problems,* and he continues:

> To those who have never given thought to the matter, it may seem irreverently presumptuous to say that it is the evident intent of the Creator that land values should be subject to taxation; that rent should be utilized for the benefit of the entire community. Yet to whoever does think of it, to say this will appear no more presumptuous than to say that the Creator has intended men to walk on their feet, and not on their hands. Man in his social relations is as much included in the creative scheme as man in his physical relations. . . . Man is driven by his instincts and needs to form society. Society, thus formed, has certain needs and functions for which revenue is required. These needs and functions increase with social development. . . . Now, experience and analogy, if not the instinctive perceptions of the human mind, teach us that there is a natural way of satisfying every natural want. And if human society is included in nature, as it surely is, this must apply to social wants as well as to the wants of the individual, and there must be a natural or right method of taxation, as there is a natural or right method of walking. We know, beyond peradventure, that the natural or right way for a man to walk is on his feet. . . . In the same way we may know that the natural or right way of raising the revenues which are required by the needs of society is by taxation of land values. The value of land is in its nature and relations adapted to purposes of taxation, just as the feet in their nature and relations are adapted to the purposes of walking.[47]

To the concept of an all embracing natural law, seen as the moving force of human progress, is added a further element of the world view of the Enlightenment, the deistic belief in a religion of reason. That is why Geiger says aptly: "To natural law and natural rights was added deism, and the 18th century synthesis in George was almost complete."[48]

To be sure, we cannot follow Geiger in his differentiation of two levels in George's thinking. He feels that George's teachings contain an ethical and an economic level, and he divides his book about the American social philosopher accordingly.[49] It is only in the synthesis that, Geiger believes, the levels of the ethical and the economic become one.[50]

Such a separation of economics and ethics, when seen from George's standpoint, however, is impossible on the face of it. The components of natural law and economics or, as Edward J. Rose formulates it, the "religio-economic"[51] unity, is fundamental to his doctrine from its inception.[52]

The reason for this dualistic interpretation of George's teachings may well lie in the previously detailed manner of presentation of his thesis, especially in *Progress and Poverty*,[53] but it may also be found in a dualistic attitude of the interpreter, who wishes to see his perception confirmed by George.

George received the intellectual impulses which were to be decisive for his life's work in his childhood and early youth, thus at a time when he had not yet heard anything about economics. There were two influences which determined his development: First, the faith in which he grew up. His parental home was filled with an atmosphere of strong piety.[54] But though George, in his strivings for pure ethics and genuine Christianity, turned away already in his youth from institutionalized religion, he was to remain faithful throughout his life to the fundamentals of the Judeo-Christian tradition.[55]

In addition, the ideas of the American Revolution had a no less significant effect on him. George was educated in the spirit of a belief in natural justice as it is manifested in the Declaration of Independence and the Bill of Rights. In this connection, Rose states:

> Nurtured by an environmental and national devotion to individual rights, expressed most powerfully in the Declaration of Independence and in the Constitution and Bill of Rights, Henry George's later social theories were deeply and continually influenced by the moral prerogatives of the Judaic-Christian consciousness.[56]

On these two cornerstones, an enlightened religious belief and an 18th century concept of natural law, George built, for the most part independently, his own social philosophy. One must, therefore, agree with Parrington when he writes about George as follows: "His major doctrines he arrived at largely independently. . . . His matured philosophy was the outcome of the meditations of a Jeffersonian idealist contemplating the divergence between the crude facts of exploitation all about him and the 18th century ideal of natural justice."[57]

When Parrington, however, describes the principals of the French Revolution as progenitors of George's doctrine, and George himself as the most original interpreter of these principles in America,[58] he probably mistakes the ideo-historical connections:[59] Just that which distinguishes the foundations of the French Revolution from their European forerunners—the strong accent on subjective-individualistic rights—is inspired by the ideological world of the American Revolution. It is true that the English settlers had already brought the concept of inalienable land rights from their homeland to the New World. But the transformation of these still historical, once conceded rights into rights which were supra-historical and grounded "only" in reason, and their sorting into a large number of claims due each individual was an independent outcome of the American Enlightenment. This era was the pioneer of the American Revolution, the schema of which may well be seen as the fertile soil for both the French Revolution and for the teachings of Henry George.[60]

Notes

1. *Cf.* Stow Persons, *American Minds* (New York, 1958), p. 76.

2. On the differences between the conceptions of natural law in the 18th and 19th centuries in general, *cf.* Persons *op. cit.*, p. 222 *ff.*; on the rejection of the idea of evolution as a characteristic of Enlightenment thought, *cf.* Fritz Valjavec, *Geschichte der abendländischen Aufklärung* (Vienna, 1961), pp. 91, 361.

3. *Social Problems,* (New York, 1898), p. 86.

4. Henry George, *The Condition of Labor* (New York, 1898), p. 92.

5. *Social Problems,* pp. 92 *ff.*

6. *Progress and Poverty,* (New York, (1879), 1898), p. 153.
7. *Op. cit.,* p. 40.
8. *Loc. cit.*
9. *The Science of Political Economy,* pp. 260 *ff.*
10. *Progress and Poverty,* p. 37.
11. *The Science of Political Economy,* p. 296.
12. George R. Geiger, *The Philosophy of Henry George* (New York, 1933), p. 259.
13. *Cf.* to this: Friedrich Georg Friedmann, "Amerika und das Problem der Geschichtlichkeit," *Speculum Historiale* (Freiburg, 1965), pp. 106–14, *passim.*
14. "The fundamental that in all economic reasoning must be firmly grasped, and never let go, is that society in its most highly developed form is but an elaboration of society in its rudest beginnings, and that principles obvious in the simpler relations of men are merely disguised and not abrogated or reversed by the more intricate relations that result from the division of labor and the use of complex tools and methods," *Progress and Poverty,* p. 26.
15. *The Condition of Labor,* p. 90.
16. *Progress and Poverty,* pp. 335*ff.*
17. On Ricardo's Law of Rent *cf.* Franz Oppenheimer, *David Ricardos Grundrententheorie,* 2nd ed. (Jena, 1927), pp. 32 *ff.*
18. *Progress and Poverty,* p. 168.
19. *The Science of Political Economy,* pp. 260 *ff.*
20. *Progress and Poverty,* pp. 333 *ff.*
21. Rip van Winkle is the leading character in a short story by the same title by Washington Irving.
22. *Progress and Poverty,* p. 336.
23. "As a man belongs to himself, so his labor when put in concrete forms belongs to him." *Progress and Poverty,* p. 332.
24. *Op. cit.,* pp. 335 *ff.*
25. *Op. cit.,* pp. 187 *ff.*
26. *Op. cit.,* pp. 261 *ff.*
27. Henry George, *Protection or Free Trade* (New York, 1966), p. 286.
28. *The Condition of Labor,* p. 11.
29. *Progress and Poverty,* p. 256.
30. *Op. cit.,* p. 403.
31. *Loc. cit.*
32. Geiger, *op. cit.,* p. 154.
33. *Cf.* Henry George, *Why the Landowner Cannot Shift the Tax on Land Values* (New York, n.d.), *passim.*
34. *Progress and Poverty,* pp. 414 *ff.*
35. Regarding the expression "Single Tax" for the tax proposd by George on land value see Henry George, "Concerning That Name 'Single Tax'," Land and Labor Library, Vol. 1, No. 39 (Endwell, N.Y., n.d.) (from a speech given in 1889 in Glasgow).
36. Henry George, *The Single Tax, What It Is and Why We Urge It,* (New York, n.d.), p. 3.
37. *Progress and Poverty,* p. 363; *cf.* also chapter "Compensation" in Henry George, *A Perplexed Philosopher* (New York, 1898), pp. 218 *ff.*
38. *Social Problems,* pp. 209 *ff.*
39. *Op. cit.,* pp. 210 *ff.*
40. *Op. cit.,* pp. 211 *ff.*
41. Oppenheimer, *Neue Freie Presse,* p. 10.

42. Parrington, *op. cit.*, p. 126: "He still remains our most original economist."
43. *The Condition of Labor*, p. 67.
44. *Progress and Poverty*, p. 523.
45. *Op. cit.*, p. 558.
46. *The Condition of Labor*, pp. 9 *ff.*
47. *Social Problems*, pp. 213–15.
48. Geiger, *op. cit.*, p. 375.
49. Thus, in Geiger, *op. cit.*, Chapter III is titled "George's Economic Solution," Chapter IX, "Economics and Ethics," and Chapter X, "George's Ethical Solution."
50. *Op. cit.*, p. 12 and *passim.*
51. Rose, *op. cit.*, p. 160.
52. In contrast, Barker, unlike Geiger, does not see two levels, but rather speaks of "two sequences of thought, distinct and separable" (*op. cit.*, p. 268). He believes that he can distinguish in *Progress and Poverty* a "moral sequence" consisting of Preface, Book X, and Conclusion, and an "economic syllogism" in Books III to IX (*op. cit.*, p. 269; Barker expresses the same view in his article "Henry George," in *The International Encyclopaedia of the Social Sciences*, Vol. VI [New York], 1968, p. 153.) This differentiation would be questionable even if one could describe as "economic" those parts of the book which are also open to an exclusively politico-economic interpretation. For in Book VII, thus in that part of *Progress and Poverty* which Barker characterizes as his "economic syllogism," George proves by argumentation based purely on natural law that the reform proposed by him is ethical. (*Cf.* above, p. 394.
53. *Ibid.*
54. *Cf.* Barker, *op. cit.*, pp. 10–13, and Anna George de Mille, (George's youngest daughter), *Henry George, Citizen of the World:* "Childhood and Early Youth," *American Journal of Economics and Sociology*, Vol. 1, No. 3, pp. 284–87.
55. Geiger, *op. cit.*, p. 338.
56. Rose, *op. cit.*, p. 20.
57. Parrington, *op. cit.*, p. 126.
58. *Op. cit.*, p. 136.
59. On the effect of the American idea on the French Revolution, in general, *cf.* A. Aulard, *Histoire politique de la Révolution française*, (Paris, 1901), pp. 19 *ff*; (p. 20: "The French Revolution, although different from the American Revolution in some regards, was to be haunted by the remembrance of that revolution."); Bernard Fay, *L'esprit révolutionnaire en France et aux États-Unis* (Paris, 1925), *passim;* (p. 176: "All the parties recognized and then proclaimed that the Americans were the model which the revolutionary idealists of France wanted to follow in 1789. . . . They thought that it contained a great lesson, and they exhibited a sort of mysticism in wishing to imitate it, to find in it a prototype, a rule, a universal truth"); and Daniel Mornet, *Les origines intellectuelles de la Révolution Française* (Paris, 1933), pp. 389*ff.*) ("La Révolution americaine").
60. *Cf.* Christian Egbert Weber, *Die Integration eines Kontinentes als Problem: Amerika, Europa* (Berlin, 1971), pp. 18 *ff.*; regarding the American influence on the authors of the Declaration of Human and Civil Rights of 1789 see George Jellinek, *Die Erklärung der Menschen-und Bürgerrechte*, 4th ed. (Munich, 1927), *passim* and pp. 8 *ff*, as well as Crane Brinton, *A Decade of Revolution* (New York, 1934), p. 41: "The Assembly [i.e. the French National Assembly of 1789] could hardly avoid issuing some kind of Bill of Rights; English and American precedent worked here with overwhelming insistence."

3

Henry George and Europe:

As Dissident Economist and Path-breaking Philosopher, He was a Catalyst for British Social Reform

By MICHAEL SILAGI*

Translated by SUSAN N. FAULKNER

ABSTRACT. *Henry George's* influence was greater in the *United Kingdom* than in the *United States.* The 80s and 90s there were particularly favorable for the reception of his revolutionary ideas. Though, thanks to such thinkers as *Alfred Russell Wallace* and *James* and *John Stuart Mill,* a *land reform* movement already existed, its sudden rise to national significance was due to George. George's writing and speaking skills and his dedication moved many serious citizens into the political *Left* and heavily influenced men and women who became leaders of *British non-Marxian socialism,* at the formation and consolidation of their movement. While George's followers broke with both the Wallace and socialist movements, George's rhetorical talents awakened the broad circles of thinking people to a *consciousness* of the full range of the *social question.*

I

George, Hyndman and Marx

THE INFLUENCE of Henry George in Great Britain, as a result of his writings and appearances there, was more profound than in the United States. Despite his fine showing in the New York mayoral elections in 1886, despite the honors paid him at his funeral by hundreds of thousands of fellow citizens, his effect in his native country remained marginal during his lifetime.[1]

A first British edition of *Progress and Poverty* appeared as early as 1880 and was soon out of print; it was followed shortly thereafter by a cheap "sixpenny edition." Four years later, about 100,000 copies of the work had been sold.[2]

A contemporary of George, the Liberal jurist, Clement M. Bailhache explains the success of the author by the extraordinary vividness and forcefulness of his exposition[3] and this is surely correct. Yet the factor responsible for the enormous response and the fruitfulness of his efforts was, in actuality, the particular period which was especially favorable for the reception of George's ideas.[4]

* [Michael Silagi, J.S.D., Ph.D. is a Senior Research Fellow at the Institute of International Law, University of Göttingen, Nikolausberger Weg 9c, 3400 Göttingen, West Germany.]

American Journal of Economics and Sociology, Vol. 48, No. 1 (January, 1989).

Toward the end of the seventies, England's industry was plagued by a severe depression.[5] But these industrial difficulties were far surpassed by the great crisis in agriculture. Since England held fast to its policy of free trade and refused to shield agriculture by protective tariffs, the British market was flooded by agricultural products from overseas, so that the farmers lost their livelihood.

This led to a rural exodus and to an overpopulation of the slum quarters in the cities. While the rural population in the decade of 1871–1881 rose by 7.42 percent, the urban population in the same period increased by 19.63%.[6] The economic distress in the countryside brought on tensions between the imperiled tenant farmers and the large landowners. The farmers soon began to place the blame for all their misery on the landlords. In the cities, too, the contrasts sharpened between the various social classes. The growing needs of the cities, particularly in regard to road construction, public transportation, and sanitation conflicted with the profit-seeking interests of the urban real estate owners.[7]

In the face of all this, Henry George's words found a resounding echo. He did not lack precursors, of course (one might mention again Thomas Spence and Patrick Edward Dove, and two others, James and John Stuart Mill), but the land reform ideas of these men had remained largely unknown. The sudden rise of the land reform movement after 1880 was due to Henry George, who—through his *Progress and Poverty* and through his personal dedication—succeeded in awakening in many thousands a deep interest in his theses regarding a just distribution of land. The British Liberal John A. Hobson is right, therefore, when he not only points to the fact that *Progress and Poverty* "struck the thinking people with convincing and dramatic force," but also emphasizes that this work by George was in effect the "first book of serious economic import which ever reached the outer circle of the English reading public."[8]

The immense influence of George on the political Left in Great Britain is the more remarkable because Karl Marx, by then already the guiding authority for the Socialists of Continental Europe outside the Romanic countries, had lived and worked in London since 1849. Nevertheless, British Socialism, in contrast to the movement on the Continent, was at this time still far from being ideologically stabilized and did not represent a potent force. D. C. Summervell found that "British Socialism was an affair of very small sects in the first 40 years of the [19th] century, and may be said to have been extinct during the 40 years that followed."[9] Hence, the revolutionary effectiveness of George's teachings was further aided by the fact that *Progress and Poverty* reached England precisely at the onset of the process of formation and consolidation of British Socialism.

Das Kapital, the first volume of which had appeared twelve years prior to *Progress and Poverty,* first became available in an English translation not before 1886. Those among the British Socialists who knew it had previously been able to read it only in the French version. George's work, on the other hand, found—as has already been pointed out—a ready market, not only among the groups familiar with French, but among the broad public. (As late as 1909, a small inquiry among 34 workers about their readings of economic and historical writings revealed that seven of those questioned had read *Progress and Poverty,* second only to Blatchford's *Merrie England* (nine readers). Only one reader had taken up Marx's writings.[10])

To be sure, the easier readability of George and his clarity of expression, comprehensible even to the untrained, further contributed to this difference in dissemination. J. A. W. Marriot, who, incidentally, was opposed to the ideas of both Marx and George, wrote about their major works as follows: "Even more persuasive than Marx's *Capital* was Henry George's *Progress and Poverty,* which was published in 1879. George wrote arrestingly with no little rhetorical power. Anyone could follow his argument, even if they refused to assent to his conclusions."[11]

Marx himself assessed George's significance highly, albeit negatively, as is reported in the memoirs of H. M. Hyndman, a doctrinaire Socialist and great admirer of Marx.[12] Hyndman was personally close to Henry George as well, perhaps closest of all English Socialists.[13] (In 1882, the author of *Progress and Poverty,* together with his family, had for some time been house guests in Hyndman's London home.[14]) Hyndman reports that Marx called *Progress and Poverty* "the Capitalists' last ditch."[15] While a Marxist would regard this as a scathing judgment, it would not be seen at all in a negative light when regarded from the standpoint of the non-Marxist Henry George. For he firmly believed that his reform proposal would serve to perpetuate the capitalistic system, though in a more refined form.

According to Hyndman, Marx feared the extraordinary persuasiveness of the American. Furthermore, he did not believe that a study of *Progress and Poverty* would lead the reader toward Socialism. On the contrary, he was afraid that for every ten readers who, enlightened by George about the evils of the prevailing system, became Socialists, there would be a hundred others who would stop at the position taken by Henry George.[16] Marx further commented on George in a letter written in 1881.[17] There he described the American as "totally backwards,"[18] although a "writer of talent,"[19] whose work, nevertheless, was important because it is "a first, albeit a failed, effort, to free himself of orthodox political economy."[20]

Hyndman rejected *Progress and Poverty* as much as did Marx. But Marx contradicted Hyndman's notion that the literary success of George contributed greatly to the dissemination of Marx's theories. In effect, the "easily read" book, as Marx called it, had, he thought, made public opinion aware of the social question and, indeed, of the entire problem of the economic situation. But that is all Marx would concede.

II

George and British Land Reformers

UNDER THE INFLUENCE of Henry George, an organization developed in England which was committed to the cause of justice regarding landownership. But its program differed significantly from the basic points of *Progress and Poverty.* This was the Land Nationalization Society, formed between 1882 and 1883, whose spiritual father was the famed naturalist Alfred Russel Wallace, co-author of the theory of evolution. Wallace advocated the nationalization of land, while George wanted to leave the land itself in private hands and merely transfer the land rent to community property through taxation. Wallace intended to compensate the expropriated landowners, a measure which George fought as a sanction, contrary to natural rights, of robbery.[22]

Wallace's outline of his plan regarding the land question appeared in 1882—three years after *Progress and Poverty.* It was titled *Land Nationalization/Its Necessity and Its Aims/Being a Comparison of the System of Landlord and Tenant With That of Occupying Ownership in Their Influence on the Well-Being of the People.*[23] The author remarked in a footnote[24] that Henry George's work (which he enthusiastically praised, by the way,[25] and cited in detail[26]) had come to his attention only after he had already completed most of his manuscript. Wallace called *Progress and Poverty* the most noteworthy and important work of the century; indeed, there can be no doubt that, although he had nearly finished his own book when he came upon George's writing, he adopted some essential thoughts from the American.[27] The title of one chapter, "Low Wages and Pauperism, the Direct Consequences of Unrestricted Private Property in Land," is obviously a formulation inspired by George.[28]

But Wallace had developed some fundamental concepts independently from George in his book. Here, however, something similar happened to him, unintentionally, as had occurred also unintentionally, in 1858 in connection with evolution. Wallace, in fact, had anticipated with his essay on the theory of human descent Charles Darwin's ground-breaking work, *On the Origin of Species.*[29] But his name is linked with Darwin's in crediting the theory only by historians.

Wallace's organization was a catch-all for those who, each in his own way, wanted to fight for the reform of landownership. Henry George's first public lecture in London was organized, under Wallace's chairmanship, by the Land Nationalization Society. In 1883 the followers of the American's ideas joined together to form a Land Reform Union as part of Wallace's Society. Initially, the activities of the Land Reform Union consisted predominantly of joint readings and discussions of *Progress and Poverty,*[30] in which not only Georgists took part, but also advocates of land nationalization, among them the Social-Democrats.

Subsequently, the Union worked out its own program which, while it was based on *Progress and Poverty,* was so formulated as to seem acceptable as well to Wallace's adherents and to Social-Democrats. Yet, the differing views could not be bridged permanently in this fashion.[31] After only one year, the Georgists took over the leadership of the Union, reorganized it strictly along the ideological lines of *Progress and Poverty,* and changed its name to "Land Restoration League." The organization is still in existence under the name, adopted in 1907, of the "United Committee for the Taxation of Land Values."[32]

The founding of the Land Restoration League brought about a sharp demarcation from those groups wishing to achieve the abolition of private monopoly of land through nationalization; it signified, at the same time, a repudiation of socialism. This complete separation from the advocates of nationalism as much as from the Socialists was to make it easier for the Georgists—after 1889—to join with the Liberals.[33]

The creation of an organization entirely dedicated to Henry George did not, however, lead to an immediate break with the followers of Wallace and with the Socialists. This circumstance was partly responsible for the fact that Henry George's program was identified in the British press until 1888 with the "land nationalization" movement and, as a result, rejected as Socialist.[34] During his first trips to England, George often spoke at public gatherings of these groups, while failing simultaneously to point out the incompatibility of many of their principles with his own. In addition, he himself described his remedy—the confiscation of land rent through taxation—as "virtual nationalization,"[35] although in actuality this means would leave the property relations entirely unchanged. George, furthermore, assured his listeners again and again of his sympathy for Socialism,[36] but not, to be sure, because of doctrinal agreement. E. J. Rose remarks in this connection: "Long right of Morris, George was ideologically not even so far left as Tolstoy, much less . . . the Fabians in England; but George found great satisfaction in their influence upon socioeconomic ideas."[37]

When English Socialists, for their part, assessed George's influence positively, they did so for the same reason: they saw his effects on the social and economic attitudes of his contemporaries as highly beneficial.

There can be no doubt that George Macaulay Trevelyan's statement is correct: "The revival of British Socialism was preceded and in some way prepared by the vogue of a different doctrine, that of the American Henry George in his *Progress and Poverty.*"[38]

But George was by no means only forerunner and pioneer; he was in an extremely direct way activator and spur as well for those men who later were to play leading roles in the English non-Marxist Socialist movement.

III

Georgism as Catalyst

BETWEEN 1870 AND 1890, many organizations for social reform developed in Great Britain. Yet of all these groups, Max Beer says, "none exerted as deep an influence, relatively, upon public opinion as the Fabian Society."[39] In turn, Edward R. Pease,[40] a co-founder of the Fabian Society, writes as follows about George and his significance:

> *Progress and Poverty* gave an extraordinary impetus to the political thought of the time. It proposed to redress the wrongs suffered by the working class as a whole: the poverty it considered was the poverty of the wage workers as a class, not the destitution of the unfortunate and downtrodden individuals. . . . It suggested a method by which the reward of labour would go to those that laboured; the idleness alike of rich and poor would cease; the abundant wealth created by modern industry would be distributed with something like fairness and even equality, amongst those who contributed to its production. Above all, this tremendous revolution was to be accomplished by a political method, applicable by a majority of the voters, and capable of being drafted as an Act of Parliament by any competent lawyer. To George belongs the extraordinary merit of recognising the right way of social salvation.[41]

Sidney Webb, who was considered by many to have been the best mind among the Fabians, and who later held several ministerial posts in Labour governments,[42] expressed similar thoughts about Henry George:

> Little as Mr. Henry George intended it, there can be no doubt that it was the enormous circulation of his *Progress and Poverty* which gave the touch which caused all the seething influences to crystalize into a popular Socialist movement. The optimistic and confident tone of the book, and the irresistible force of its popularization of Ricardo's Law of Rent, sounded the dominant "note" of the English Socialist party of to-day.[43]

In March of 1889, at a time when George was encountering evergrowing opposition among Socialists, Webb wrote in a letter to the American:

> I want to implore your forbearance. When you are denounced as a traitor and what not, by Socialist newspapers; and 'heckled' by Socialist questioners, or abused by Socialist orators, it will be difficult not to denounce Socialism in return. But do not do so. They will be only the noisy fringe of the Socialist Party who will do this, and it will be better for the cause which we both serve, if you can avoid accentuating your difference with Socialists.[44]

Leading figures of the English Left have given interesting reports about their truly having been awakened to the social question by George. The noted novelist and popular historian H. G. Wells writes in his autobiography as follows:

> It seems improbable that I did not then [c. 1883] encounter the opposition of Socialism and individualism, but oddly enough I cannot recall having thought at all about Socialism until I read Henry George at Midhurst.[45]

Even more impressive is the testimony given in a letter of 1904 by probably the most famous Fabian, George Bernard Shaw, regarding the contribution made by George to his own "conversion" to Socialism. He describes his conversion through George in his reply to an invitation to a "Progress and Poverty Dinner" in New York, and his description lends support to Anne Freemantle's opinion that George's influence on him was attributable more to his personality than to his book.[46] Shaw writes:

> One evening in the early eighties I found myself . . . in the Memorial Hall, Farrington St., London, listening to an American finishing a speech on the Land Question. . . . He spoke on Liberty, Justice, Truth, Natural Law, and other strange 18th century superstitions and . . . explained with great simplicity and sincerity the views of the Creator. . . . I noticed also that he was a born orator. . . . Now at that time I was a young man not much past 25, of a very revolutionary and contradictory temperament, full of Darwin and Tyndall, of Shelley and DeQuincey, of Michael Angelo and Beethoven, and never having in my life studied social questions from the economic point of view, except that I had once, in my boyhood, read a pamphlet by John Stuart Mill on the Irish Land Question. The result of my hearing that speech and buying from one of the stewards a copy of *Progress and Poverty* for sixpence . . . was that I plunged into a course of economic study, and at a very early stage of it became a Socialist. . . . When I thus swept into the great Socialist revival of 1883, I found that five-sixths of those who were swept in with me had been converted by Henry George. This fact would have been far more widely acknowledged had it not been that it was not possible for us to stop where Henry George stopped. . . . But I am glad to say that I never denied or belittled our debt to Henry George.[47]

Even twenty-four years later, Shaw expressed similar views in the preface to the American edition of his book *The Intelligent Woman's Guide to Socialism and Capitalism:*

> I wonder this book of mine was not written in America by an American fifty years ago. Henry George had a shot at it; indeed it was his oratory (to which I was exposed for forty-five minutes forty-five years ago by pure chance) that called my attention to it. . . . Still, America can claim that in this book I am doing no more than finishing Henry George's job.[48]

The surpassing importance of the, as it were, catalytic effect of George's influence, which Shaw credits with the Socialist revival of 1883, is extended by Max Beer to the eighties in general: "Four-fifths of the Socialists [in Great Britain] who came to Socialism in the eighties had gone through the Henry George school."[49] In Hobson's words, *Progress and Poverty* was for these people "a stepping-stone to a more or less formal Socialism,"[50] and Henry Pelling thinks that it was only due to the influx of former Georgists that the previously tiny Social-Democratic Federation became a permanent organization.[51]

Indeed not only the Fabians, but also British Socialists of other orientations, confirmed the tremendous impact of the American and his works, even while rejecting his views. William Morris[52] wrote in 1883 that it was certain that Henry George's book was being received in England, as in America, like a "new Gospel."[53] Tom Mann[54] shows his great appreciation for the illumination he had found in George's ideas when he conveys to us this vivid impression of the spiritual state of young Socialists after 1880:

> In 1881 I read Henry George's *Progress and Poverty*. This was a big event for me; it impressed me as far the most valuable book I had so far read, and, to my agreeable surprise at the time, it seemed to give an effective answer to Malthus. I was greatly interested in the book. It enabled me to see more clearly the vastness of the social problem, to realize that every country was confronted with it, and the capable and comprehensive analyses of the population question supplied me with what I had not then found in any book in this country before. . . . His book was a fine stimulus to me, full of incentive to noble endeavour, imparting much valuable information, throwing light on many questions of real importance and giving me what I wanted—a glorious hope for the future of humanity, a firm conviction that the social problem could and would be solved.[55]

In summary, the historical development confirms Hyndman's views, not those of Marx: The great rhetorical talents of George were needed to awaken the broad circles in England to a consciousness of the full range of the social question. Yet the majority of those stirred up by George did not remain Georgists, but became Socialists; Anne Fremantle's remark, meant for Shaw, is as valid for many others: George had won them *with* his teachings, but not *for* his teachings, rather for Socialism.[56] To this point, Geiger writes:

> It is true that the majority of George's English converts soon turned from the land question to the growing socialist movement, but the impetus for the consideration of social reform had been supplied by the stocky red-bearded American orator with the religious vision and almost fanatical confidence of some chosen prophet.[57]

George, to be sure, had proposed only an unsentimental, matter-of-fact solution though he described and scourged passionately the prevailing injustices. As passionately as he called for their elimination, as wholly devoid was his remedy of pathos, filled only with sparse simplicity and cool rationality. This could neither satisfy, nor maintain a hold on, the aroused masses. What remained, ultimately, was the enduring effect of George's writings and personality on the entire British Left and his decisive contribution to the formation of the Fabian Society and the Social Democratic Federation, and thereby as well, though indirectly, to the later founding of the Labour Party.

Notes

1. The American historian Sidney Fine reports, citing substantial evidence from the beginnings of Progressivism through the period of the New Deal: ". . . Henry George had not fought his battle in vain. Not only did he establish himself as an important figure in the realm of American economic thought and as an influence on the movement for tax reform, but as the era of Progressivism was to demonstrate, his ideas served as a stimulant to the reform movement as a whole." *Laissez Faire and the General-Welfare State: A Study of Conflict in American Thought, 1865–1901* (Ann Arbor: Univ. of Michigan Press, 1956), p. 295.

2. Elwood P. Lawrence, *Henry George in the British Isles* (East Lansing: Michigan State Univ. Press, 1957), p. 34.

3. Clement M. Bailhache describes the effect in *Practical Land Reform* (London: 1904), p. 85: "Henry George, with a clearness and force which no other possesses, with illustration on illustration and argument on argument, demonstrated to us what it now seems extraordinary we could not see for ourselves."

4. On this, John A. Hobson comments, "A certain dramatic opportuneness attending the advent of *Progress and Poverty* gave to Henry George the public ear." See Hobson, "The Influence of Henry George in England," *Fortnightly Review,* 62 (New Series), 1897, p. 838.

5. R. C. K. Ensor, *England, 1879–1914* (Oxford: Oxford Univ. Press, 1936, 1952), p. 111.

6. *Op. cit.*, p. 103.

7. *Cf.* Hobson, *op. cit.*, p. 839: "The rising standard of sanitation and of other civic needs was driving home to municipal reformers a sense of conflict between the public interest of the town and the private interest of the owners of town land."

8. *Op. cit.*, p. 837.

9. In his *English Thought in the Nineteenth Century* (London: 1929, 1964), p. 202. Also see Julius Braunthal, *Geschichte der Internationale,* Vol. 1 (Hanover: 1961), pp. 209*ff.*

10. Derek Hudson, "Reading," *Edwardian England, 1901–1914,* Simon Nowell-Smith, ed. (London: 1964), p. 312.

11. J. A. R. Marriot, *Modern England* (London: 4th ed., 1948), pp. 230*ff.*

12. H. M. Hyndman, *The Record of an Adventurous Life* (London: 1911), p. 282.

13. George Raymond Geiger, *The Philosophy of Henry George* (New York: Macmillan, 1933), p. 236.

14. Hyndman, *op. cit.*, p. 290.

15. *Ibid.*, p. 281.

16. *Ibid.*, p. 282.

17. Quoted in F. A. Sorge, *Briefe und Auszüge aus Briefen von Joh. Phil. Becker, Jos. Dietzgen, Friedrich Engels, Karl Marx u. A. und F. A. Sorge und Andere* (Stuttgart: 1906), pp. 174*ff.* (The relevant parts of the letter are also reprinted in F. A. Sorge, "Die Arbeiterbewegung in den Vereinigten Staaten 1877–1885," *Die Neue Zeit,* 10th year, 1891–92, Vol. 2, pp. 201*ff.*)

18. *Ibid., Briefe,* p. 76; *Neue Zeit,* p. 201.

19. *Ibid.*, p. 77 or p. 203.

20. *Ibid.*, p. 77 or p. 202.

21. Hyndman writes: "Nevertheless, I still hold that George's temporary success with his agitatory fallacies greatly facilitated the promulgation of Marx's own theories in Great Britain, owing to the fact that the public mind had been stirred up to consider the social question, and political economy generally, by George's easily read book." *Op. cit.*, p. 282.

22. *Progress and Poverty* (New York: Robert Schalkenbach Foundation, 1979), p. 365. George devoted a whole chapter to the question: Book VII, Ch. 3, pp. 358–67. *Cf* Heinrich Niehuus, *Geschichte der englischen Bodenreform theorien* (Leipzig: 1910), pp. 141*ff.*

23. Quoted from the 3rd edition (London: c. 1890).

24. *Op. cit.*, p. 9.

25. George Jr. quotes a letter from his father: "I see, too, by the English papers that Alfred Russel Wallace has been indorsing *Progress and Poverty* which he says 'is undoubtedly the most remarkable and important work of the present century.' " (*The Life of Henry George,* New York: Robert Schalkenbach Foundation, 1960, p. 353).

26. See especially Wallace, *op. cit.*, pp. 165*ff.*

27. Rose calls *Land Nationalisation* by Wallace "a book clearly in debt to Progress and Poverty," (Edward J. Rose, *Henry George,* New York: Twayne Publishers, 1968), p. 100.

28. Chapter VII.

29. *Cf.* also Karl Schewe, *Bodenreform und Bodenreformpartei in England* (Jena: 1925), p. 10.

30. Lawrence, *op. cit.*, p. 32.

31. *Ibid.*, p. 34.

32. *Loc. cit.*

33. On this, Lawrence points out: "By separating themselves from socialism, George's followers laid the foundation for their eventual cooperation, beginning in 1889, with the Liberal Party" (*op. cit.*, p. 37).

34. *Ibid.*, pp. 52*ff.*

35. In Henry George and H. M. Hyndman, "Socialism and Rent Appropriation: A Dialogue," *Nineteenth Century*, February, 1885, p. 378.

36. *Ibid.*, pp. 377*ff.*

38. George Macaulay Trevelyan, *British History in the 19th Century and After, 1782–1919* (London: 1937, 2nd ed., 1956), p. 402.

39. Max Beer, *Geschichte des Sozialismus in England* (Stuttgart: 1913, p. 461); on the significance of the Fabians see also Trevelyan, *op. cit.*, p. 403.

40. (1857–1955). See Margaret Cole, "Edward Reynolds Pease," *Dictionary of National Biography, 1951–1960* (London: 1971), pp. 799*ff.*

41. Edward R. Pease, *The History of the Fabian Society* (London: 3rd ed., 1963), p. 20.

42. (1859–1947). See Mary Agnes Hamilton, "Sidney James Webb," *Dictionary of National Biography, 1941–1950* (London: 1953), pp. 935–940.

43. Sidney Webb, *Socialism in England* (London: 1890), p. 21.

44. Quoted in Charles Albro Barker, *Henry George* (New York: Oxford Univ. Press, 1955), p. 526.

45. H. G. Wells, *Experiment in Autobiography* (London: 1934), Vol. 1, p. 168.

46. Anne Fremantle, *This Little Band of Prophets* (London: 1960), p. 157; J. Morris Davidson, a contemporary of George, assessed author and work as follows: "In most cases of brilliant authorship the writer is markedly inferior to his literary offspring; but this could not be said of Henry George." In *Concerning Four Precursors of Henry George and the Single Tax* (London: 1899), p. 2.

47. Quoted in Archibald Henderson, *Bernard Shaw* (London: 1932), pp. 149*ff.*

48. George Bernard Shaw, *The Intelligent Woman's Guide to Socialism and Capitalism* (New York: 1928), p. xi; see also a letter by Shaw in the same year to the American Georgist, J. Rupert Mason, published in *Land & Liberty*, 55 (London: 1948), p. 198. Before expressing his reservations about George's theories, Shaw emphasized here: "I have never repudiated Henry George, nor denied my indebtedness to him for making an economist of me."

49. Beer, *op. cit.*, p. 439.

50. Hobson, *op. cit.*, p. 842.

51. Henry Pelling, *America and the British Left* (New York: 1957), p. 56.

52. (1834–1896). See J. W. Mackail, "William Morris," *Dictionary of National Biography*, 1st Suppl. VI, III (London: 1901), pp. 197–203.

53. "It is certain that Henry George's Book has been received in this country as a new Gospel." Quoted in J. W. Mackail, *The Life of William Morris*, Vol. II (London: 1912), p. 110.

54. (1856–1941). See J. S. Middleton, "Thomas Mann," *Dictionary of National Biography*, 1941–1950 (London: 1959), pp. 568–570.

55. *Tom Mann's Memoirs* (London: 1967), pp. 16*ff.*

56. "Shaw's conversion by Henry George—though not to him," Freemantle, *op. cit.*, p. 34.

57. Geiger, *op. cit.*, p. 232.

4

Henry George and Europe:

Ireland, the First Target of His Efforts to Spread His Doctrines Internationally, Disappointed Him

By MICHAEL SILAGI*

Translated by SUSAN N. FAULKNER

ABSTRACT. *Henry George* made several crusading forays into the *British Empire* at the time of its zenith. But the first, to *Ireland,* proved a disappointment. George saw Ireland as an object lesson in the *land question* and at first it was uppermost in the minds of the 600,000 *tenant farmers.* But the 20,000 *landlords* agreed to an amelioration, and for decades, *republicanism* replaced *land reform* in Irish *social history.* George misread the temper of the times; he saw Ireland's political future better served by becoming a self-governing unit of a *league of British nations.* "*Integration*" was the trend of the times, the American *social philosopher* insisted. Ireland (with the exception of Ulster) became a *dominion* in 1921 but it withdrew from the *British Commonwealth* in 1949 to become a *sovereign republic.* George was not wholly wrong in emphasizing *economics* over *politics.* In 1955 Ireland, now Eire, entered the United Nations where it wielded influence all out of proportion to its resources and economic *development* became its over-riding issue.

I

Introduction

HENRY GEORGE'S NAME is associated with Ireland's struggle for freedom from British imperialistic domination. Only at the end of the first quarter of the next century did the struggle—now waged by guerilla warfare—begin its march toward total victory. In the 19th century the Irish Revolution began as an agrarian rising by the landless against their landlords.

Naturally a rebellion over the land question won the sympathy of the American economist and social philosopher, who brought together into a coherent system classical economics and the ideas of the Enlightenment philosophers, the ideas of Thomas Jefferson and his followers who laid the foundations of the American republic. George seized upon the issue, regarded abroad as a local one, and

* [Michael Silagi, J.S.D., Ph.D., is a Senior Research Fellow at the Institute of International Law, University of Göttingen, Nikolausberger Weg 9c, 3400 Göttingen, West Germany.]

American Journal of Economics and Sociology, Vol. 46, No. 4 (October, 1987).

argued in his writings that it was typical of the land question everywhere else in the world where land was subject to absolute private ownership.

George's intervention in Irish affairs, however fruitless, led to his crusades in Great Britain and the empire, missions which were to spread the American land reform movement in several parts of the world. The impact he was to make elsewhere contrasted with the interlude in Ireland, which was, to say the least, disappointing.

The policy of free trade had led to an agrarian crisis and flight from the land in England. It brought to the majority of the British urban population, on the other hand, the advantage of cheaper agricultural products. In Ireland, on the contrary, the disastrous effects of this policy were felt by the entire population. In 1870, more than 90 percent of the Irish made their living—directly or indirectly—from agriculture.[1] Farming was given over almost wholly to tenant farmers, more than 600,000 in number, as against about 20,000 landlords.[2]

When the Irish farmers lost their British markets, both because of cheap American competition and because of the decreasing purchasing power of the English people, they still had to continue paying the same amount of rent to their landlords.[3] This caused an exacerbation of the class antagonism which had been smoldering in Ireland already for centuries, but which had been pacified somewhat only a few years before, in 1870, with Gladstone's Land Act. Gladstone's legislation had improved the situation of the tenant farmers by making their arbitrary expulsion by the landlords more difficult, and by providing that the tenant must be compensated after termination of the tenure relationship for improvements undertaken by him.[4]

Toward the end of the seventies, however, the situation became truly catastrophic. To the effects of the British economic policies now were added the consequences of the weather conditions of the years 1877 to 1879. These were devastating for the farmers so that the situation of the Emerald Isle soon came to resemble the time of the Great Famine of 1845–1847—the "Hungry Forties."[5]

II

Davitt and the Irish Land League

In 1879, THE ECONOMIC DISTRESS of the Irish reached its climax. It was then that a period ensued of unparalleled agitation and unrest. This so-called "New Departure" was connected primarily with the name of Michael Davitt, son of a Catholic farmer, who as a small child had been expelled with his father from the latter's tenant farm. At the age of eleven he became a worker in a cotton spinningmill, where he lost his right arm. In 1865, Michael Davitt joined the secret Irish Republican Brotherhood, for which he was imprisoned from 1870 to 1877.[6] He was the moving force of the most important Irish organization of those days, the Irish Land League, and soon rose to become leader of the entire Irish national movement.

Earlier organizations had fought England as a military occupation force and political oppressor. Davitt effected a break with this tradition. The Land League made use of a battle cry which not only could mobilize momentary hatred, but which promised enduring, far-reaching results, and in any case presented an irresistible attraction for the mass of tenant farmers: "The land for the people!"

Thus, Davitt placed the land question in the center of his political agitation, a question which naturally touched the farmers threatened by eviction notices and expulsions more closely than the fight for national independence.[7] After some hesitation, the parliamentary leader of the Irish Nationalists, the Protestant landowner Charles Stewart Parnell, joined the Irish Land League; indeed, in 1879 he took over its leadership.

The League solicited support as well in the United States for its objectives, and promoted the founding of an American Land League. In the U.S., it was especially Patrick Ford's New York weekly *Irish World* which fought for the cause of the Irish Land League, and at the end of 1881 the *Irish World* sent Henry George to Ireland as its correspondent.

George took advantage of the opportunity which, he felt, the Irish movement offered him for the dissemination of his ideas. After all, in *Progress and Poverty* George had already cited the economic situation in Ireland as evidence for the correctness of his thesis.[8] At the end of 1879, he wrote an article for a California periodical about "The Irish Land Question."[9]

When Davitt a short time later traveled through America to win support for the League, he met with George and suggested that the League make an effort toward a wider propagation of *Progress and Poverty* in Great Britain.[10] Since George was afraid, however, that his book would be too voluminous and difficult for the rural members of the Land League, he decided to rework his ideas not only in a simpler and more direct form, but also with special application to the existing circumstances in Ireland. For this purpose he rewrote the previously cited article into a book of about a hundred pages, entitled *The Irish Land Question/What It Involves and How Alone It Can Be Settled.* Of course, the author still had as his main goal the proclamation of general truths. Ireland was merely a concrete example, evidence which served to provide illustrations, but these illustrations could just as well have been taken from anywhere else.[11] (The book could, therefore, appear in later editions without the adjective "Irish" in the title, as *The Land Question,* and be distributed in other countries as well.[12])

The [Irish] Land Question was, as already stated, a simplified presentation of the proposals detailed in *Progress and Poverty* for the solution of the social question, and a guide to the application of these proposals to the concrete case of Ireland.

But George was somewhat critical, in this work, of the program of the Irish Land League, particularly of Parnell's formulations. On one hand, George objected to transferring the land, as Parnell and his followers were planning to do, to ownership by the tenants, thereby eliminating rent altogether. This would be an action taken on behalf of only one social class, as George saw it.[13] It would have the effect of merely supplanting the class of the landlords with another, though more numerous, class, namely that of peasant proprietors.[14] George's other objection to the policies of the Land League addressed itself to its nationalistic and anti-British position.

George suggested to the Irish leaders that, on the contrary, the League should unite with the English working class against the landowners.[15] As far as the nationalistic strivings were concerned, he felt that of course the Irish had the same inalienable right to self-determination as any other nation, but that this did not necessarily need to lead to separation from Great Britain: "It must be remembered that the tendencies of the time are not to separation, but to integration,"[16] George stressed. For this reason, he demanded from those he was addressing: "Let them be Land Leaguers first, and Irishmen afterwards."[17]

III

"Equal Justice for All"

IT IS NOT SURPRISING, therefore, that the efforts of the American on behalf of Ireland turned out to be unproductive. Basically, he was not ready for any compromise whatsoever, even verbally, regarding that which to him appeared fundamental and decisive. To him, the demand for equal justice for all was primary, and he wanted to subordinate all special interests, including nationalist ideals, to this principle. For two reasons, this fundamental, two-fold divergence did not at first become clear either to him or to his Irish friends.

For one thing, not all Irish leaders shared Parnell's opinion regarding the question of the transfer of land to common property; in fact, the leaders of the Land League could not even agree among themselves on this point. Before Davitt, for example, met with George, he had already thought about nationalization of land.[18] Under the influence of the author of *Progress and Poverty,* he propagated a solution that followed in the footsteps of the theses of this book,[19] but with this stumbling block: Davitt—similar to the "Land Nationalization Society" of A. R. Wallace,—wrote the compensation of the landlords on his banner.

Secondly, George saw in Davitt only the passionate land reformer, for whom, he thought, since his meeting with the American the watchword "The Land for the People" had become synonymous with the demand for nationalization of landed property.[20] But here, too, a serious misunderstanding existed: George and Davitt, it is true, agreed on the demand for land reform. For both, too, land reform was only the means to an end; however, the reformers differed profoundly in their ultimate objective. For George, the solution to the Irish land problem was a step in the direction toward universal justice—for Davitt toward national independence.[21]

Davitt was more radical than Parnell not only on the question of land, but also on that of nationalism. Parnell strove for Ireland's having home rule within the United Kingdom, while Davitt demanded complete independence from London.[22] It was, thus, Davitt's radicalism which engendered the illusion of agreement with Henry George, an illusion which, however, could not last long. But for the time being, both agreed on a rejection of the Kilmainham treaty.

By this treaty, the detention of Parnell and his co-fighters who had been arrested in October, 1881, ended in May of 1882. In exchange for the freeing of the detainees and a much-needed remission of debts for a hundred thousand Irish tenant farmers, Parnell promised to restrict anti-British agitation.[23] George took a strong stand against this compromise because he saw in the economic concessions by the English a strengthening of the tenure system. This, George felt, would postpone even further the abolition of "landlordism," and thus of the root cause of the economic and social ills. Davitt, for his part, condemned the agreement because he saw in it a blow to the cause of nationalism.[24] Indeed, when he deplored the fact that the nationalization of land desired by him had been rendered more difficult, he did so because—as he saw it—this move would have been a step forward in the march toward national independence.

IV

Davitt's Break from George

GEORGE BELIEVED DAVITT to be a fellow-combatant and thought that the Irishman, who had read *Progress and Poverty* four times,[25] would prove to be an apostle of the land reform movement. This incorrect appraisal by George[26] is even perpetuated in some of the literature.[27]

Davitt, for his part, probably saw their incompatibility more clearly. A possible motive, on the Irishman's side, for the numerous meetings held between the two men during George's last years may well have been his expectation that George's support would be useful to him in his many trips through the United States.[28] However, Davitt gave a speech in the United States as early as 1882, in which he denied having been influenced by George;[29] and in 1886, while again in America, he wrote George that he could not support him in the latter's campaign for mayor of New York, because he did not want to involve himself in the American elections, and because he did not, moreover, see George's victory as desirable.[30]

Precisely to the extent that the land reform goals of George and Davitt resembled each other, they produced no practical results. Davitt's proposals for nationalization met with deaf ears on the part of the tenant farmers, while Henry George's interest in the Emerald Isle dwindled in turn.[31] During two European trips in 1884 and 1885, he gave 75 speeches in England and Scotland, but only two in Ireland.[32]

George hoped Ireland would lead the way in abolishing land monopoly. But his hopes were dashed against the unyielding rocks of history by a rising tide of nationalism as the country's 20,000 landlords agreed to amelioration of the lot of the 600,000 tenants under a scheme voted by the British Parliament.

Through guerilla warfare the Irish won dominion status in 1921. Withdrawing from the British Commonwealth of Nations in 1949, Ireland, as Eire, became a sovereign republic. It has become a leading figure in the United Nations and in world diplomacy. But George was not wholly wrong in emphasizing economics over politics. Successive administrations in the young republic have made economic development their top priority issue. Yet the land question remains an issue, marked by mass unemployment as in other developing democracies.

Notes

1. Norman Dunbar Palmer, *The Irish Land League Crisis* (New Haven, 1940), p. 2.
2. *Ibid.*, p. 9.
3. *Ibid.*, p. 56.
4. *Ibid.*, pp. 41*ff.*
5. *Ibid.*, pp. 64*ff.*
6. R. C. K. Ensor, *England, 1870–1914* (Oxford, 1936, 1952), p. 111.
7. Palmer, *op. cit.*, p. 108.
8. Henry George, *Progress and Poverty,* (1879) (New York, 1979), pp. 123*ff.*
9. Charles Albro Barker, *Henry George* (New York, 1955), p. 320.
10. "Davitt pledged the Land League to push it (*i.e., Progress and Poverty*) in Great Britain." Henry George, quoted in Henry George Jr., *The Life of Henry George* (New York, 1960), p. 341.
11. George wrote: "In speaking with general reference to the case of Ireland, I have, so far as general principles are concerned, been using it as a stalking-horse." *The Land Question* (New York, 1898), p. 73.
12. In the preface to the 1898 edition we read: "In order better to indicate the general character of this subject . . . the title was subsequently changed to *'The Land Question,'* " *op. cit.*, p. 3.
13. *Ibid.*, p. 59.
14. Palmer says, "The displacement of the landlord, by peasant proprietors meant simply the substitution of one landowning class for another; for a peasant proprietor, as Lord Montagu once remarked, was 'a landlord written small.' " *Op. cit.*, p. 14.

15. *The Land Question,* p. 60.
16. *Ibid.,* p. 62.
17. *Ibid.,* p. 63.
18. F. Sheehy-Skeffington, *Michael Davitt* (London, 1967), pp. 70*ff.*
19. Barker, *Henry George,* p. 367.
20. *Cf.* F. S. L. Lyons, "Introduction" to Sheehy-Skeffington's *Michael Davitt,* (London, 1967), p. 9.
21. Palmer calls it "a social revolution with political ends." *Op. cit.,* p. 128.
22. "Throughout his life he was a crusader in the national cause." *Ibid.,* p. 129.
23. Ensor, *op. cit.,* pp. 74*ff.*
24. Michael Davitt, *The Fall of Feudalism in Ireland* (London, 1904), p. 363.
25. George, quoted by George Jr., *op. cit.,* p. 380.
26. Palmer is right when he writes, "To expect a pure land movement under such leadership would be fantastic and absurd." *Op. cit.,* p. 129.
27. Thus in Elwood P. Lawrence, *Henry George in the British Isles* (East Lansing, MI, 1957), p. 10.
28. Davitt says the goal of these propaganda tours was "to organize auxiliary movements in other lands," *op. cit.,* p. xiii.
29. George Jr., *op. cit.,* pp. 384*ff.*
30. Barker, *Henry George,* p. 471.
31. George's resignation concerning Ireland is reflected in the beginning of Chapter 10 of Part III of his *Perplexed Philosopher.* There he complains that his stance got him between two chairs: "In this confusion of thought we who hold that the right of property is an absolute right . . . are looked upon by one side as deniers of the right of property, and by the other . . . as not radical enough," p. 209.
32. Lawrence, *op. cit.,* p. 35.

5

Henry George and Europe:

George and His Followers Awakened the British Conscience and Started a New, Freer Society

By MICHAEL SILAGI*

Translated by SUSAN N. FAULKNER

ABSTRACT. Henry George played a tremendous role in the development and growth of the British Liberal party and of British Liberalism, one no less significant than his role in that of British non-Marxian socialism. One of the Liberal leaders who gained a place in history, Joseph Chamberlain, had already been a land reformer before he learned about Georgism. Chamberlain used the Georgist analysis, but he and the other 19th century Radical Liberals worked up a program for a broader distribution of landed property, not for the abolition of the private land monopoly. The same tactic in Ireland entrenched private land monopoly thereby making many renters small holders. But George also supplied the analysis and the context of the Liberal campaign. And later Liberal leaders—notably David Lloyd George, Winston Churchill (as well as Liberals in the Labour Party, Philip Snowden, Herbert Morrison, Ramsay MacDonald and Josiah Wedgwood)—came close to making the taxation of land values the law of the kingdom.

I

Joseph Chamberlain, Land Reformer

HISTORICALLY, Henry George played a significant role in the development of the characteristically British, non-Marxian variety of individualist and collectivist socialism. But no less significant was the role he played in the development and growth of the British Liberal party and of British Liberalism. In the Liberals' program, the demand for land taxation, based on George's analysis of the causes of poverty, was to play a tremendous role. And that politician who, more than anyone else, fought to place the land question foremost among the later policies of the Liberals was Joseph Chamberlain (1836–1914).

Chamberlain's interest in the land problem was arrived at independently and stemmed from years before his acquaintance with Henry George's theories. Since the publication of *Progress and Poverty,* however, he had come to be

* [Michael Silagi, Dr. jur. et phil., is senior research fellow at the Institut für Völkerrecht der Georg-August Universität, Platz der Göttingen Sieben 5, Blauer Turm, D-3400 Göttingen, Germany.]

American Journal of Economics and Sociology, Vol. 50, No. 2 (April, 1991).

dependent in two contrasting ways upon the American social philosopher. On one hand, he was utterly fascinated by George's description and analysis of the prevailing conditions, especially in regard to landownership; but he was repelled, on the other hand, by George's proposed solution. While in his speeches he relied heavily on the arguments contained in *Progress and Poverty* and came increasingly under the spell of George's thought processes, he nevertheless developed his own practical land reform program out of an ever sharpening sense of contradiction to George. Yet in reality, Chamberlain's impact on the Liberal Party was to come about as a result, not of his anti-Georgist suggestions, but of his Georgist arguments.

Chamberlain's interest in the law of landed property, particularly in regard to the lot of the farmworkers, awakened in the time of his communal-political activities in Birmingham, where, from 1873 to 1876, he held the post of mayor. In the early 70s, Chamberlain began his collaboration with the reformers who, under the leadership of John Stuart Mill, had joined together to form the Land Tenure Reform Association.[1]

At a meeting of this Association in 1872, he supported a motion demanding a change of the laws concerning tenure. As he explained, to begin with, city dwellers and agricultural laborers had to be given, by means of electoral reforms, proportionate parliamentary representation, so that they could influence legislation. Then he continued: "If I were to write the heading of the next chapter of the Liberal programme I would write 'Free Schools,' 'Free Land,' and 'Free Church.' . . . In this country and this alone the agricultural labourer is entirely divorced from all interest in the soil he tills."[2]

But when soon thereafter, under the leadership of Joseph Arch, the "National Agricultural Labourers' Union," a unionized farmworker organization was formed, small farmers were denied the right to associate. It was Chamberlain who took their side and protested sharply against a union which locked out co-workers.[3] His espousal of the cause of the agricultural labourers became known far beyond the borders of Birmingham through his contributions to the *Fortnightly Review,* the periodical, founded in 1865, of the progressive forces within British Liberalism.[4]

In 1874, Chamberlain summarized his views in the *Review.* He noted the most urgent of all reforms was a change of the electoral system. But after that, an alteration of the existing agrarian order was the one measure which would be of the greatest direct use to the community at large. In this connection, he said:

> Sooner or later, laws which have no parallel in any other part of the world, which were elaborated in the interest of a small minority of the nation, and which failed to secure even their advantage, will certainly be remodelled. An absolute tenant-right will have to be conceded

to the English farmer; the Game Laws must be abolished or reformed; the rights of entail and settlement will have to be restricted within the narrowest limits; and some provision made for securing to small cultivators more frequent opportunities of proprietorship.[5]

II

Chamberlain's Position vs. George's

As a Radical Liberal politician, who, already half a decade prior to the publication of *Progress and Poverty,* had emphatically rejected the existing agrarian order, Chamberlain of course had to take George's theses into account after 1879. After all, these had found a substantial echo among just those whose lot the British Liberal wanted to ameliorate. The Georgist remedy of confiscation, through taxation, of the land rent was, however, fundamentally different from the proposals which Chamberlain and the co-authors of a "Radical Programme" began to spread at about that time. Among the most important points of this Radical Programme of the eighties belongs the assurance of "commensurate living space" for the urban proletariat,[6] as well as the improvement of the conditions of the agricultural laborers,[7] and the creation of a new class of independent, small farmers ("a new race of yeomen").[8]

As far as urban reorganization was concerned, this was to take place exclusively at the expense of the real estate owners: "The expense of making towns habitable for the toilers who dwell in them must be thrown on the land which their toil makes valuable, and without any effort on the part of the owners."[9] These owners, for their part, were to be prohibited from wringing disproportionately high increases in value from their land through a utilization both excessive and contrary to the interests of the community. Failing this, the land would have to be expropriated, in which case the owners could be compensated only for the actual, present value ("with no allowance for prospective value").[10]

The second objective, the creation of a healthy agricultural class, was to be attained through expropriation of the landlords against appropriate compensation and through support of the new yeomen by means of favorable government credit.[11]

In the final analysis, then, Chamberlain's plans called for a broader distribution of landed property, not the abolition of private land monopoly. George's effect on the "Radical Programme" is, nevertheless, unmistakeable; the influence of *Progress and Poverty* was, in fact, evident in just those comments with which Chamberlain warned against the American and his writings: The Radical Liberals regarded the urban and rural land reforms as "the two greatest and most pressing needs of [their] time,"[12] not least because they thus hoped to counter successfully the Georgism which they saw as 'dangerous.'

Pointing to the wide dissemination of *Progress and Poverty* and its radiating effects on the workingclass, Chamberlain called on the owners to recognize their responsibility for the lot of the poor. Otherwise these, stirred up by George's teachings, would demand measures just as cutting and unjust as the American's proposals. As antidote, he therefore urgently suggested the distribution of real property among those farmers who were working the fields. Chamberlain's views are illustrated here by two excerpts, one from an article in the *Fortnightly Review,* the other from a letter, both written in 1883. In the periodical, he writes as follows:

> The needs of the poor are gradually finding expression; the measures proposed for their relief are coming under discussion. The wide circulation of such books as *Progress and Poverty,* of Mr. Henry George, and the acceptance which his proposals have found among the working classes, are facts full of significance and warning. If something be not done quickly to meet the growing necessities of the case we may live to see theories as wild and methods as unjust as those suggested by the American economist adopted as the creed of no inconsiderable portion of the electorate.[13]

And in the letter, Chamberlain writes:

> Have you read two books lately published—*Progress and Poverty,* by Henry George, and *Land Nationalisation,* by A. Walton [sic—*i.e.* Wallace]? They come to the same conclusion, "L'ennemi, c'est le propriétaire," and they advocate the same remedy, namely, the confiscation of property in land. I am told that these books are being eagerly read by the working classes in London, and that the feeling in favour of drastic measures is growing. In all seriousness, if I were a large landowner I should be uneasy. They are so few, and the landless are so many. *There is only one way of giving security to this kind of property, and that is to multiply the owners of it.* Peasant proprietorship in one form or other, and on a large scale, is the antidote to the doctrines of confiscation which are now making converts.[14] (Emphasis supplied.)

In short, George wanted to eliminate land monopoly. But Chamberlain wanted to perpetuate it by creating additional small land monopolists: getting more allies for the hitherto limited number of landed proprietors, he hoped to secure them from expropriation. On the other hand Chamberlain did learn and adopt a great many ideas from George, and he was (according to his biographer J. L. Garvin) a thorough admirer and student of the American. Chamberlain also met George personally at a dinner of the Reform Club in April 1882,[15] and he was as profoundly shaken by George's description of the contrasts between the rich and the poor in *Progress and Poverty* as he previously had been through his contacts with Joseph Arch. Garvin reported:

> Chamberlain read it [*Progress and Poverty*] electrified. . . . A decade had passed since he had been moved by Joseph Arch, as now more potently by Henry George's eloquent pictures of the contemporary contrasts, and they were glaring, between the wealth of the few and the distress of the many.[16]

In fact, although Chamberlain recommended the plan of dividing up the large estates as a counter to Henry George's proposals, he followed *Progress and Poverty* extensively in his presentation of the social ills and their causes, most especially at public meetings where he was appealing directly to potential voters.

Thus, in a speech he gave in 1885 in Inverness, he said the following: "I have sometimes speculated upon what would have happened in this country if it had been possible to establish private property in air,"[17] and: "I read the other day that within recent years many valuable public rights had been lost beyond recovery. Lost! Gentlemen, do you not think that it is a very mild way of putting it? But why beyond recovery? I hope that the people will never admit that doctrine so dear to pilferers of every class that a theft is to be condoned because it escapes detection at the time."[18] In this speech, too, Chamberlain described "the sacred right of the landowners" as a fetish. All this sounds like *Progress and Poverty,* whether the talk is about the hypothetical consequences of establishing private property in air, or whether it is about the perception that the theft contained in the private acquisition of land is still robbery, because the statute of limitation does not apply to it.[19]

Equally reminiscent of George is Chamberlain's famous "Ransom" speech, in which he commented, that in the early years of the English social system every man had been born with natural rights, one of these being a claim to a part of his native soil; and that it was only later that communal ownership of this native earth was replaced by private landownership. And, Chamberlain continues, this arrangement, now that it had become institutionalized, might perhaps not be retractable. But then he asks what "ransom" the owners are willing to pay for the security they enjoy.[20]

Garvin describes Chamberlain's dilemma by saying that he was stirred by George's spirit; although he rejected George's dogmatic campaign, his crusade was against the system of the ownership of large landed properties. In vain, however, the English politician repeated that his ideal ("a new race of yeomen") represented the opposite of the nationalization of land.[21] The Radical Liberals and the Georgists were thrown into one pot by the speakers of the right wing of the Liberal Party and, even more so by the Conservatives. The Radicals were accused of making common cause with George, and were told that they were basically undistinguishable from the avowed followers of the American. Thus warned Lord Salisbury in 1884: "We are on an inclined plane leading from the position of Lord Hartington to that of Mr. Chamberlain and so on to the depths over which Mr. Henry George rules supreme,"[22] In the same vein, Lord Stanley of Alderley declared in the following year that a brochure about the land question from the pen of the radical candidate for the House of Commons, A. C. Fyffe, was "of the same nature though less in degree than the publications of Mr. Henry George."[23]

III

The Report of the Royal Commission

THE FACTORS which caused public opinion to classify the Radicals as moderate (or masked) Georgists were not any common elements as to the contents of their practical proposals, but the parallels in their presentation of the existing land order. Here Chamberlain's opponents forgot that he wanted to eliminate the miseries so forcefully described in *Progress and Poverty,* not by the introduction of the Single Tax, but by the creation of a broadly-based peasant proprietorship. The Radicals of the 19th century shared only George's view that the appropriation of the land (*i.e.,* of the land rent) by private persons was against natural law. But they did not draw the inference from this—despite Chamberlain's comment that a theft not immediately discovered was not therefore to be condoned—that a community could freely take back that of which, in contravention of natural law, they had been deprived: "In the largest number of cases the wrongful possession has been sanctified by time."[24] George, on the other hand, insisted that no custom contrary to natural law, however long in existence, could establish a new prerogative, and that private appropriation of rent by landowners was nothing more than indefinitely repeated theft. In George's view, as has already been discussed in detail, only confiscation of the land rent through taxation could abolish poverty and need, as well as reinstate social conditions in accord with natural law.[25]

The Radical Liberals regarded the latter view of the American as "visionary,"[26] while at the same time seeing the opposing viewpoint, that landownership should not be changed at all, as misguided. The same Fyffe (who was reproached by Stanley of Alderley for differing from George only in degree) objected to the reform suggested in *Progress and Poverty* on the grounds that it was "beyond practical politics."[27] On the other hand, Fyffe characterized his own project of creating a broadly-based peasant proprietorship as "the middle ground of the practicable."[28]

But despite this supposed incompatibility, repeatedly stressed by the Radicals, of their intention of dividing up large estates with George's Single Tax plan, all Radical Liberal reform proposals are, in fact, permeated by the spirit of *Progress and Poverty.* With good reason, therefore, R. H. Gretton says, "his [George's] theories coloured the whole of the Radical Programme."[29] Chamberlain's opponents were really not mistaken in believing that the author of *Progress and Poverty* had supplied more than merely the impetus for the development of the

Radical points concerning the land question. He had done so by persuading the Liberals of the injustice of the existing social arrangements and of the need for changing the applicable land law.

For the reformation of land law, the Radical Liberals demanded, in addition to the peasant proprietorship, a tax reform which had undeniable Georgist features: The "Radical Programme" speaks of "vexatious and restrictive taxes which press heavily upon industry,"[30] of the complexities and high cost of the collection of indirect taxes, taxes which the Radicals did not wish to abolish entirely, but to lower by increasing, simultaneously, taxes on real property.[31] In order to prevent, however, valuable land (*i.e.,* land urgently needed by the community) from being withheld from proper use, the radicals proposed to tax uncultivated land not according to its actual yield, but according to its market value.[32]

The latter principle—an unheard-of, yes, revolutionary, new, purely Georgist principle—was first mentioned in 1885, a short time after George's third trip to England. This was in the House of Commons. It found acceptance in the same year, in the concluding report issued by the "Commission on the Housing of the Working Classes" appointed in 1884. (One member of this Commission was Cardinal Henry Edward Manning who was to play a significant role favorable to Henry George at the intra-church discussion of *Progress and Poverty.*[33]) With the consent of Cardinal Manning, and at the instigation of another member of the Commission, Jesse Collings, a co-author of the "Radical Programme," a resolution was adopted which recommended the taxation of uncultivated, urban real property at a level of 4% of its value, for the following reason reminiscent of *Progress and Poverty:*

> At present, land available for building in the neighbourhood of our populous centres, though its capital value is very great, is probably producing a small yearly return until it is let for building. The owners of this land are rated, not in relation to the real value, but to the actual income. They can thus afford to keep their land out of market, and to part with only small quantities, so as to raise the price beyond the natural monopoly price which the land would command by its advantages of position. Meantime, the general expenditure of the town on improvements is increasing the value of their property. If this land were rated at, say, 4 per cent, on its selling value, the owners would have a more direct incentive to part with it to those who are desirous of building. . . . Their competition with one another would bring down the price paid for land which is now levied on urban enterprise by the adjacent landowners—a tax, be it remembered, which is no recompense for any industry and activity of the townspeople themselves.[34]

This paragraph from the report of the Royal Commission on Housing could have been taken straight out of a Georgist tract. It shows the extent to which Henry George's ideas had become accepted by 1885 in English politics, through the intercession of Liberal members of the House of Commons. Not without admiration, a George biographer, Charles A. Barker, remarks in this connection:

"Henry George's ideas had reached farther into the policy-making of Parliament than they ever had into the policy of the legislative [sic] of California."[35]

IV

The Consequences of the Commission's Report

THE CITED 1885 REPORT of the Commission became the point of departure for a systematic examination of the land problem in Great Britain's political circles. The propelling force behind the land reform efforts was the Liberal Party. Even after Joseph Chamberlain had parted from the Liberals, the demands for the reform of land law, which he had brought into the "Unauthorized Programme" of 1885, continued to exert an influence on the Liberal Party. Indeed, in 1889, the Liberal Party Congress passed a resolution calling for the taxation of land value.[36] The influence of Georgist ideas was still in the ascendancy.

The previously mentioned, noted Liberal publicist John A. Hobson (incidentally himself an opponent of the Single Tax, which he designated as "obvious injustice"[37]) thus assessed Henry George's effect in 1897, the year of the American's death: "Henry George may be considered to have exercised a more directly powerful formative and educative influence over English Radicalism of the last fifteen years than any other man."[38]

Following this campaign of enlightenment regarding land reform, there were numerous attempts during the final five years of the 19th century to shift the tax burden on real property to land alone. The beginning was made in Glasgow in 1895 when the corporate bodies of 518 communities demanded the power to impose taxes on land value only, apart from buildings and improvements.[39]

A Royal Commission was appointed in 1896 to examine the then existing system of community taxation and to make proposals for a fairer distribution of personal and property taxes. In 1901, a minority within the Commission proposed leaving the communities free to impose local land taxes.[40] From then on, a series of legislative proposals to this end were laid before the Lower House, but these were turned down consistently by the Conservative majority until 1906.[41]

In 1906, however, the Liberal Party won the majority in the House of Commons, and it appeared that things would be different. Among the Liberal M.P.'s, a "Land Value Parliamentary Committee" was formed (called, for short, the "Land Values Group"), which at Easter of 1906 had no less than 280 members.[42] Even then, however no bill instituting land tax became law. Despite the majority in the Lower House, all attempts at a Georgist-inspired tax reform were foiled by the vetoes in the House of Lords.[43] The far-reaching effects of these failures were to be seen later.

In 1909, the Liberals tried to evade the intervention of the House of Lords by means of a trick. David Lloyd George, then Chancellor of the Exchequer, tied the proposals for tax reform to the Budget estimate, and placed both together within the Budget bill before the Lower House. Now, the Budget had traditionally been the sole domain of the House of Commons for a quarter of a millennium. For 250 years, no Upper House had denied its approval to any Budget estimate. Confident of this custom hallowed by time, the Liberals sought to put through land value taxation.[44]

With his "People's Budget," as the proposal has gone down in British parliamentary history, Lloyd George had to close a budgetary gap of 15 million pounds, which had developed primarily because of the costs of a rapid buildup of the navy and of an old-age pension law passed the previous year. The needed funds were to be obtained through an increase in existing taxes and the imposition of new ones. Among the taxes to be introduced were those to be based on land assessments, particularly an "undeveloped land duty," a duty of ½ penny per pound of the value of unenclosed or fallow land, as well as an "increment value duty," a value increment tax, which was to be imposed at the time of property exchange and which was to amount to 20 percent of the difference between the value of the estate at the target-date, April 30, 1909, and the date of the exchange of property.[45]

The explanation offered by Lloyd George for the introduction of these new taxes is, actually, non-Georgist,[46] yet does utilize Georgist argumentation: "The country is in need of money and we are looking out for somebody to tax. . . . We don't want to tax industry. We don't want to tax enterprise. We don't want to tax commerce. What shall we tax? We will tax the man who is getting something that he never earned, that he never produced, and that by no law of justice and fairness ought ever to belong to him."[47]

The fiscal significance of these taxes would have been minimal to begin with, since the Liberal government shrank from a consistent application of their land reform ideas. (The Georgist A. W. Madsen wrote, not without bitterness, about the "undeveloped land duty": "That tax is made almost a dead letter by numerous restrictions and exemptions."[48]) All new land taxes would have brought in, during 1909, if actually collected, 500,000 pounds. Their great significance lay in the fact that their actual imposition would have necessitated a reassessment of all land values throughout Great Britain, something which Geiger has perceptively labeled "a tremendous undertaking, comparable to the Domesday Book of William the Conqueror."[49] The ensuing, dogged opposition of the landlords, in fact, was not aimed so much at the planned taxes as at this general land value appraisal. They saw in it, perhaps not unjustifiably, the first step toward an all-embracing land reform; such reassessment would, after all, have ascertained the actual land value—without the value of the installations, buildings, and improvements of each parcel of land.

This, in turn, would have created the basis for a separate tax on the bare land, as well as the possible basis for the introduction of a more or less Georgist-oriented system of taxation.

In 1911, Lloyd George openly expressed himself about this problem: "When it [*i.e.,* the valuation] is accomplished it will be very great piece of work. It will be of enormous value, not merely for the taxation we imposed under the Budget of 1909, but the reconsideration of the problem of local as well as Imperial taxation."[50]

In 1909, then, the great question was whether the Lords would again reject the plan for new land taxes, in spite of its being part, this time, of the Budget. They did so. In 1909, they broke the tradition of 250 years because they wanted to thwart the government's intention of land reform. The Upper House turned down the "People's Budget."

V

Greater Democracy Through a Constitutional Crisis

THE CONSEQUENCE was a constitutional crisis. The attention of the stirred-up public, however, was turned only secondarily to the problem of whether the Commons should have introduced a land value tax through the back door of budgetary legislation. Now, it was fundamentally the prerogatives and authority of the Upper House that became the central question. In the Lower House, in answer to the veto in the House of Lords which basically had been directed at the land reform section, a bill was introduced and passed which demanded a drastic curb of the power of the Upper House.

In consequence, two elections for members of the House of Commons were held in 1910. Both times, the majority of the electorate voted against the Lords. The outcome of these elections was, in effect, a popular referendum in favor of the Commons and against the Lords. After the first ballot in early 1910, the Budget was passed. Furthermore, in December after the second election a Parliament Act became law which conceded to the House of Lords only a deferred veto—but not for fiscal proposals, for "money bills". According to this Act, money bills could be enacted immediately, if necessary without the assent of the Lords.[51]

Clearly, then, the decision of Lloyd George to tax real property more heavily and in a manner based on land reform principles led to a severe conflict, at the end of which stood a democratic constitutional revolution in favor of the Commons. Haldvan Koht said: "Thus a whole revolution was brought about. . . .

The ideas of Henry George proved capable of stimulating far-reaching practical measures."[52]

Yet in fact no practical measures resulted along the lines of the Georgist program. Already in 1920, even before the end of the land reassessment, which had been delayed by the war, the regulations for land taxation were annulled.[53] A further attempt by the Labour Chancellor of the Exchequer Philip Snowden, to push through the land value assessment and land tax together with the Finance Act of 1931, was unsuccessful,[54] even though it was thoroughly supported by liberals in the Labour party, including Herbert Morrison, Ramsay MacDonald and Josiah Wedgwood.

It is evident that just as much as Georgism proved to be a catalyst within the political Left of the process leading to the development of the Labour Party, it acted, within the area of Liberal Party politics, as ferment for the constitutional crisis culminating in the weakening of the House of Lords.

It should be mentioned at this point that Georgism was more successful in the overseas territories of the British Empire than in Europe, in the mother country. In particular, in some provinces of Australia and New Zealand, laws were enacted, for the most part in the closing years of the 19th century, which provided for a land tax on net value. This thereby created as well the foundation for the prerequisite general land value assessment. It is true that George's guidelines were altered, mostly by supposed improvements, and nowhere did the new tax laws bring with them the abolition of other taxes as George had sought. In each case, rather, it was simply a matter of the introduction of an additional kind of tax which appeared especially just—in conformity with natural law—but which was intended to replace at most one or two other—unjust—types of land tax.[55] But it would be a mistake to conclude that because the Georgist movement in Great Britain has yet to achieve the taxation of land values it has been a failure. The movement can be charged with underestimating the political power of the land monopolists and the resources they command; indeed, this is true of its assessment of all monopolists.

But besides the greater democratization of the British oligarchy, George and his followers also achieved the recognition of the social question in a country dominated by an aristocracy, a nobility and a plutocracy. This domination was responsible for the decline in the British economy and British culture. "The true measure of George," said a perceptive historian,[56] "is found in the effect of his crusade against suffering in the minds and hearts of the British people."

"George had helped start a new society," he added, "though neither he nor his followers were able to lead it." At least not then.

Notes

1. Elsie E. Gulley, *Joseph Chamberlain and English Social Politics* (New York, 1926), pp. 197, 200.

2. Quoted in J. L. Garvin, *The Life of Joseph Chamberlain,* (London, 1932), Vol. I, pp. 149 *ff.*

3. Gulley, *op. cit.*, pp. 201 *ff.*

4. See "*Fortnightly Review*" in the *Oxford Companion to English Literature,* 4th ed. (London: 1967), p. 309.

5. Joseph Chamberlain, "The Next Page of the Liberal Programme," *Fortnightly Review,* 16 (N.S.), 1874, p. 419.

6. [Frank Harris]. (The authors of the anonymously published "Radical Programme" are named in Joseph Chamberlain, *A Political Memoir* [London, 1953, p. 109]). See also "The Radical Programme, III.-The Housing of the Poor in Town," *Fortnightly Review,* 34 (N.S.), 1883, pp. 587 *ff.*

7. Jesse Collings, "The Radical Programme, IV.-The Agricultural Labourer," *Fortnightly Review,* 34 (N.S.), 1883, pp. 609 *ff.*

8. Garvin, *op. cit.,* Vol. II, p. 79.

9. Joseph Chamberlain, "Labourers' and Artisans' Dwellings," *Fortnightly Review,* 34 (N.S.), 1883, p. 775.

10. *Loc. cit.*

11. (Francis Adams), "The Radical Programme, Vii. Taxation and Finance," *Fortnightly Review,* 38 (N.S.), 1885, pp. 133 *ff.*

12. Garvin, *op. cit.,* Vol. I, p. 552.

13. *Loc. cit., Fortnightly Review,* 34 (N.S.) 1883, pp. 761 *ff.*

14. Dorothy Nevill, *Under Five Reigns,* 5th ed. (London, 1911), pp. 206 *ff.*

15. Henry George Jr., *The Life of Henry George,* New York, 1960, p. 371.

16. Garvin, *op. cit.,* Vol. I, pp. 305 *ff.*

17. *Ibid.,* Vol. II, pp. 385 *ff.*

18. *Loc. cit.*

19. *Cf. Progress and Poverty,* (New York, 1979), pp. 333 *ff.*, 363.

20. "What ransom will property pay for the security it now enjoys?" Quoted in Garvin, *op. cit.,* Vol. I, p. 548. On the historical discussion in the 'Ransom' speech, compare the parallel passages in *Progress and Poverty,* Book VII, Ch. 4, "Private Property in Land Historically Considered," pp. 366 *ff.*

21. Garvin writes, "Stirred up by the spirit, rejecting the dogma of Henry George's *jehad* against landlordism, (Chamberlain) often pointed out that his ideal, a new race of yeoman, was the opposite of land nationalization." *Op. cit.,* Vol. II, p. 79.

22. Quoted by Garvin, *op. cit.,* Vol. I, p. 462.

23. Stanley of Alderley, "Radical Theorists on Land," *Fortnightly Review,* 37 (N.S.), 1885, p. 297.

24. Adams, *op. cit.,* p. 133.

25. *Progress and Poverty,* p. 363.

26. C. A. Fyffe, "The Coming Land Bill," *Fortnightly Review,* 37 (N.S.), 1885, p. 284.

27. *Loc. cit.*

28. *Loc. cit.*

29. R. H. Goetton, *A Modern History of the English People,* 2nd ed. (London, 1913), Vol. I, p. 143.

30. Adams, *op. cit.,* p. 135.

31. *Op. cit.,* pp. 134 *ff.*

32. Gulley, *op. cit.*, p. 218.
33. Charles Albro Barker, *Henry George* (New York, 1955), pp. 487–88.
34. Quoted from P. Wilson Raffan, *The Policy of the Land Values Group in the House of Commons* (London, 1912), pp. 3 *ff.*
35. Barker, *op. cit.*, p. 414.
36. Raffan, *op. cit.*, p. 3.
37. John A. Hobson, *The Taxation of Unearned Incomes* (London, 1908), p. 8 and *passim.*
38. Hobson, "The Influence of Henry George in England," *Fortnightly Review,* 62 (N.S.) 1897, p. 844.
39. Raffan, *op. cit.*, p. 6.
40. George Raymond Geiger, *The Philosophy of Henry George* (New York, 1933), p. 409.
41. Raffan, *op. cit.*, p. 6.
42. A. W. Madsen, "Great Britain," *Single Tax Yearbook* (New York, 1917), pp. 103 *ff.*
43. See Lawrence, *op. cit.*, p. 129.
44. *Ibid.*, pp. 140 *ff.*
45. H. Köppe gives a detailed description of the new taxes in the "People's Budget" in "Die englische Bodensteuerreform," *Jahrbuch der Bodenreform,* VI (1910), pp. 1 *ff.*, 34 *ff.*
46. The English Labour party politician Lord Douglas of Barloch (*Who's Who,* London, 1972, p. 894) says about Lloyd George: "He never showed any understanding of the principle of the taxation of land values." ("Is No Bread Better Than Half a Loaf?" *Land & Liberty,* 79 (1972), p. 39.
47. David Lloyd George, *The Lords, the Land and the People* (London, 1909), p. 50.
48. Madsen, *op. cit.*, p. 96.
49. Geiger, *op. cit.*, p. 413; the Domesday Book was put together in 1086 on orders of William the Conqueror. It contains statements about property conditions, size, and value of the entire English land and real estate.
50. Quoted in Raffan, *op. cit.*, p. 16.
51. R. C. K. Ensor, *England 1870–1914* (Oxford, 1936, 1952), pp. 424 *ff.*
52. Haldvan Koht, *The American Spirit in Europe* (Philadelphia, 1949), p. 203.
53. Geiger, *op. cit.*, p. 414.
54. Lawrence, *op. cit.*, p. 180.
55. On this, see *The Operation of Land-Value Rating in Various Countries* (Memorandum of Evidence submitted by the United Committee for the Taxation of Land Values, Ltd., to the Enquiry Committee appointed by the British Government), (London, 1949), *passim,* and E. J. Craigie, "Australia" in *Land-Value Taxation Around the World,* eds. H. G. Brown *et al.* (New York, 1955), pp. 3–24, as well as Roland O'Regan, "New Zealand," *op. cit.*, pp. 27–36. (One is strongly tempted to present a more detailed discussion of the Georgist successes in the British overseas territories but they fall outside the scope of this work.)
56. Lawrence, *op. cit.*, p. 191.

6

Henry George and Europe:

Precursors of Land Reform in Germany; Marx and the Land Question; the Beginnings of the Georgist Movement in the Empire

By Michael Silagi*
Translated by Susan N. Faulkner

Abstract. Henry George's *Progress and Poverty* was translated into German and published in Germany in 1881, a little more than a year after its publication in America. But it was not through George's own words that his ideas first became known there. Germany already had *land reformers,* organized in small societies. They made his teachings known. However, unlike the case in Britain, Germany's leftists did not welcome George's land reform ideas. True, *Karl Marx* recognized and wrote about the role the land question played in the exploitation of labor and in his third volume of *Capital* took basic positions parallel to George's; it was published long after *Progress and Poverty.* The hostility of *Wilhelm Liebknecht* toward land reform reflected the German public's disinterest in the land question and may explain why Marx concentrated on appealing to the urban industrial worker.

I

Arnd, Gossen, Stamm and Other Precursors

The dissemination of Henry George's ideas in Wilhelmian Germany took a less stormy course, and their effects a totally different direction, than in Victorian and Edwardian England. In contrast to Great Britain, where the study of *Progress and Poverty* strongly influenced the Liberal and Leftist circles, in Germany the teachings of the American social philosopher had only an indirect influence—via the organized land reformers. These publicists at first banded together in small, more or less short-lived societies.

In 1898, Adolf Damaschke founded the Union of German Land Reformers and eventually developed it into the largest land reform association in the world. Damaschke, similar to the leaders of the German land reform movement before 1898, was a keen student of George's social philosophy. The Georgist doctrine, though altered and diluted, was to influence in no small measure, thanks to

* Michael Silagi, Dr. jur. et phil., is a senior research fellow at the Institut für Vökerrecht der Georg-August, Universität, Platz der Göttinger Sieben 5, Blauer Turm, D-3400 Göttingen, Germany.

American Journal of Economics and Sociology, Vol. 51, No. 2 (April, 1992).

Damaschke's Union's proddings, legislators and administrators in both the German Empire and the Weimar Republic.

The differing reception of George's works in Germany from that in Great Britain was due, first of all, to quite different economic situations. In 1876, Bismarck had initiated in the German Empire a change from free trade to a regime of national protectionism.[1] He thereby avoided the bloodletting among agriculturalists such as had taken place in the British Isles. This period in Germany was marked too by the beginnings of the "first great socio-political formation of the modern industrial-capitalistic society."[2]

Just as important as the economic differences, however, were the divergent ideo-historical assumptions in both countries. Unlike in Great Britain, when the first translation of *Progress and Poverty* appeared in Germany in 1881 there already existed a well-organized, ideologically established Left—the Socialist Workers Party. But land reform ideas did not play a role in its development, as will be shown subsequently, since its ideology ascribed no particular importance to land.

Before discussing this point further, however, we shall comment briefly on Henry George's German "precursors."

German authors who had published proposals for land value taxation (such as Karl Arnd[3]) or for land nationalization (such as Hermann Heinrich Gossen[4]) elicited no response from the public.

The only forerunner of Henry George who is of some significance is the physician August Theodor Stamm (1822–1892). To be sure, he had no practical influence on the development of the German land reform movement; yet through shocking accusations of plagiarism against George, he caused the latter to take a position which cleared up the question of George's own originality. Besides, his attempt—though unsuccessful—to win the Socialists' support for land reform goals is interesting for the history of land reform ideas in Germany.

In 1871, Stamm had published a book with the title (translated), *The Salvation for Needy Mankind.*[5] In it, he called, *inter alia,* for the nationalization of land.[6] (He also took up in great detail such matters as control of epidemics,[7] limitation of the variety of languages[8] and the fight against the "greed of the churches for property."[9])

For the propagation of the objectives stated in his book, among them that of land reform, he founded in 1874 a Society for Humanism. But it was dissolved four years later, since, as Stamm himself stated, "it simply could not have succeeded for the time being."[10]

In the preface to the third, revised and expanded edition of his book issued in 1884, Stamm made the following assertion about George's *Progress and Poverty:*

"*Progress and Poverty* was published . . . as a result of the previously initiated movement [i.e., through the Society for Humanism founded in 1874]. The main conclusions of *The Salvation for Needy Mankind,* published already in 1870/71, and of the resultant theses of the Society for Humanism are rendered here in the terminology of the old school of political economy."[11]

To imply that George had merely repeated Stamm's own conclusions, with which he was supposed to have become acquainted through the propaganda of the Society for Humanism, is absurd on the face of it. Firstly, according to Heinrich Freese, land reform leader and author of a history of the movement, the activities of this "modest Society . . . were known only to the inner circle of the membership."[12] Secondly, George already had published his first treatise, *Our Land and Land Policy,* three years before the founding of the Society.[13]

But beyond that, a comparison of the two books shows that the authors have little in common. In Stamm's case, the land reform ideas are intermingled with a series of philanthropic and socialistic goals, such as the previously mentioned epidemic control and a demand for the creation of "national industries."[14]

The symbiosis of natural law and economics, in other words, the core of George's tenets, is completely lacking in the theories of the German physician. *The Salvation for Needy Mankind* is not grounded in natural law, nor does the author make any effort to introduce, where necessary, a politico-economic perspective.

At the same time, when Stamm does describe facts related to political economy—without, throughout, defining his terms—he enmeshes himself in contradictions.[15]

Stamm's insinuations against Henry George in the preface of the third edition of *The Salvation for Needy Mankind* can be explained only by his idea, one that must be called pathological, that he was being plagiarized by other land reformers. To this point, Stamm did, in fact, suggest in the same preface that Alfred Russel Wallace[16] was indebted to him for his work about land reform.[17] Furthermore, he carried on a fight lasting many years, which even went through the courts,[18] with the founder of the German land reform movement, Michael Flürscheim, about the question of priority of authorship.

In 1887, George responded to the physician's accusations with an open letter to the German land reformers. This letter was published the same year in the land reform periodical *Deutsch Land* (German Land) in a "rather awkward" translation. [The text is here translated back into English with no effort to follow the supposedly "awkward" rendering—tr.]

"At the time when I wrote *Progress and Poverty* (and in fact until quite recently), I had never heard of Dr. Stamm; but I am ready to grant Dr. Stamm the honor of having gone into battle before me. When I spoke in Oxford, England,

Mr. Marshall, the Professor of Economics, declared that there was nothing in *Progress and Poverty* that was both new and true. I replied that I was quite willing to accept this characterization of my book, since what is true cannot be new. And that which gives me the certainty that the conclusions I have reached are essentially true is the fact that so many persons have independently reached the same ones."[19]

II

German Marxists and Land Reform

AUGUST THEODOR STAMM is of interest for the history of land reform in Germany, not because of his writings, but because of his activities among the Social Democrats, since, as mentioned earlier, he tried to convince the socialists of the paramount importance of land nationalization. For this purpose, he joined the Social Democratic Workers Party,[20] in whose Sixth Party Congress in Coburg, in 1874, he participated as delegate. There, he moved that the following sentence be placed at the end of the party platform decided upon in 1869, in Eisenach, a platform which, incidentally, made no mention whatsoever of the land reform question[21]: "A very significant part of unearned income is derived from private real property; we therefore demand the total abolition of private landownership through a just process of expropriation."[22] By a vote of 49 to four, the party conference refused to even discuss this motion.[23]

The Marxist, Wilhelm Liebknecht, who had founded the Social Democrats in 1869, commented as follows at the Congress on the proposed motion: "Stamm's proposals . . . are based on a fundamentally false view. The land does not have any economic value without human labor. To make human labor free, that is the goal of Social Democracy. When labor is free, land will also be free."[24]

In the following year, 1875, at the merger convention at Gotha, the Socialist Workers Party (as it called itself now, dropping the qualifier "Democratic") passed a new program which, despite some concessions to the undogmatic Lassalleans, carried the imprint of the "Eisenachers" and was composed largely by Liebknecht.[25] At the beginning of the program one finds again his emphasis of the previous year on the central position of labor: "Labor is the source of all wealth and of all culture,"[26] and the statement continues: "In today's society, the means of production are monopolized by the capitalist class; the consequent dependence of the working class is the cause of all misery and of slavery in every form."[27] The motion put forward by a few delegates from Leipzig, to expand this sentence to include the word "landowners" to those monopolizing the means of production, was defeated.[28]

In the explanation of the causes of economic poverty, which became part of the Gotha program, there is no word about the importance of private land monopoly for the capitalistic system. This may well be because this program was tailored quite deliberately for the urban workers. It sought to explain "misery and slavery" of only the industrial proletariat, and in fact in the cities the land-ownership question did not, at first glance, play a decisive role. In the foreground here was the confrontation between the working class and industrial capital. It was for this reason that Liebknecht failed to realize that the dependence of the working class was brought about at least equally by the monopolistic position of the landowners.

In contrast to Liebknecht, Karl Marx was thoroughly convinced of the special significance of land for production, and of land-ownership conditions for the capitalistic economic order. In his "Margin Notes to the Program of the German Workers Party,"[29] a critique of the Gotha program, he wrote as follows about Liebknecht's thesis that labor was the sole source of wealth and culture:

"Labor is not the source of all wealth. Nature is equally the source of commodities (which is, after all, what actual wealth consists of!) as labor, which is itself but the manifestation of a force of nature."[30] Marx here held a view similar to Henry George, who entitled one chapter of *Progress and Poverty* "The Enslavement of Laborers the Ultimate Result of Private Property in Land."[31]

It followed for Marx, according to his critique of the first sentence of the Gotha program, "from the natural exigence of labor that the man who has no other property than his working power will have to be the slave of other men who have made themselves owners of the objective working conditions,"[32] first and foremost the slave of landowners.[33]

Marx, furthermore, sees in the monopoly of landowners, the foundation of the capitalistic monopoly. He comments thus on the statement in the Gotha program that the monopoly over the means of production lies in the hands of the capitalistic class:

"In today's society, the means of production are monopolized by landowners (the monopoly of landed property is actually the basis of the capitalistic monopoly) and of the capitalists."[33]

Equally critical of the statement regarding capitalistic monopoly, Friedrich Engels wrote in a letter in 1875 to August Bebel, co-founder of the Social Democrats in 1869, about the Gotha program: "The whole matter is utterly disorganized, confused, incoherent, illogical, and disgraceful. If there were, among the bourgeois press, even a single critical mind, he would have gone through this program sentence by sentence, examined each one for its real content, exposed all the nonsense to the light of day, developed the contradictions and economic blunders (for example: that the means of labor are today under 'the monopoly of the capitalistic class,' as if there were no landowners; that talk about 'liberation of work,' rather than of the working-class—actually, work is, on the contrary, much too free today!), and would have made our Party horribly ridiculous."[34]

With regard to the "Margin Notes to the Program of the German Workers Party," these were not thoughts developed *ad hoc.* (These "glosses" were labeled as the sum total of Marx's entire work by the publishers of the edition cited here.)[35] Marx's views about the significance of landownership conditions are also detailed in *Capital:*

The 24th chapter of the first volume, entitled "The So-Called Original Accumulation," is taken up, to a large extent, by the land question. The author writes about the origin of the capitalistic class: "The expropriation of the rural producer, the farmer, from the land is the foundation of the whole process."[36] In the third volume, Marx speaks no longer only of the expropriation of the farmer, but also of the "expropriation of the great mass of the people from the land" as the prior condition for capitalistic production. He stresses, moreover, that the monopoly of landownership is not merely a "historical" presupposition, for it "remains the continual foundation of the capitalistic production method as well as of all previous production methods which rest on the exploitation of the masses."[37]

Similar to George, Marx also sees the difference between capitalist and landowner as lying in their different relationships to the production process. In the third volume of the *Capital,* he says: "To the same degree to which [the production of value added and product added] develops, the capacity of real property develops so as to snatch away an ever-increasing part of this value added by means of its monopoly over land. . . . The capitalist at least is an independent functionary in the development of such value added and product added. But the landowner has merely to take possession, without any effort on his part, of this incremental share of the value added and product added."[38]

No doubt Franz Oppenheimer had in mind these comments by Marx regarding the nature and effects of the landowner's monopolistic position when he wrote: "Marxists scoff at Henry George and all other 'land reformers' because they indict the monopoly of the soil alone. They are pained when I quote certain sentences of their own master, proving him to be one of us heretics."[39]

This analysis of the social ills[40] would have led one to expect that the mature Marx would have placed, among the first items in his catalog of demands, the expropriation of the landowners. But in actuality, Marx's position closely resembled the Gotha program of 1875 in practical terms. His fight, too, was directed primarily against industrial capital, while in his work as a whole the subject of land monopoly, which he recognized as playing a special role in capitalistic exploitation, receded far into the background.[41]

The Anglo-American historian Francis Neilson tried to give a psychological explanation for this fact: Marx had come to the realization only after completion of 700 pages of his chief work, and he did not have the strength to start over again.[42]

In reality, Marx, already at the beginning of writing *Capital,* saw in the land the "universal means of labor," the "*locus standi,*" the "area of operations" for the workers.[43] If he did not draw the expected conclusions from these observations, it may have been because of the consideration that tenant farmers and agricultural laborers, who felt the burden of land monopoly most directly, were hardly accessible to his ideas.[44] For a revolutionary movement one could win over only an urban proletariat; this seemed capable of being mobilized against industrial capital, but hardly against landed property.

But the fact is that, aside from such tactical considerations, Marx was thoroughly in agreement with Henry George regarding the theoretical assessment of the production factor, land. The teachings of both see the private monopoly of land as the ultimate cause of the virtual enslavement of the workers and demand (according to the formulation of the Communist Manifesto) the "utilization of land rent for national expenditures."[45]

Still, George wanted only land values to be confiscated; Marx and his followers espoused the nationalization of capital as well as of land. In their propaganda, capital played, as already discussed, the leading role, indeed for Liebknecht the only one. George regarded land rent as the only legitimate source of revenue for the State; capital wealth and interest as well as wages were to remain untaxed private property. The socialist program, in contrast, saw "in the private property arrangements no limits whatsoever for the objectives of taxation policy . . . but rather [viewed] the diminution of private property as a path toward the desired form of 'Economic democracy.' " (Johannes Messner[46]).

To achieve this goal, German socialism advocated the imposition of a tax, the source of which was to be the yield from the land *and* from capital *and* from labor, namely the "total product of the production processes in the state."[47] In the Gotha program of 1875, as had been the case in the 1869 Eisenach program,[48] a "single, progressive income tax for state and communities instead of all prevailing . . . taxes"[49] is called for, a tax which had only its singleness in common with Henry George's "Single Tax."[50]

Notes

1. Wilhelm Treue, *Deutsche Geschichte von 1806 bis 1890* (Berlin, 1961), p. 113.
2. *Op. cit.,* p. 115*ff.*

3. Karl Arnd (1788–1877; on the biography *cf.* Peter Fuchs, "Arnd, Karl," *Neue Deutsche Biographie,* (NDB) I (Berlin, 1953), p. 357, and Louise Sommer, "Arnd, Karl," *Encyclopaedia of the Social Sciences,* II (New York, 1953), p. 218). He proposed in his book *Die naturgemässe Steuer* (Frankfurt, 1852) a single land tax (*passim*). But, unlike George, he believed such a tax would result in maintaining a low wage level (*op. cit.,* p. 321).

4. Hermann Heinrich Gossen (1810–1877; on his biography see Alexander Mahr, "Gossen, Hermann Heinrich," NDB VI (Berlin, 1964), p. 649*ff,* and Friedrich A. Hayek, "Gossen, Hermann Heinrich," *Encyclopaedia of the Social Sciences,* VII (New York, 1953), p. 3)), in his work *Entwicklung der Gesetze des menschlichen Verkehrs und der daraus fliessenden Regeln für menschliches Handeln* (Braunschweig, 1854), Gossen also demanded the nationalization of land with compensation of the owners (p. 250ff.)

5. August Theodor Stamm, *Die Erlösung der darbenden Menschheit* (Zurich, 1871); in 1873, a second edition appeared there which was enlarged by an appendix, but was otherwise unchanged.

6. *Op. cit.,* p. 128ff.

7. *Op. cit.,* p. 190ff.

8. *Op. cit.,* p. 258ff.

9. *Op. cit.,* p. 50ff.

10. August Theodor Stamm, *Die Erlösung der Darbenden Menschheit* [sic], 3rd rev. and enlarged edition (Stuttgart, 1884), p. XXVI.

11. *Op. cit.,* p. xxvii; *cf.* also Stamm, *Die sozial-politische Bedeutung der Bodenreform* (Minden, 1885), p. 11.

12. Heinrich Freese, *Die Bodenreform* (Berlin, 1918), p. 46.

13. *Cf.* Silagi, *American Journal of Economics and Sociology,* 45 (1986), p. 207.

14. Stamm, *Die Erlösung* . . ., 1st ed., p. 167*ff.*

15. Two examples of contradictions in the *Erlösung der darbenden Menschheit:* 1) Stamm disputes that capital is "accumulated labor," and this because its acquisition rests largely on "unpaid surplus labor" (1st ed., p. 110) and thus on an unjust basis; as if unpaid ("surplus") labor were not also some kind of labor. 2) Stamm writes: "Individual property is a blessing. . . . The goods which man acquires through labor he may keep as his property as far as he wishes." (*op. cit.,* p. 133). Accordingly, the individual should also, if he wished, be permitted to keep the interest-bearing portion of the goods produced by him. But precisely that the author denies a few pages later, where he condemns "interest created without labor by the capital owner" (*op. cit.,* p. 136).

16. *Cf.* Silagi, AJES, 48 (1989), p. 116*ff.*

17. Stamm, *Die Erlösung* . . ., 3rd ed., p. XXIX f.

18. *Cf.* [Michael Flürscheim], "Wer ist der erste deutsche Vorkämpfer für die Bodenreform?" *Deutsch Land,* II (Bubenheim, 1888), pp. 51–55.

19. "Ein Brief von Henry George," *Deutsch Land,* I, 1887, p. 68 f.

20. Adolf Damaschke, *Geschichte der Nationalökonomie,* II, 13th ed. (Jena, 1922), p. 410.

21. *Protokoll über die Verhandlungen des Allgemeinen Deutschen Sozialdemokratischen Arbeiterkongresses zu Eisenach am 7., 8. und 9. August 1869* (Leipzig, 1869), *passim.*

22. *Protokoll über den sechsten Congress der Sozial-demokrati-schen Arbeiterpartei abgehalten zu Coburg am 18., 19., 20. und 21. Juli 1874* (Leipzig, 1874), p. 76; the original, longer form of Stamm's proposal can be found in the same work, p. 6f.

23. *Op. cit.,* p. 80.

24. *Op. cit.,* p. 79.

25. *Cf.* Ludwig Bergsträsser, *Geschichte der politischen Parteien in Deutschland,* 8/9th ed. (Munich, 1955), p. 170.

26. "Protokoll des Vereinigungs-Kongresses der Sozialdemokraten Deutschlands, abgehalten zu Gotha, vom 22. bis 27. Mai 1875," in *Die ersten deutschen Sozialisten-Kongresse* (Frankfurt, 1906), pp. 68–148.

27. *Loc. cit.*

28. *Op. cit.*, p. 74.

29. Karl Marx, "Randglossen zum Programm der Deutschen Arbeiterpartei," *Kritik des Gothaer Programms,* 3rd ed. (Berlin, 1946), pp. 14–34 (initially published incomplete under the title "Zur Kritik des sozialdemokratischen Parteiprogramms" in *Die Neue Zeit,* IX, 1, 1890–91, pp. 561–575.

30. "Randglossen . . .," p. 14.

31. *Progress and Poverty,* p. 345.

32. "Randglossen . . .," p. 15.

33. For Marx, the "objective working conditions" are not the "things which mediate between the effect of labor and its object" (Karl Marx, *Das Kapital,* I, Vol. 23, of the Marx-Engels joint edition, published, Inst. für Marxismus-Leninismus beim ZK der SED, 7th ed. (Berlin, 1972, p. 195)). Thus, they are not the "means of production" but the "objective conditions which are required for the [labor] process to take place. They do not enter into this process directly, but without them it cannot go on, or only incompletely. The general means of labor of this kind is . . . the land itself, for it gives the worker his *locus standi* and to his process the field of employment. Means of labor of this sort which are mediated through work are, *e.g.,* edifices of labor, canals, streets etc." (*Loc. cit.*) The concept of the objective working conditions, therefore, stands for the classical production factor, land, and Marx here includes the improvements with land, rather than with capital, the "means of production." "Owners of the objective working conditions"—consequently—are for Marx in foremost place the landowners.

34. "Randglossen . . .," p. 17.

35. The letter is reprinted by August Bebel, *Aus meinem Leben,* II (Stuttgart, 1911), p. 277 f. (278).

36. *Kritik des Gothaer Programms,* p. 3.

37. *Das Kapital,* I, p. 741*ff.*

38. Karl Marx, *Das Kapital,* III, Vol. 25, of the Marx-Engels Joint Edition, publ., Inst. für Marxismus-Leninismus beim ZK der SED, 4th ed. (Berlin, 1970), p. 630.

39. *Op. cit.*, p. 651.

40. Franz Oppenheimer, "Communism and the World Crisis, IV," *American Journal of Economics and Sociology,* II, 1942–43, p. 61.

41. On similar statements by other socialists *cf.* Max Hirsch, *Democracy versus Socialism,* 2nd ed. (Leeds, 1924), p. 452*ff.*

42. "Marx focuses his attention primarily on the factory, and only incidentally and accidentally on the land on which the factory was built." (John Haynes Holmes, "Henry George and Karl Marx," *American Journal of Econ. and Sociology,* VI, 1946–47, p. 162.

43. "When Marx and Engels became conscious of this phenomenon it is difficult to say. But no one that I have read has explained why Marx put the cart before the horse in the first seven parts of his work. Not until the chapter on 'The So-called Primitive Accumulation' does he give the reader the full story of the expropriation of the tillers of the soil and, consequently, the congestion of labor in towns. How different his work would have been if he had dealt with the cause of the evil conditions before he touched the effect. It seemed as if he was suddenly struck—after writing more than 700 pages—by the fallacy of his own creation, for he says: 'The expropriation of the agricultural producer, of the peasant, from the soil is the basis of the whole process.' Surely it is amazing that our authors did not see the significance of the historical evidence

they turned up about primitive communities. . . . It seems to me that they learned the cause of the trouble too late and they had not the wit or courage to reconstruct the work upon a sound economic basis." (Francis Neilson, "The Twilight of Marx," *American Journal of Economics and Sociology,* VIII, 1948–49, pp. 13–15.

44. *Das Kapital,* I, p. 195; *cf.* note 33, above.

45. *Cf.* Hans Georg Lehmann, *Die Agrarfrage in der Theorie und Praxis der deutschen und internationalen Sozialdemokratie.* (Tübingen, 1970), p. 1*ff.*, espec. p. 7.

46. Karl Marx, Friedrich Engels, *Manifest der Kommunistischen Partei* (Berlin, 1948), p. 32; see also Oscar J. Hammen, "Marx and the Agrarian Question," *American Historical Review,* 77, 1972, pp. 679–704, *passim,* and p. 683: "From a theoretical point of view Marx and Engels always felt that the peasant, farm tenant, and agricultural worker were subjected to the same nightmare of exploitation by the bourgeois, capitalist society as were the proletariat, even if in a less apparent, direct, and massive manner."

47. Johannes Messner, *Das Naturrecht,* 5th ed. (Innsbruck, 1966), p. 906.

48. Arno Auerswald, *Beiträge zur Lehre von der einzigen Steuer* (Greifswald, 1922), p. 87.

49. "Protokoll . . . Eisenach . . .," p. 37.

50. "Protokoll des Vereinigungskongresses . . . zu Gotha," p. 69.

51. On this problem *cf.* Adolf Damaschke, *Marxismus und Bodenreform* (Jena, 1922), *passim,* and Frank McEachran, *Henry George and Karl Marx* (New York, 1936), *passim.*

7

Henry George and Europe:

Early Efforts to Organize Germany's Land Reformers Failed, But the Pioneers Won a National Demonstration

By MICHAEL SILAGI*

Translated by SUSAN N. FAULKNER

ABSTRACT. *Michael Flürscheim,* an industrialist, sought in 1885 to organize in *Germany* a society of *land reformers.* Only 20 responded to his call. Soon afterwards two journalists, did respond and organized a group called the *Land League.* It disbanded in 1887. *A. T. Stamm,* who had previously tried to start an organization he called "The Society for Humanism," then sought to form a society, "The All-Weal Union." These efforts came to naught until Flürscheim launched in *Frankfort* the "*German Union for Land Ownership Reform.*" It gained 600 members. It was called by a government official, *Wilhelm Schrameier,* himself a land reformer, "a small sect." But these educational efforts convinced officials of the imperial government and navy of the usefulness of the *land value tax* for ending *land speculation* and provided for 16 years a practical demonstration of that in a large colonial territory, *Kiaochow, China.*

I

The Beginnings of the German Land Reform Movement

IN 1885, MICHAEL FLÜRSCHEIM, an entrepreneur, distributed several thousand copies of an appeal for the founding of a union of Germany land reformers. But when he received only about 20 applications for membership, he set the idea aside for the time being.[1]

Two journalists, Martin Hildebrandt and Max F. Sebald, editors of a journal of opinion described as supra-partisan, *The Echo,* the Berlin "Weekly [Review] of Politics, Literature, Art and Science," shortly afterward heeded Flürscheim's call. On their initiative, nine land reformers met on July 4, 1886, in Berlin, to organize such a group. In imitation of the name which the English Georgists had adopted—Land Restoration League—the new group called itself the Land League ('Land-Liga')[2] and their program contained only this one point:

> In order to abolish poverty, to combat economic decline, and to free labor . . . the German Land League advocates the community ownership of land, the nature-given communal property

* [Michael Silagi, Dr. jur. et phil., is a Senior Research Fellow at the Institut für Völkerrecht, Georg-August-Universität, Platz der Göttinger Sieben 5, Blauer Turm, D-3400 Göttingen, Germany.]

American Journal of Economics and Sociology, Vol. 52, No. 1 (January, 1993).

of all men. Alongside private property, the Land League demands the creation of community property, and it demands community ownership for such property which [now] gives the single individual a monopoly over the whole. That is landownership. The Land League wants no monopolies at all, but that which constitutes a monopoly by nature—landed property—it demands for the community.[3]

The League's founders not only gave themselves a Georgist name, with the declaration just cited, they also adopted a Georgist demand along with a Georgist argument. Furthermore, just a week after their founding, they wrote their American teacher—George—a letter composed by the newly designated secretary, Max Sebald:

> It is a good 'omen' that the foundation of the league took place on the 4th of July, the date of the independence of the United States. May it be in the future the date of the declaration of German independence from the land-slavery. We greet you as our master and wish that you will gain in America the same enthusiasm as we [have] in Germany.[4]

It was Michael Flürscheim who brought the Georgist ideas to the Land League. Jan Stoffel, founding member of the League, called him the "scientific founder of the principles of the Land League."[5] Similar testimony is given by *Die Gesellschaft, The Society,* a periodical founded in 1885 in Munich by the naturalistic writer Michael Georg Conrad.[6] As an "organ of contemporary literary youth," it achieved "a prominent position."[7] This periodical, in an editorial introduction to an article by Flürscheim about the program of the Land League, commented that this program was "the first step to a practical realization of the great reform proposed in Flürscheim's article."[8]

But Flürscheim, because of his bad experiences with the appeal of the previous year, stayed away from the League's founding meetings. He did, it is true, join the Land League a few weeks after its inauguration, but because he remained skeptical of the entire undertaking, he refused to become a member of its board of directors.[9] In fact, in 1886, he resigned from its membership for reasons of personal and ideological differences with his colleagues.[10] This meant the loss of a source of the support that, according to Stoffel, the League could hardly afford.[11]

Flürscheim's pessimism proved to be wholly justified. Six weeks after its founding only 26 people had joined the League, a fact which Hans Wehberg called "extremely depressing."[12] Only 14 members took part in the first annual meeting in 1887, and at the year's end the League suspended its activities entirely.[13]

II

The Land Reformers Organize in Frankfurt

After the breakup of the Land League, August Theodor Stamm founded with a few followers a new organization called the All-Weal Union ('Allwohls Bund'), a "strange" name in Heinrich Freese's view.[14] (Initially, Stamm had intended to call the group "Union of the Pioneers of the All-Weal."[15]) This organization[16] never had more than 80 members[17] and maintained a "precarious existence" (Wehberg[18]). For the further development of the land reform idea in Germany it remained just as insignificant as Stamm's previous group, the Society for Humanism.

But more significant for the future destiny of the land reform idea in the German Empire was the land reform association called into existence by Flürscheim at the same time. On September 16, 1888, the first meeting of the Union for Landownership Reform took place in Frankfort on the Main. (After 1889, in order to distinguish itself from organizations with similar sounding names in foreign countries, the group adopted the name, "German Union for Landownership Reform.") The initial organizational meeting had been preceded by Flürscheim's appeal, in March of the same year, in the land reform periodical he edited *Deutsche Land* (*German Land*),[19] and by intense propagandistic efforts on his part.[20] These had the effect of bringing together 188 followers of the land reform idea in Frankfort.[21]

The meeting was chaired by the materialist philosopher Ludwig Büchner. He was an admirer of Henry George[22] and had been won over to the movement by Flürscheim.[23] Twenty-five years earlier, on May 17, 1863, in the same hall, he had presided at the Frankfort Workers Day, which was to be decisive for the founding of the General German Workers Association.[24]

Michael Flürscheim, initiator of the land reform union, was unanimously offered the chairmanship, but he refused to accept this conspicuous position because he feared that his being a Jew would give ammunition for antisemitic propaganda.[25]

Thereupon, at his suggestion, Heinrich Wehberg (1855–1912), the father of the biographer of A. T. Stamm, Hans Wehberg, an international lawyer, was elected chairman. He was the first of three leaders of the German land reform movement until 1935, all of whom came to the land reform idea through George's student Flürscheim. Heinrich Wehberg had learned about Flürscheim through Ferdinand Gilles' *Democracy and Bismarck,*[26] as he stated in a work of his own published posthumously.[27] He was, incidentally, as critical as Flürscheim of Henry George's position regarding the question of interest on capital.[28]

The Dutch manufacturer and lumber dealer Jan Stoffel became vice-chairman. He was a devoted admirer of Henry George. The introduction and conclusion of his first letter to the American author, written in 1884, demonstrate that: "Friend of humanity, bearer of the New Evangelium, author of *Progress and Poverty,* I am considering it my duty to thank you for your work" and "I am thanking you again for the light you have spread in my mind and that of thousands and thousands of others. May your idea soon pass into reality and humanity be saved from misery, avarice and crime. Your devoted pupil Jan Stoffel."[29]

It is true that he adopted Flürscheim's modifications of Henry George's teachings,[30] but this fact did not alter in any way his esteem for the American, whose *Social Problems* he had translated into Dutch. His objections to some of George's theses, formulated in a letter to his teacher in 1892, are preceded by the sentence: "We are convicted [sic]; we are your followers, your disciples."[31]

Ludwig Büchner, along with Jan Stoffel, was also elected a vice-chairman of the Union. Michael Flürscheim took over the post of secretary.[32]

The platform adopted by the land reformers[33] had also been written by Flürscheim.[34] Like Henry George, he demanded the abolition of unearned land rent income, but beyond that the elimination in addition of interest on capital. As means to these twin ends the program considered appropriate either the nationalization of land or the community appropriation of only the land rent. Through keeping the second alternative open, one could "satisfy equally those who wanted to nationalize land and those who—with Henry George—wanted to win back only the land rent." (Freese[35])

To this extent the program was still thoroughly Georgist. As for the demand for abolition of interest on capital, the reason has already been given why George would have no fundamental objection against it as long as this goal did not have a negative effect on the main path to be taken, the "remedy." Nor was the first alternative, Flürscheim's preference, land nationalization, in contradiction to George's principles. George himself had written in *Progress and Poverty* explaining the option: "We should satisfy the law of justice . . . by at one stroke abolishing all private titles, declaring all land public property."[36]

He preferred the "simpler, easier and quieter way"[37] of the land rent tax, the land value tax, only out of practical considerations. Since the Union's program, moreover, completely ignored the question of compensation, in which the views of the German and the American land reform leaders were in conflict, it was no wonder that the name of Henry George could be found at the top of a list of the members.[38] It was, however, only a year later that, in a 35-point enumeration of the "Principles of the Union for Landownership Reform," the "imposition of the land tax" was given preference over nationalization of land, but "after compensation to the owners."[39]

In addition to the nationalization of land, *i.e.* of land rent, already this initial program of the Union for Landownership Reform contained a demand, an un-Georgist one, in this form: "As the first step, and one to be realized immediately, the Union sees the confiscation of the increase in urban land rent income."[40] That which was advocated here—only as a first step—was the limitation, firstly, of increases in land values, and secondly, of city real estate speculation. But the espousal of this point was to thrust increasingly into the background, as we shall see, the basic land reform objectives, the gaining of all land, or all land rent, for the community.

III

Discord Presses Immediate Goals on the Reformers

THE FIRST PROGRAM of the Union stayed in force for only two years. Discord caused a change, in 1890, in the Union's leadership,[41] and at the same time in the platform.

Heinrich Freese, a factory owner, was elected chairman. He had become acquainted with Henry George and land reform in 1886, through Michael Flürscheim. In 1907, he described the process by which he became a land reformer: "A speech by the founder of the Gaggenau Iron Works, Michael Flürscheim, a man who was wise in the ways of the world, about the teachings of Henry George, made the scales fall off my eyes; my eyes were opened to the land question."[42]

Under Freese's chairmanship, the Union began to concentrate more and more on the so-called "demands of the present," on, as it was stated in the platform, "the demands soonest to be realized."[43] There were three of these among the new tenets: 1. The inalienability and most feasible augmentation of present-day state and community lands; 2. an appropriate communal taxation of the increased value of land, unearned by the owner; 3. the abolition of private mortgage rights over land."[44]

True, the avowed, ultimate objective of the Union still remained the "nationalization or community appropriation of land or of land rent." But Freese, upon whose motion the "demands of the present" had been added to the platform,[45] regarded the formulation of this aim as merely a utopian declaration of intention without actual, practical relevance. For, according to Freese, "the proposals made by either Henry George or Flürscheim offered little hope for [timely] success. . . . For practical policies, these programs have the significance only of a remote goal which indicates the direction in which one wishes to move."[46]

Freese dedicated himself predominantly to an objective not at all mentioned in the platform, and one in no way connected with land reform, *i.e.,* safeguarding the claims of construction workers. To secure their demands against the builders, they were to be granted legal mortgages prior to those securing bank loans.

The most outspoken opponent of this "construction workers land reform"[48] was Bernhard Eulenstein, a German-American and decidedly a follower of Henry George and the Single-Tax doctrine. As he wrote to George, "I am a strict Landleaguer in your terms and agree with your plans for introducing the great

Land-Reform to the very letter."[49] In 1892, he had translated into German the American's open letter to Pope Leo XIII regarding the latter's Encyclical *Rerum novarum.* In the following years, he discussed George's teachings in several works[50] and defended these theories against attacks, whether it be from land nationalizers of Flürscheim's persuasion[51] or from opponents of any kind of land reform.[52]

Eulenstein practically idolized his mentor, whom he addressed in his letters as "our beloved prophet."[53] Together with a few members of the Union of Landownership Reform, who saw, as he did, the land reform aims adulterated by Freese's campaign for the rights of construction workers, he founded, at the end of 1894, a Henry George Association. This, however, broke up after a few months because of internal conflicts.[54] (Eulenstein did not notify Henry George of the founding of this organization. Only after the fact, on December 3, 1895, he wrote to George about the unsuccessful undertaking: "I had collected quite a number of S[ingle] T[ax] men. But after a certain time the activity of most men did slacken."[55])

Eulenstein was not the first person to leave the Union because of conflicts about the direction to be taken, because of the setting up of priorities in the program, or because of dogmatic problems. Disagreements were the order of the day,[56] starting with the already mentioned conflict that led to Heinrich Wehberg's resignation from the chairmanship. This disagreement had arisen over the question whether "the land rent will decline when organic reform is put through"[57]—Wehberg's view—or not, as Flürscheim (with George) supposed.[58]

The German Union for Landownership Reform, founded by Flürscheim, had a (temporarily) high membership in 1892 when compared to the Land League, All-Weal Union and Henry George Association. It had attained a maximum membership of 600.[59] After that year it declined. But how little the Union was able to generate effective publicity is shown in an episode which took place in 1893. At that time, elections were held for the Reichstag. The land reformers put up a few candidates in Berlin but they could not obtain more than 257 votes there.[60]

In his brief description of the land reform movement in Germany until 1912, Wilhelm Schrameier believes that the Flürscheim Union achieved "only a shadowy existence"; it lacked "inner vitality" so that the disintegration of this "small sect" was inevitable.[61]

IV

A New Phase in the German Land Reform Movement

THE GERMAN UNION for Land Ownership Reform ceased to exist, for all practical purposes, in 1896. This ended the first phase of the land reform movement in the Empire.

But in contrast to the other land reform organizations cited, whose activities had no impact whatsoever and which dissolved virtually without a trace, there grew from the remnants of the Union for Landownership Reform two years later a new organization.

With members of the defunct union, Adolf Damaschke, a schoolteacher, founded, in 1898, his Union of German Land Reformers. This organization preserved to the utmost a continuity with its predecessor. Thus, the periodical of the new Union, first called *German People's Voice,* then *Land Reform,* counted its annual editions from the first publication of *Free Land* [1890], the older union's journal. It continued to carry that title as its subtitle. Similarly, the annual conventions of the land reformers were counted from the initial organizational meeting of Flürscheim's Union in Frankfort in 1888.

The same year, 1898, also saw an event no less important for the history of the land reform idea and of the land reform movement in Germany, as for the world-wide effort to promote understanding and implementation of the economic and social philosophy of the American reformer, Henry George. It was the proclamation of the Land Order of Kiaochow, China, the successful application of complete land reform through a land value tax in a substantial jurisdiction, that colonial territory of the German Empire.

It ended land speculation and was the basis of a program for redistributing land to users for 16 years until the first world war ended German dominion. It demonstrated the practicality of Henry George's basic proposal. Thereafter only ignorance of it permitted American opponents of George's ideas to maintain that his ideas were never applied on a national scale.

The land reformers before 1898 were few, disseminating their ideas in a few periodicals and in speeches at meetings. But they made an impression in the government's colonial office and among top officers of the Imperial Navy who were struggling to control land speculation in the government's colonies in China and Africa. The officials tried out the proposal—and it worked. A handful of reformers achieved what masses failed to achieve elsewhere.

Notes

1. Hans Wehberg, *A. Theodor Stamm und die Anfänge der deutschen Bodenreformbewegung* (Bonn, 1911), p. 20.

2. *Ibid.,* p. 24.

3. Heinrich Freese, *Die Bodenreform* (Berlin, 1918), p. 355.

4. Max F. Sebald to Henry George, July 10, 1886, Henry George Collection, New York Public Library (hereafter HGC). At the end of the pamphlet written by Heinrich Wehberg, "Was Will die deutsche Land-Liga?" (Berlin, c. 1886), a series of publications are recommended, intended for those "who wish to become acquainted in greater detail with the goals of the Land League." Here mention is also made of the two works by George then available in German, *Fortschritt und Armut* and *Soziale Probleme.*

5. Quoted in Wehberg, *Stamm, op. cit.*, p. 31.

6. On Conrad (1846–1927), see Hedwig Reisinger, *Michael George Conrad* (Würzburg, 1939), *passim*, especially p. 29*ff.*

7. Joachim Kirchner, *Das deutsche Zeitschriftwesen: Seine Geschichte und seine Probleme*, Vol. II (Wiesbaden, 1962), p. 345.

8. Michael Flürscheim, "Die Grundbesitz-Reform," *Die Gesellschaft*, Vol. II, No. 2 (Munich, 1886), pp. 42–49, especially p. 42.

9. Wehberg, *Stamm, op. cit.*, p. 26.

10. [Michael Flürscheim], "Die Landliga," *Deutsch Land*, Vol. 1, 1887, pp. 121–124, *passim.*

11. Hans Wehberg, *A. T. Stamm*, p. 31.

12. *Op. cit.*, p. 27.

13. Freese, *Die Bodenreform*, p. 85.

14. *Op. cit.*, p. 45.

15. Rudolf Görnandt, *Zur Entwicklung des Bodenreformgedankes in Deutschland* ('On the development of the land reform idea in Germany') (Berlin, 1914), p. 8.

16. His program is reprinted in Freese, *Die Bodenreform*, p. 355*ff.*

17. Hans Wehberg, *Stamm*, p. 37.

18. *Op. cit.*, p. 45.

19. Michael Flürscheim, "Aufforderung behufs Gründung eines Vereins zur Förderung der Bodenreform," *Deutsch Land*, II, 1888, p. 50*ff.*

20. Hans Wehberg, *Stamm*, p. 39*ff.*

21. Michael Flürscheim "Gründungsversammlung des 'Bundes für Bodenbesitzreform,'" *Deutsch Land*, II, 1888, pp. 193–195.

22. Ludwig Büchner, *Darwinismus und Sozialismus* (Leipzig, 1894), p. 55.

23. Freese, *Die Bodenreform*, p. 90.

24. Franz Mehring, *Geschichte der deutschen Sozialdemokratie*, III, 6th/7th ed. (Stuttgart, 1919), p. 66*ff.*

25. In this regard, Flürscheim writes in his report about the "Gründungsversammlung . . . ," *Deutsch Land*, II, p. 194, that he rejected the chairmanship. He did so "because—despite lack of religious adherence and despite his family's being part of the German Fatherland for probably more than a thousand years—the absence of aryan blood in his veins could hurt the cause if he were to head the Union." Indeed, an antisemitic organ had already asserted that in this movement, too, the Jews were trying to get their representatives to the top.

26. Ferdinand Gilles, *Demokratie und Bismarck* (Düsseldorf, 1885); the cited reference is to be found on p. 116, note 2.

27. Heinrich Wehberg, *Die Bodenreform im Lichte des humanistischen Sozialismus* (Munich, 1913), p. IX.

28. *Op. cit.*, p. 63*ff.*

29. Stoffel to George, Sept. 11, 1884, HGC.

30. Stoffel to George, Dec. 23, 1892, HGC.

31. Stoffel to George, Jan. 2, 1892, HGC.

32. Flürscheim, "Gründungsversammlung . . . ," *Deutsch Land*, II, p. 195.

33. "Satzungen des 'Bundes für Bodenbesitzreform,'" *Deutsch Land*, II, 188, p. 195*ff.*

34. Freese, *Die Bodenreform*, p. 125.

35. *Loc. cit.*

36. Henry George, *Progress and Poverty,* p. 401.

37. *Op cit.,* p. 402.

38. Freese, *Die Bodenreform,* p. 92.

39. "Grundsätze des Bundes für Bodenbesitzreform," *Deutsch Land,* III, 1889, pp. 66–74 (72).

40. "Satzungen . . . ," *Deutsch Land,* II, p. 195*ff.*

41. Hans Wehberg, *Stamm,* p. 54.

42. Heinrich Freese, *Bodenreform!* (Gotha, 1907), p. 5; on Freese's biography (1853–1944) see Hans-Henning Zabel, "Freese, Johannes Carl Heinrich," Neue Deutsche Biographia, V (Berlin, 1961), p. 389*ff.*

43. "Die Generalversammlung," *Frei Land,* I (Düsseldorf, 1890), No. 22.

44. *Loc. cit.*

45. Freese, *Die Bodenreform,* p. 208.

46. *Op. cit.,* p. 207.

47. *Op. cit.,* p. 260*ff.*

48. Adolf Damaschke, *Aus meinem Leben,* p. 328.

49. Eulenstein to George, Dec. 2, 1891, HGC.

50. These are: the already cited *Nur eine einzige Steuer!* (Berlin, 1895); *Der Bund der nützlichen Berufe* (Kiel, 1896); and *Die Entschädigung der Grundeigentümer* (Leipzig, c. 1895)-(Reprint of the article with the same title from *Die Gesellschaft,* XI, 4, 1895, pp. 1567–1589). The brochure *Die Entschädigung der Grundeigentümer* also contains a "programmatic draft after Henry George," entitled "Die Grundrentensteuer" ('The Land Rent Tax'), in which Eulenstein pleads in his own words for the initiation of Georgist reforms (*op. cit.,* pp. 23–28). As introduction, a German letter by Leo Tolstoy to Eulenstein is reprinted (pp. iii–v) which had first been published as "Thoughts about Henry George's reform efforts" in the *Gesellschaft,* X, 2 (1895), pp. 856–859. There the Russian writer declares himself for Henry George's teachings.

51. Bernhard Eulenstein, *Henry George und die Bodenbesitzreform deutscher Richtung* (Leipzig, c. 1894), Part I, pp. 3–44 (this first part of the discussion is a reprint from *Die Gesellschaft,* X, 2 [1894], pp. 431–472.).

52. *Op. cit.,* Part II, pp. 45–61 (from *Die Gesellschaft,* X, 2, pp. 634–650) and the paper *Die soziale Frage dennoch eine Grund- und Bodenfrage/Eine Replik* (Leipzig, 1896).

53. Eulenstein to George, September 4, 1893; Nov. 18, 1893; March 24, 1894; Dec. 3, 1895, and Feb. 29, 1896; HGC.

54. Freese, *Die Bodenreform,* p. 273*ff.*

55. Eulenstein to George, Dec. 3, 1895, HGC.

56. *Cf.* the section about the "Austritt der Sozialdemokraten" in Freese, *Die Bodenreform,* pp. 207–230.

57. Hans Wehberg, *Stamm,* p. 54.

58. The dispute was reflected in the Union journal *Freie Land:* [Heinrich Wehberg] "Editorial Comment," 1890, No. 6, and Michael Flürscheim, "Wird die Grundrente nach der Bodenverstaatlichung steigen?" ('Will land rent increase after nationalization of land?'), 1890, No. 8.

59. Freese, *Die Bodenreform,* p. 217.

60. *Op. cit.,* p. 238.

61. Wilhelm Schrameier, *Die deutsche Bodenreformbewegung* (Jena, 1912), p. 6.

8

Land Reform in Kiaochow, China:

From 1898 to 1914 the Menace of Disastrous Land Speculation was Averted by Taxation

By MICHAEL SILAGI*

Translated by SUSAN N. FAULKNER

ABSTRACT. Mistaken land policies in overseas possessions of the *German Empire* resulted in disastrous *land speculation.* The small *German Land Reform League* vainly petitioned the Chancellor for a rational *colonial land policy.* Von Wissman, East African Governor, stopped the selling of crown lands, ordering their leasing. The speculators and the press denounced him. But the League supported him and the *Colonial Office* distributed its periodical to leading officials. The articles reached the *Navy Department* and high officers were won to the cause of *land reform.* When *Admiral von Diederichs* occupied *Kiaochow* in 1898, he was determined, as was his superior, *Admiral von Tirpitz,* to prevent land speculation. The *Kiaochow Land and Tax Statute,* in force from 1898 to 1914, achieved their goal. Inspired by *Henry George,* it was written by *Wilhelm Schrameier,* a young colonial officer who became Imperial Commissioner.

I

Equality of Opportunity

WHEN POLITICIANS of the Third World discuss underdevelopment, blame is usually laid on external factors; hence, a 'New International Economic Order' has recently been propagandized as the precondition of economic progress and of a more equitable distribution of wealth, worldwide as well as within the single countries. Only a few nations, among them the Chinese of Taiwan (Formosa), have tried to narrow the gap between rich and poor by internal reforms. The reforms introduced by the Republic of China government of Taipei have led to a marked improvement of living conditions for the majority of Taiwan peasants and industrial workers.

* [Michael Silagi, J.S.D., Ph.D., is a Senior Research Fellow at the Institute of International Law, University of Göttingen, Nikolausberger Weg 9c, 3400 Göttingen, West Germany. Susan Newlander Faulkner, Ph.D., a specialist in English literature, and former faculty member, City University of New York, is a writer and translator, 70-35 Broadway, Jackson Heights, N.Y. 11372.]
The author acknowledges with thanks a grant from the Robert Schalkenbach Foundation which funded the translation.

American Journal of Economics and Sociology, Vol. 43, No. 2 (April, 1984).

It has been noted that the land reform carried through under the slogan of *equalization of opportunities* by the Taipei authorities "reflected concepts very similar to the thought of Henry George."[1] This is very true, and the similarity is by no means accidental. Ideas of the American social philosopher have deeply influenced modern China; the chief mediator of those ideas was the very father of the 1911–12 revolution, Sun Yat-sen.

Chen Cheng, then governor of the island, rightly emphasized in 1961 that anyone studying Taiwanese land reform must start with the teachings of Sun.[2] Indeed, as early as 1905, Sun proclaimed the equalization of land rights as one of the four main planks of his revolutionary platform.[3] This is, of course, common knowledge, but it is little known that among the Western doctrines from which Sun derived his land program, the teachings of Henry George had the strongest impact during the Chinese leader's formative period. The theory of Sun's land reform was developed along the lines drawn by Henry George and, to a lesser extent, by John Stuart Mill; and it was the administration of Kiaochow that "showed him how that theory could be put into practice."[4]

II

Land Reform in Kiaochow

THE CASE of Kiaochow is remarkable and unique. Land Value Taxation legislation has been passed in several parts of the world on the municipal and provincial level. The German protectorate (*Schutzgebiet*) of Kiaochow was the only State-like territory to introduce a Single Tax on land in response to George's campaign.

Kiaochow was formally a leasehold territory of the German Empire held under the jurisdiction of the German Navy Department. The 400 square mile territory on the north-eastern coast of China was occupied for Germany on November 14, 1897, by Admiral Otto von Diederichs. The conquest of Kiaochow was presented to the world public as retaliation for the murder of two German missionaries. But at the same time it was no secret that the area had been seized in order to gain a foothold for the German Empire in the Far East, as the other great powers had done before.

The combined effects of several circumstances resulted in the institution of a land-reform-styled economic order for Kiaochow. The British historian W. O. Henderson, in his *Studies in German Colonial History,* scores the heads of the Colonial Office in Berlin (responsible for the overseas possessions of the Reich with the exception of Kiaochow) for having committed two serious errors: firstly, the frequent use of officials unsuited to their tasks in the administration of a territory, and secondly, an entirely mistaken land policy.[5]

The splitting up of the area among the real estate companies quickly led to wild land speculation in the colonies. Two petitions by the then so-called *Bund für Bodenbesitzreform,* the German Land Reform League, to the Chancellor of the Reich for a change in the colonial land policy[6] (in 1894 and 1895) were completely ignored.

But in the colonial administration itself many were taken aback at the aggressiveness of the land speculators. Governor Hermann von Wissmann—whom Henderson counts among those producing the "brighter side of German colonial administration"[7]—tried to put an end to land speculation in German East Africa by certain land reform measures. He ordered that the crown lands no longer be made available for interested buyers, but only for leasing.[8] With this decree he drew upon himself the wrath of the groups with special interest in real estate; and in the press, too, the debate raged about the pros and cons, the prestigious *Vossische Zeitung* siding with the governor.[9]

At this time, the small German Land Reform League, led by Heinrich Freese,[10] in which the young Adolf Damaschke was already active, intervened in the controversy and published in its organ, *Frei Land,* two articles in which Wissmann was ardently supported. The author of one article was Freese, the second was written by Damaschke.[11] *Frei Land* was a periodical with an extremely limited circulation. It was completely ignored by anyone outside the tight circle of the organized land reformers. But, evidently, support even from this corner was welcome to the distressed von Wissmann. Anyway, the Colonial Office ordered several copies of that particular edition of *Frei Land* for distribution among the leading political circles in Berlin.[12]

Thus the articles reached the Navy Department. There the arguments contained in these essays were taken up by a number of naval officers, foremost among them the officer who was later to become Grand Admiral—Alfred von Tirpitz, then Secretary of the Navy. He was not a mere seaman, but a leader who entertained advanced socio-political notions, and he was closer in spirit to the liberal bourgeoisie at times than to the old conservatives.[13] He also showed some sympathy for the basic conceptions of the land reformers, as will be shown shortly. As a matter of fact, subsequently, the Navy Department became a sort of stronghold of land reform ideas.

The salon of Mrs. Hildebrand, wife of Captain Walter Hildebrand, became the meeting-place for navy personnel interested in land reform. Adolf Damaschke was invited there to give speeches, and he was able to win over a number of high naval officers to the cause of land reform. As a result, Admirals Iwan Oldekop and Max Plüddemann, as well as Otto von Diederichs, who conquered Kiaochow, became members of the *Bund deutscher Bodenreformer* (as the League was called after 1898).[14]

Kiaochow was leased in 1898 for a period of 99 years from China.[15] Von Tirpitz had succeeded in preventing the territory from being placed under the jurisdiction of the Colonial Office, and it remained under the auspices of the Navy Department.[16] The Secretary of the Navy was determined to prohibit the land speculation that was so usual in other colonies.[17] "Accordingly, Admiral von Tirpitz formulated his intentions that even individuals of modest means should be able to purchase land to settle on."[18] Admiral von Diederichs shared these views: "It was our firm conviction from the outset that land speculation with all its consequences, as we experienced them in other East-African coastal areas, had to be made impossible," he stated to Adolf Damaschke in 1902.[19]

III

The Role of Wilhelm Schrameier

WITH THIS INTENTION in mind, von Diederichs, on the very day Kiaochow was occupied by his forces, issued a decree which made every transfer of landed property subject to prior consent of the German Governor. Wilhelm Schrameier, Imperial Commissioner and responsible for land policy, reports about that decree in his book *Aus Kiautschous Verwaltung,* and von Tirpitz, in a marginal comment in the copy Schramaier had dedicated to him personally, added that it had been "ordered by telegraph from Berlin."[20]

The realization of von Diederichs' ideas was in the main the work of Dr. Wilhelm Schrameier. Ludwig Wilhelm Schrameier (1859–1926) had entered the foreign service of the Reich upon graduation and functioned as a Chinese language expert in various consulates throughout China. When Kiaochow was occupied, he was interpreter for Admiral Diederichs. The Admiral, in his statement to Adolf Damaschke mentioned before, also talked about Schrameier: "When I think back to those great days in Kiaochow, it becomes clear to me that a young colonial officer, an interpreter, Dr. Schrameier, whom we had on board, contributed substantially to the land reform through the Kiaochow Land Statute. For this purpose [i.e. for the implementation of that Statute] Schrameier's proposals appeared to us to be the best."[21] Subsequently, Schrameier became Imperial Commissioner and was entrusted with the administration of land affairs in the territory. For his services he received the honorary title of Privy Councillor of the Admiralty. In 1910, bad health forced him to retire prematurely, but he remained active in the Union of German Land Reformers.

In early 1924, he returned to China on an invitation of Sun Yat-sen to become consultant for questions regarding land reform and reform of land taxes. He was sent to Canton, where Sun Fo, the son of the leader of the Chinese revolution, was then mayor. Sun Fo had numerous conversations with Schrameier regarding the land problem before he was sent to Mukden as Sun Yat-sen's Special Emissary.[22]

When Schrameier was killed in a traffic accident in 1926 in Canton, Sun Fo had a monument erected to him in the municipal cemetery, and he himself formulated the inscription.[23] The text of the inscription was communicated to the editors of the German land reform periodical, *Bodenreform,* by the press section of the Foreign Office in Berlin. Its beginning reads as follows:

> Dr. Ludwig Wilhelm Schrameier was born in Essen on October 2, 1859, and studied theology and oriental languages. These studies led him into the Foreign Office as a career interpreter for Chinese in 1885. In November of the same year, he came to China with German minister Brandt. On December 23, 1889, he was appointed interpreter at the Consulate in Canton which he also headed subsequently several times. In 1897, Schrameier, then principal interpreter at the Consulate General in Shanghai, was attached to the German Admiral von Diederichs as consultant, and in 1898 he was transferred to the administration of the leased territory of Tsingtao as Commissioner for Chinese affairs. In this position, Schrameier gained decisive influence on the development and organization of the port and of the city which was founded by the German administration in the Bay of Kiaochow. His main objective was the model land order he elaborated and in which for the first time the ideas of Henry George on land reform were realized.[24]

For Schrameier, the paramount problem in administering the new German territory appeared to be the following:

> To attract German capital and labor to barren lands fighting powerful foreign competitors. The chances for successful colonization primarily depend on cheap urban and rural lands. Now, all achievements by the municipal and imperial governments tend to increase real estate values; and as soon as land is utilized, individual greed raises its value in a way to depress living conditions and to decrease competitive capacity.
>
> Hence, the most important goal of all colonization is to protect the soil, as indispensable for human endeavours as air and sun, from being abused or withheld selfishly, and at the same time not to impede individual enterprise.[25]

According to Schrameier, the prevailing tax system which encumbered industry and trade was incompatible with that goal. Instead, "as a natural consequence, not labor, which ought to be encouraged by every possible means, but rent, which constitutes unearned income, must be used for the needs of the community."[26]

IV

The Kiaochow Land and Tax Statute

IN 1898, SCHRAMEIER PRESENTED to the Governor of Kiaochow a "Memorandum Concerning Land and Tax Matters," which was the basis of the Kiaochow Land and Tax Statute,[27] published in late 1898.

The core of this statute was a land tax assessed at 6 per cent per annum of the land value to be re-ascertained at regular intervals, deducting, of course, the value of all improvements made by the owner (Article 8). In Schrameier's words, this was a

> tax on the value of the naked land equalling the potential rent that could be realized in each case, since the sales value represents the capitalized amount of the possible rent.[28]
>
> In its primitive form, this land tax satisfies the conditions set down as the general principles for tax imposition; it is by far lower than the tax on the actual rent in our neighbouring towns; it requires no large apparatus to be collected, since it can be ascertained and imposed without difficulty through the Land Register. Its distribution is just: revenues from this tax will increase at the same rate as the development of the territory.[29]

The Land Statute also provided for an increment tax to be levied in case of transfer of property or at least every 25 years, if a parcel of land had not been sold within that period. This tax amounted to one-third of the increase in value of the "naked" land (Articles 6 and 7).[30] Taxing the increment was not considered to be a fiscal measure, but was intended to prohibit land speculation harmful to the community. According to Schrameier, the goal of that increment tax would be reached completely when the tax no longer needed to be imposed.[31]

It is true that after some time the Kiaochow administration abandoned its policy of complete freedom from customs duties, but except for a few minor levies and duties, including a dog licence, there was only a tax on land.[32] It remained "the only significant tax aimed at the Europeans."[33] Thus, by and large, the Georgist program of a Single Tax on land values had become a reality in Kiaochow.

The comments of Schrameier quoted earlier could have been taken straight out of Henry George's works. As a matter of fact, the American physician and missionary, W. E. Macklin, head of a hospital in Nanking who translated George's chief works into Chinese, reported in 1917: "Some years ago, Mr. Karl Schmidt boarded with me and I got him to read *Progress and Poverty.* He was a friend of Dr. Schrameier [. . .] and got him to adopt it to prevent speculators from destroying the colony."[34] (Karl Schmidt became known as an enthusiastic supporter of Georgism; he wrote several works on land reform topics, such as in 1892 the pamphlet *Der kleine George/Des grossen Amerikaners Meisterwerk "Fortschritt und Armuth" gemeinfasslich bearbeitet.*[35]

Therefore, it was not surprising that circles familiar with land reform and Henry George considered the Kiaochow Land Statute as applied Georgism. Poultney Bigelow, for example, U.S. delegate at the 7th International Congress of Geographers in Berlin, in a speech delivered to the scientists from many parts of the world on October 3, 1899, had the following remarks on Kiaochow:

"Here, for the first time the principles of Henry George, *i.e.* of land reform, have been put into practice."[36] Similarly, Chr. von Bornhaupt told the First Colonial Congress in Berlin on October 10, 1902: "In Kiaochow a land order is actually in force complying essentially with the theories of Henry George as developed in his *Progress and Poverty.*"[37]

V

Schrameier and George

WILHELM SCHRAMEIER HIMSELF always showed esteem for Henry George, even speaking of him with highest praise. But, at the same time, he claimed the Kiaochow Land Statute, the legislation conceived in concrete articles and put into force by the German administration, to be his, Schrameier's, own achievement worked out independently. Nonetheless, his position in this respect changed in a rather odd manner over the course of the years.

In 1903, Schrameier published a pamphlet titled *Wie die Landordnung von Kiautschou entstand?* ("How the Kiaochow Land Statute came into being"). There the author stated that, at the time of the occupation of Kiaochow (1898), he had "already heard of Henry George"; but George's doctrine was not yet as familiar to him as to have had any immediate influence upon the elaboration of the Kiaochow Land Statute.

> Although the thesis was known to me, [he goes on] that the increase of land values, as far as it is created by the labor of the community, *i.e.* the increment rent, remains the natural property of all, this doctrine did not, as a matter of fact, offer any support for the practical realization of the project in the new German protectorate. The Land Statute of Kiaochow though considered as the first application of Henry George's teachings, was not influenced by him directly.[38]

Thus, Schrameier claims sole authorship for the piece of legislation known as the Kiaochow Land Statute and he does so probably with justice. But while he denies twice that he had been influenced directly by Georgism, he actually admits to have been familiar in 1898 with its basic principles.

In effect then, Schrameier confirmed in 1903 that George's teachings had been familiar to him in 1898, but at the same time he insisted that he had worked out the Kiaochow Land Statute by himself. In 1911, however, he published an essay on "Landpolitik in Kiautschougebiet" in the German Land Reform Yearbook. (He republished it later as a chapter of his book *Aus Kiautschous Verwaltung.*) Here, we look in vain for any indication that he had already heard of Henry George at the time he formulated the Statute. On the contrary, some rather wordy and tortuous remarks are made to prove his pretended independence from the American social philosopher.

But still, in 1911, Schrameier only denies any *direct* influence, and he stresses that the formulation of the Statute had been determined by the practical necessities facing the administration of the territory. The following sentences of the long text seem to be the crucial ones:

> It is really a strange coincidence that shortly after the restless champion of a sensible land policy [Henry George] had closed his eyes in America, the new German possession on the Chinese coast should witness the experiment to solve, for the first time, generously those questions to which he had devoted a life's work. [. . .] There was no direct connection between the teachings of the land reformers, particularly of Henry George, and the Kiaochow Land Statute. Often as this Land Statute has been considered afterwards as the first practical application of the teachings of this reformer, it must be stressed emphatically, that it was not influenced by him directly. [. . .] To Henry George and his followers goes the credit for having drawn attention to the just demand and having worked towards its realization; but for its practical elaboration they did not develop any guidance of general value, this having to be adjusted, of course, to the special circumstances of every individual case.[39]

The real turning point concerning questions of authorship came in 1912: In Schrameier's pamphlet *Die deutsche Bodenreformbewegung,* one finds the truly astounding sentence: "It should be pointed out that the only really consequent application of 'Single Tax' can be found in Germany, namely in Kiaochow; it is a complete execution of Henry George's principles, but without knowledge of Henry George and his doctrine."[40]

While in 1903, Schrameier had, *en passant,* admitted to have heard of Henry George and to have known at least the fundamental ideas of his doctrine, this had been repressed, as a psychoanalyst would say, by 1912. Withal, even in this brochure, Schrameier called Henry George the "father of land reform."[41] He spoke of George's "superior genius,"[42] and even emphasized George's principles when talking about Kiaochow.[43] But just here we find the Land Statute appraised as an event "alien to the German Land Reform League and completely independent from it."[44]

In later secondary writings, we find rather far-reaching conclusions drawn from this rather ambiguous presentation. Adolf Damaschke speaks of the "truth which he [Schrameier] had found independently."[45] George R. Geiger writes: "The Kiaochow land value tax seems to have had little connection with any economic theory, much less with the work of Henry George,"[46] and Joseph Danziger, in the 1917 *Single Tax Yearbook,* gives his fantasy free rein. Danziger compares Schrameier's discovery of the solution of the land question with George's description of his "illumination," to be found in *The Life of Henry George*[47]: "Then [1897/98] it was that the Great Idea burst in upon Dr. Schrameier just as Henry George tells of its suddenly being revealed to him."[48] Danziger presents the reader this version despite the fact that the Navy Department had already discussed land reform ideas and Schrameier himself had admitted to having heard of Henry George previously.

Not only concerning the question of prior knowledge of Georgism, Schrameier, in his efforts to distance himself from Henry George, involved himself in strange contradictions. In his previously mentioned essay on the land policy in Kiaochow (1911), he defines the 6 per cent land value tax levied in Kiaochow as a tax amounting to the land rent obtainable in each case,[49] in other words, the exact equivalent of the Georgist Single Tax. One year later, in the introduction to his book *Die deutsche Bodenreformbewegung,* he strictly denies that it amounted to a land value tax.[50] But Schrameier trips over his own arguments when he concludes this book with the statement already quoted above: "It should be pointed out that the only really consequent application of 'Single Tax' can be found in Germany, namely in Kiaochow; it is an exact realization of Henry George's principles."[51]

The question of who depended on whom, who influenced whom, apparently had become an obsession for Schrameier after his retirement. Again and again he referred to this matter, writing sentences as tortured as the following:

> If Henry George epitomized his doctrine to mean essentially prevention of mass exploitation through socializing land by means of taxation, then in a young colony as Kiaochow, any thoughtful person would necessarily have to cope with the problem of eliminating from the outset the many ills caused by private land speculation that was complained of in the Chinese neighborhood, in order to make a peaceful development possible.[52]

This sentence with all its awkward conditional clauses, if it has any meaning at all, can only be interpreted to mean that Henry George's doctrine gave the first impetus to finding a solution of the urgent problems in Kiaochow.

In 1915, Schrameier published a book and an article on Kiaochow.[53] Now, no mention whatsoever is made of Henry George. Maybe it seemed improper to Schrameier to refer to an American social philosopher after the outbreak of the World War. After all, even English names of movie houses and cafés were "Germanized" now, and a campaign was started against everything foreign.

For Sun Fo, who knew Schrameier's views from many discussions about land questions, Schrameier put into practice the ideas of Henry George.[54] Never did Sun hear any critical comment about George from his German consultant. Whether Schrameier considered himself a Georgist he does not know; but, according to Sun Fo, the German expert founded his land reform efforts on Henry George's theories.[55]

VI

The Reichstag Adopts the Statute

THE LAND STATUTE formulated by Wilhelm Schrameier remained in force, without substantial changes, during the whole period of the German occupation. It turned out to be extraordinarily successful,[56] and it helped the German land reform movement at home in what seemed then a decisive breakthrough. In its session of May 13, 1914, the Reichstag passed a resolution calling for a similar statute for Cameroon, the West African *Schutzgebiet* of the Reich. The German Parliament resolved that "the authorities administer and assess the expropriated lands according to the Kiaochow Land Statute."[57]

Only a few months later, the outbreak of World War I put an end to the German rule over Kiaochow, and, at the same time, to the Georgist Land Order and the colonial hopes cherished by German land reformers after their initial successes.

Notes

1. A. M. Woodruff, "Five lessons for land reformers," *Land & Liberty,* 1980, pp. 42 *ff.*
2. Chen Cheng, *Land Reform in Taiwan* (Taipe: 1961), p. 10.
3. H. Schiffrin, "Sun Yat-sen's Early Land Policy," *Journal of Asian Studies* 16 (1956/57), pp. 549 *ff.*
4. *Ibid.,* p. 561.
5. W. O. Henderson, *Studies in German Colonial History* (London: 1962), p. 7.
6. The text of those two petitions can be found in Heinrich Freese, *Die Bodenreform* (Berlin: 1918), pp. 390 *ff.*
7. Henderson, *op. cit.,* p. 118.
8. Paul Lautwein, *Wissmann* (Lübeck: 1933), p. 37.
9. Freese, *op. cit.,* pp. 287 fn.
10. For Freese and the German land reform movement, see M. Silagi, *Henry George und Europa* (Munich: 1973), pp. 78 *ff.*
11. The two articles were Freese, "Kolonialspekulanten," and Damaschke, "Bewährte Grundsätze—ein Wort an unsere Kolonialverwaltung," *Frei Land,* 1896, No. 13/14; *cf.* Freese, *op. cit.* pp. 387 fn.
12. *Ibid.,* p. 288.
13. Alfred von Tirpitz, *Erinnerungen,* 5th ed. (Berlin, 1927), p. 2.
14. Adolf Damaschke, *Zeitenwende* (Leipzig: 1925), pp. 236 *ff.*
15. *Cf.* Wilhelm Schrameier, *Kiautschou: seine Entwicklung und Bedeutung,* (Berlin, 1915), pp. 21 *ff.*
16. Von Tirpitz, *op. cit.,* p. 66.
17. *Ibid.*
18. Schrameier, *Aus Kiautschous Verwaltung* (Jena: 1914), p. 70; chapter 1 of this book was first published under the title "Die Landpolitik im Kiautschougebiete" in the *Jahrbuch der Bodenreform,* 7 (1911), p. 1 *ff.*
19. Damaschke, *Zeitenwende,* pp. 239.
20. Tirpitz' own dedicated copy with marginal notes by the Admiral is to be found in the Bavarian State Library, signature H.As. 4501 a.
21. Damaschke, *Zeitenwende,* pp. 238 *ff.*
22. Letter to the author by Dr. Sun Fo of August 28, 1972.
23. "Kuo Min Tang und Bodenreform," *Jahrbuch der Bodenreform,* 23 (1927), pp. 166 *ff.*

24. Complete text in *Bodenreform,* 1927, No. 7, col. 51.

25. Schrameier, *Aus Kiautschous Verwaltung,* p. 70.

26. *Ibid.,* p. 72.

27. For a complete text of the "Landordnung" and the "Verordnung betreffend die Erhebung von Steuern und Abgaben in dem deutschen Kiautschougebiete" *cf.* "Die Landfrage in den Kolonien," *Jahrbuch der Bodenreform,* 1 (1905), pp. 66 *ff.*

28. Schrameier, *Aus Kiautschous Verwaltung,* p. 55.

29. *Ibid.,* p. 77.

30. According to George R. Geiger, *The Philosophy of Henry George,* New York, 1933, p. 452, that tax "was a tax on the total increment [. . .] of the sale and not levied on the land value itself, and therefore a 6 per cent exemption was deducted from the gross increment as an allowance for the improved value." But Geiger does not render correctly the pertinent article 6, which stated that in case of resale the buyer of a piece of land was to pay .33⅓ per cent of the net gain to the Government. For calculation of the net gain, the value of improvements undertaken by the owner (adding 6 per cent interest) had to be deducted from the price realized at the resale.

31. Schrameier, *Aus Kiautschous Verwaltung,* p. 110.

32. *Ibid. Kiautschou: seine Entwicklung und Bedeutung,* pp. 82 *ff.*

33. Speech by von Tirpitz in the German Parliament on January 31, 1899 concerning the Kiaochow budget (*Stenographische Berichte über die Verhandlungen des Reichstags. X. Legislaturperiode. I. Session 1899/1900* Vol. I) (Berlin: 1899), p. 550.

34. W. E. Macklin, "China," *The Single Tax Year Book,* (New York: 1917), p. 188 *ff.; cf. id.,* "China," *Single Tax Review* I, 3, New York 1902, p. 47.

35. Karl Schmidt, *Der kleine George* (Dresden: 1892).

36. Schrameier, *Aus Kiautschous Verwaltung,* p. 64.

37. *Ibid.,* p. 65.

38. Wilhelm Schrameier, *Wie die Landordnung von Kiautschou entstand?,* Berlin 1903, p. 16.

39. *Id., Aus Kiautschous Verwaltung,* pp. 64 *ff.;* see note 18 above.

40. *Id., Die deutsche Bodenreformbewegung* (Jena: 1912), pp. 63 *ff.*

41. *Ibid.,* p. 4.

42. *Ibid.,* p. 15.

43. *Ibid.,* p. 19.

44. *Ibid.*

45. Damaschke, *Die Bodenreform,* 19th ed. (Jena: 1922), p. 389.

46. Geiger, *op. cit.,* p. 542.

47. Henry George Jr., *The Life of Henry George* (New York: 1900), p. 210.

48. Joseph Danziger, "Germany," *Single Tax Year Book,* 1917, pp. 145 *ff.*

49. Schrameier, *Aus Kiautschous Verwaltung,* p. 55.

50. *Id., Die deutsche Bodenreformbewegung,* p. 21.

51. *Ibid.,* pp. 63 fn.

52. *Ibid.,* p. 19.

53. *Kiautschou: seine Engwicklung und Bedeutung* and "Kiautschou," in *Süddeutsche Monatshefte,* Vol. 12, No. 11 (August 1915), pp. 762 *ff.*

54. According to the epitaph quoted in note 24, above.

55. Sun Fo in a letter to the author: "He was basing his land reform operations on the theories of Henry George." (August 28, 1972).

56. Schrameier, *Aus Kiautschous Verwaltung,* pp. 142 *ff.*

57. Damaschke, *Zeitenwende,* p. 244.

9

Henry George and Europe:

An Industrialist and Pioneer Social Reformer, Michael Flürscheim, Publicized George's Ideas in Germany

By MICHAEL SILAGI*

Translated by SUSAN N. FAULKNER

ABSTRACT. *Henry George's land reform* ideas became known in *Germany* not through his writing or speaking but through the efforts of *Michael Flürscheim,* an industrialist and pioneer social reformer, who first presented those ideas to the public. The American's idea that the *land value tax* was the only legitimate source of *government revenue* as the only *economic surplus* had found no acceptance among German socialist leaders. It was a capitalist, Flürscheim, who was inspired by George's theories and wrote and spoke about them. Flürscheim brought about the foundation of the first German land reform organization. Though it failed, a successor became the largest such association in the world.

I

Flürscheim and the German Land Reform Movement

GERMANY'S SOCIALIST LEADERS had no interest in the Georgist idea that a land value tax was the only legitimate source of government revenue, being based on an economic surplus. Karl Marx sought to dismiss the theory as "the capitalists' last ditch" and George as a panacea monger, while Wilhelm Liebknecht was concerned only with the fate and the future of the industrial worker. It was an industrial magnate, Michael Flürscheim (1844–1912) who, inspired by George's theories, publicized them in his writings and speeches. He promoted the foundation of the first German land reform organization.

The pacifist and international law expert Hans Wehberg[1] wrote in his book, *A. Theodor Stamm and the Beginnings of the German Land Reform Movement,* that it was Flürscheim who, through his "long, industrious and certainly unselfish activity,"[2] brought the idea of land reform to the notice of the German public.

Michael Flürscheim was the son of a Jewish business magnate of Frankfurt. He learned the banking business in America and, after his return in 1872, took over the Iron Works Gaggenau in Baden, which at the time had about 40 em-

* [Michael Silagi, Dr. jur. et phil., is a Senior Research Fellow at the Institut für Völkerrecht, Georg-August-Universität, Platz der Göttinger Sieben 5, Blauer Turm, D-3400 Göttingen, Germany.]

American Journal of Economics and Sociology, Vol. 51, No. 4 (October, 1992).

ployees. When he disposed of the business 16 years later in order to live solely for the propagation of land reform, the number of workers had grown to over a thousand.[3]

From the beginning, Flürscheim had dedicated himself to solving the social problems of his workers. He especially saw to the construction of workers' housing and to the creation of consumers' cooperatives.[4] In 1881, A. Theodor Stamm became his family doctor, and it was the physician who brought Henry George's *Progress and Poverty* to the businessessman's attention.[5]

George's work had an enormous effect on the industrialist. Through his readings he became convinced that private land monopoly was the root of social ills and that it had to be fought. Therefore, in 1884, he published his first book, *In a Peaceful Way,* at the center of which stood the demand taken straight from *Progress and Poverty:*[6] "We must turn real property into community property."[7]

Again and again the author referred to the American book, which he described to the reader in the following words: "This strange, excellent book, to which we shall return often in the course of this treatise, is best characterized by the words of an American newspaper, the *Philadelphia Evening Star:* 'Mr. George has written a work which not only represents a daring and exhaustive examination of the whole question of our modern civilization, but which also delights by its style.' And these are the translator's comments in his preface: 'No one will read it without gaining the impression that it is one of those original works which, appearing only once in a great while, give new directions to our thoughts and open the arena for a new war of ideas.' "[8]

Frequently, Flürscheim takes over word for word[9] passages several pages long from *Progress and Poverty,* and in fact concludes his book with an exact reproduction of its last chapter, "The Central Truth."[10] Toward the end of his book he calls George's work "his most powerful inspiration."[11]

The American's book was significant, indeed, fateful, for Flürscheim, who presented himself to Henry George in a letter written in 1884 as "one of your most enthusiastic admirers in Europe."[12] He himself described his reaction to the book in detail six years later, in 1890, in his second, larger publication, *The Only Road to Salvation.* In the preface to this book, which is dedicated to "his friend Henry George with great esteem and gratitude,"[13] he says:

"Six years have passed since I published my first socio-political work *In a Peaceful Way!* It was Henry George's marvelous book *Progress and Poverty* that gave me the courage and the enthusiasm needed for a simple businessman, a stranger to literary efforts, to decide on such a step.

"Reading George's book constituted a turning-point in my life, as in that of thousands. I, like so many others, had always felt for the sufferings of my fellowmen. But, also like many others, I had long ago come to the conclusion that philanthropy could not heal these sufferings, yet that the path to self-healing, that of 'laissez-faire,' had until now led only deeper into the morass.

"Then came George and traced with the magic rays of a poet and seer the picture of new possibilities. These possibilities suddenly showed a straying wanderer a path through the wilderness, through the hopeless labyrinth, which he had hardly hoped to find.

"George's book was like a revelation, and I shall never be able to repay the debt of gratitude which this perceptive author had laid on my shoulders. A new world opened up before me."[14]

II

Flürscheim's Difference Over Capital Theory

THE "SIMPLE BUSINESSMAN," in other words, sensed this "marvelous book"[15] of Henry George as a revelation. Yet even while he took from it important parts either verbatim or in paraphrase, he did think it necessary to correct his master in other no less important matters. The German land reformer commented to the following effect a quarter century later: "The chief purpose of *In a Peaceful Way* was to place the most popular points from George's book before the German public so as to create enthusiasm in wider circles for this great idea. But here I had not counted on the critical strain, highly developed within me, which now began to meddle in the affair."[16]

Flürscheim did agree with George that "the growing poverty in the midst of increasing wealth is due to private landownership."[17] Similarly, Flürscheim retained the "same objective,"[18] namely, the transfer of land rent to communal property.

But although, according to Flürscheim, private appropriation of land values was the "ultimate root cause"[19] of social deprivation, he found its "real cause"[20] to lie in the income surplus of the large capitalists which is not utilized for employment,[21] that is, invested as venture capital. The source of this income surplus he thought to be primarily capital simple interest and compound interest.[22] For these made it worthwhile not to use capital for employment of workers, but as it were, to withhold it from them. That was why Flürscheim felt that it was important to destroy the ability of capital to maintain its value over a long period of time, even to multiply it. The means to achieve this was for him nationalization of land. For "only through the support of land property rights can a single individual conserve, over an extended period of time, capital property and capital worth. Without this crutch these would be lost to him."[23]

For Flürscheim, this hypothesis argues for a bond of common interest between landowner and capitalist. Both have "the same interest, to depress wages to a minimum."[24]

Thus, while George believed that wages as well as interest on capital were depressed, contrary to natural law, by the private appropriation of land rent, the German industrialist regarded interest on capital, rather than land rent, as the "most dangerous thief of the share due to it [*i.e.*, labor]"[25] Being just a consequence of reform of private land monopoly, this interest on capital would of necessity disappear, along with land monopoly: "As soon as interest on capital loses its foothold in land rent, it will have to shrink continually."[26] In contrast to George, Flürscheim wanted, through the abolition of private land rent, to strike at the capitalist as well as at the landowner.

He believed that the basic difference between his conceptions and those of his American teacher consisted of the question regarding capital interest.[27] In reality, however, these differences about the question whether capital interest was a just income or not carried much less weight than he thought. For from this differing analysis of the role of capital and of the derivation of capital interest from land rent he did not deduce its corollary, a path of reform to be taken. The "remedy" was to remain George's alone. Flürscheim merely believed that there would be decreases in the interest rate as a consequence of land nationalization.

George himself did not regard this difference of opinion as in any way so fundamental as did his German student. In 1888, he wrote about it to Flürscheim: "The difference between us in relation to interest, while it may be of great theoretical importance, is a matter which for the present time, at least in the United States, is of no practical significance."[28]

George's attitude toward his correspondent's theory regarding interest also clears up an incident which occurred in 1893, one which Flürscheim describes in his book *Need from Excess:* Both land reformers had met at George's invitation at an open debate in the New York Manhattan Single-Tax Club. At the end of a lively discussion, the American told his opponent that he was not persuaded by the other's statements about capital interest. If, however, the German's thesis were proven correct, that interest would disappear through the proposed landownership reforms, he (George) could only say: "So much the better!"[29]

How could George give in to such an extent on a question of such apparent importance? His yielding here can only be explained by his basic position's having been founded in the principles of natural law. In the presentation of George's theories, the "secondary production factor," capital, was given short shrift because it played a rather subordinate role in the foundations of his system. Henry George repeated again and again the reason why natural law mandated the transfer of land values into community property, while labor and its products were to remain untaxed. That was why he espoused the "Single Tax." In an economic order consistent with the laws of nature, labor and capital would inevitably receive what was legitimately theirs. But George did not believe, as has already been pointed out, that labor alone was deprived of its fair share of the production of goods by capital and landownership, but rather that both labor *and* capital were so deprived. He believed that, in an economic order according to the laws of nature, capital interest, as well as wages, would rise. But even if the level of interest were to fall, George had no objection to that, for it would indicate simply that such lowering of interest corresponded to an order based on natural law. In other words, while he regarded Flürscheim's view as mistaken, it did not impinge on the core of his thinking, the principle of natural law.

III

George Confronts Again the Compensation Issue

BUT MORE IMPORTANT for the comparison between the two land reformers are their differing answers to the question whether the expropriated landowner was to be compensated. As we have shown, George saw in private appropriation of land rent a continual robbery of the values which were due the community. He denied any justification for it, even on the basis of long-standing custom. Flürscheim, in contrast, supported compensation for the landowners.[30] While he regarded his differences with George's theories on this point, contrary to the capital interest question, as "a side issue" and "unimportant,"[31] the disparity in this case was in fact a much more significant one, a disparity which shook the very foundations of George's system of natural law. For on the question of compensation, the American was not willing to give an inch.[32]

These differences of opinion did not, however, harm the good personal relationship between the two reformers. The correspondence between Flürscheim and George, which, as already mentioned, went back as far as 1884, always remained cordial despite all factual disagreements.

A copy is extant of a letter written by George to Flürscheim in 1891, in which the writer shows a warm interest in the family affairs of the recipient, and advises him in the friendliest way against participating in a settlement project in the Mexican state of Sinaloa,[33] but his advice was disregarded.[34]

The next year, however, Flürscheim appears to have become annoyed at a piece of negative criticism of Flürscheim's *The Only Way to Salvation* which appeared in George's New York periodical, *The Standard,* and at the American's silence following several letters written by him. In any case, the Netherlander Jan Stoffel, a friend of Flürscheim as well as a great admirer of the author of *Progress and Poverty,* wrote George at the end of 1892: "He [Flürscheim] is under the impression that you have broken off the connection between the two of you," and he pleaded with him: "Write, I pray you with all my heart, to Mr.

Flürscheim."[35] Yet only a month later George ended all doubt as to his attitude toward Flürscheim. He expressed his displeasure about the article in the *Standard* and invited the German to the open debate in New York[36] which was referred to earlier.[37] In his reply, Flürscheim calls George's *Progress and Poverty* "the finest poem in prose the English language ever produced."[38] At the end of the same year he suggested that the author send in to Maximilian Harden's important periodical *Die Zukunft (The Future),*[39] those works of his not yet translated into German.[40]

Finally, it should be noted that Flürscheim wrote in October 1894 to the American about his debt of gratitude: "I shall never as long as I live forget the debt of gratitude I owe you for having with your inspiring words engrafted the truth in my heart forever. We may differ in details, we shall always remain united on the bottom plank of all reforms."[41]

Notes

1. Hans Wehberg (1885–1962), son of Heinrich Wehberg, the first Chairman of the German Union for Landownership Reform, was professor of international law in Geneva. A friend of Alfred Fried and Ludwig Quidde, he undertook in 1924 publication of the *Friedens-Warte* ('Peace Observer'), founded in 1899 by Alfred Fried, the "most prestigious German pacifist organ" (Paul Guggenheim, "Hans Wehberg als Völkerrechtler," *Die Friedens-Warte,* LVI, 1961–66, p. 298), which he maintained till his death. (On Alfred Fried see Hans Wehberg, "Fried, Alfred Hermann," (NDB), V, Berlin, 1961, pp. 441 *ff.*)

2. Hans Wehberg, *A. Theodor Stamm und die Anfänge der deutschen Bodenreformbewegung* (Bonn, 1911), p. 18.

3. A. Damaschke, *Nationalökonomie,* II, p. 412; see also Friedrich Lütge "Flürscheim, Michael," NDB, V, Berlin, 1961, p. 262 *f.*

4. Damaschke, ibid.

5. Michael Flürscheim, *Not aus Überfluss* (Leipzig, 1909), p. 1.

6. *Progress and Poverty,* p. 326.

7. Michael Flürscheim, *Auf friedlichem Wege* (Baden-Baden, 1884), p. 179.

8. C. D. Gütschow was translator of the first German edition, published by Staude in Berlin.) *Op. cit.,* p. 60.

9. E.g., pp. 22 *ff.*, 147 *ff.*, 179 *ff.*, 266 *ff.*, 347 *ff.*

10. *Op. cit.*, p. 368 *ff.*

11. *Op. cit.*, p. 362.

12. Flürscheim to George, October 28, 1884, Henry George Collection of the New York Public Library (HGC).

13. Michael Flürscheim, *Der einzige Rettungsweg,* 3rd ed., (Dresden, 1894), p. I.

14. *Op. cit.*, p. iii, *ff.*

15. Flürscheim, *Auf friedlichem Wege,* p. 143.

16. Flürscheim, *Not aus Überfluss,* p. 1.

17. Flürscheim, *Auf friedlichem Wege,* p. 143.

18. Flürscheim, *Der einzige Rettungsweg,* p. iv.

19. *Loc. cit.*

20. *Loc. cit.*
21. *Op. cit.*, p. v.
22. *Loc. cit.*
23. Flürscheim, *Auf friedlichem Wege,* p. 70.
24. *Op. cit.*, p. 142.
25. Flürscheim, *Der einzige Rettungsweg,* p. v.
26. Flürscheim, *Auf friedlichem Wege,* p. 290.
27. Flürscheim, *Der einzige Rettungsweg,* p. v; *cf.* also [Flürscheim] "Die Zinsberechtigung des Kapitals," *Deutsch Land,* I, 1887, p. 73 *ff.*, and "Nochmals Henry George und die Zinsfrage," *op. cit.*, p. 105 *ff.*
28. The German version, (translated back) is together with Flürscheim's answering letter reprinted in "Ein Briefwechsel mit Henry George," *Deutsch Land,* II, 1888, p. 250 *ff.* (251). The English original cannot be found. Flürscheim's answer is to be found in the Henry George Collection (Oct. 19, 1888). *Inter alia,* Flürscheim writes here: "You have done more for humanity in these ten years than all the benevolent societies of the whole world," and "You are the general, I am proud to follow."
29. Flürscheim, *Not aus Überfluss,* p. 213.
30. Flürscheim, *Auf friedlichem Wege,* p. 209 *ff.*
31. Flürscheim, *Der einzige Rettungsweg,* p. v.
32. *Cf.* Geiger, *op. cit.*, p. 144*ff.*
33. George to Flürscheim, August 26, 1891, HGC; of George's letters to Flürscheim, except for the letter quoted above, only a copy of the letter of October 25, 1890, exists in the Henry George Collection.
34. On Sinaloa and Flürscheim *cf.* Freese, *Die Bodenreform,* p. 121.
35. Stoffel to George, December 23, 1892, HGC.
36. The original text of this letter has not survived; its content and date can be inferred from Flürscheim's answer of January 28, 1893 (HGC), in which he expresses his thanks for George's "kind and welcome letter" of January 12, and voices his relief at having found that his ill-feeling was based on a "wrong impression."
37. The pertinent records refute the view expressed by C. A. Barker in *Henry George,* p. 596: "Probably in 1891 and perhaps earlier he [George] broke with Flürscheim permanently."
38. Flürscheim to George, January 28, 1893, HGC.
39. On the *Zukunft* ('Future') see B. Uwe Weller, *Maximilian Harden und die 'Zukunft,'* (Münster, 1969), *passim.*
40. George did not react to this request and published nothing in the *Zukunft.*
41. Flürscheim to George, October 4, 1894, HGC.

10

Henry George and Europe:

In Germany, George's Followers, headed by Adolf Damaschke, Won Several Statutes and A Constitutional Revision

By MICHAEL SILAGI*

Translated by SUSAN N. FAULKNER

ABSTRACT. *Adolf Damaschke,* a Berlin schoolteacher, played a 'fateful' role in developing a large *land reform* constituency in Wilhelmian *Germany.* By chance he heard a lecture by *Michael Flürscheim,* Henry George's follower. And by accident he was won to the movement. He built the *Union of German Land Reformers* into an active organization of 100,000 dedicated members from all classes. For tactical reasons what Damaschke pushed was his version of the '*Single Tax* Limited,' though he never lost sight of George's *philosophy of freedom.* There was a "German Fatherland" emphasis in his advocacy. Yet he despaired of building a mass constituency for that philosophy.

I

Damaschke's Union of German Land Reformers

AT ABOUT THE SAME TIME as the German Imperial Commissioner of the Kiaochow, China, Territory, Ludwig Wilhelm Schrameier, composed his memorandum about the land and tax problems in the Far Eastern colony, the Berlin primary schoolteacher Adolf Wilhelm Ferdinand Damaschke (1865–1935) founded, with a few members of the defunct Flürscheim group, a land reform organization, which, beginning in 1904, called itself the Union of German Land Reformers—a second organization with that name. The significance of Adolf Damaschke for the further development of the land reform idea in Germany is described by Theodor Heuss in the *New German Biography* as "fateful."[1]

As leader of, and spokesman for, the German land reformers until his death in 1935, Damaschke gained for himself, after Henry George, the greatest name in this movement. It was due to his great political and propagandistic achievements that, instead of another sectarian land reform group, which prior to 1898 could only bring up their memberships to at best a few hundred (but for the most part only to a few dozen), a union was formed which, at the time of its greatest development, counted around 100,000 members.[2]

* [Michael Silagi, Dr. jur. et phil., is a Senior Research Fellow at the Institut für Volkerrecht, Georg-August-Universität, Platz der Göttinger Sieben 5, Blauer Turm, D-3400 Göttingen, Germany.]

American Journal of Economics and Sociology, Vol. 52, No. 3 (July, 1993).

Yet it was only a coincidence which made Damaschke acquainted with the idea of land reform. He describes in his memoirs how, one day in August of 1890, the thought occurred to him of attending a meeting of the Flürscheim Union at which its founder was to speak:

"August 16, 1890, was a dull day. Some appointment had gone awry. I was free and wandered aimlessly through the streets. Then I read on a poster for the first time the words 'land reform.' A speech by Flürscheim was announced. I decided to listen to the new doctrine."[3]

Damaschke, who "on that August evening . . . knew [nothing] of land reform,"[4] developed through this lecture "some interest in the matter,"[5] but felt "no inclination"[6] yet to join the League.

But without actually having wanted to do so, he did become a member of the German Union for Landownership Reform. This happened as follows: Damaschke had given the organizers of the meeting his name and address, and this, as he had been assured, without any obligation, merely to have pamphlets and invitations of the Union sent to him. But, asks Damaschke in his memoirs, "was it a mistake, or was it gentle violation—suffice it to say that I was entered as member of the German Union for Landownership Reform. A short time thereafter, when I happened not to be at home, a messenger came and asked for the membership dues. He was paid because it was assumed that the request was correct."[7]

Damaschke remained a member of the Union. After a short time he rose to the leadership of the small organization: in 1891, he became Secretary, in the following year Third Director, and in 1893 Second Director of the Union.[8] At that time he also published the Union's organ, *Free Land.* Soon he became the actual leader of the Union instead of Heinrich Freese, who was still nominally First Director. Indeed, when Damaschke moved for some time from Berlin to Kiel in 1896, this meant in practice the end of the German Union for Landownership Reform.[9]

When Damaschke subsequently, at Easter in 1898, revived the movement with his Union of German Land Reformers, 140 like-minded adherents from the old Union could still be found. From this small circle he created within a few years a powerful special interest group, which in the first decades of the 20th Century came to represent a significant political factor. That the 100,000 members it claimed existed not only on paper is proven by the outcome of two petition initiatives. In 1901, the Union was able to collect 94,000 signatures for a petition to the Prussian Legislature "for the protection of the new canal shores against artificial price increases through land speculation."[10] In 1919, within a short time, more than 80,000 signatures were obtained for the candidacy of Damaschke for President of Germany, after his friend and co-campaigner Adolf

Pohlmann had popularized the idea that the "leader of the land reform and homestead movement" should become the national leader of the new Republic.[11] It was proof as well of Damaschke's personal popularity. (These figures should be compared with the less than 300 votes which had been cast in Berlin, in 1893, for the land reform candidates for the Reichstag.[12]

As Union head, Adolf Damaschke was able to make the land reform movement, which actually sought the reconstruction of the prevailing social order, somehow acceptable and fit for good society or, as Flürscheim once expressed it, "fit for government"[13] within the Wilhelmian environment.

A statistic published in 1905 in the *Year Book of Land Reform* about the composition of the Union reveals that, among the first thousand members, the "state and local officials" represented the largest group with 142 (plus 27 judicial officers). The officials were followed by factory owners and businessmen (139), primary schoolteachers (112), teachers of secondary schools and farmers (80 each), physicians (71), and private scholars and students (57).[14] Among the members of the National Assembly, which met in 1919 in Weimar, there were, according to information given by the Union leader, 76 Union members, "and these of all parties."[15]

II

The Platform of 1898 Appeals to the Public

THE BASIS FOR THIS UPSWING was the platform accepted in 1898, from which can be deduced as well the attitude of its author Damaschke:

> The Union of German Land Reformers sees in the land question the principal part of the social problems. It advocates that land, this foundation of all national existence, should be placed under a law which will promote its use as work and living site, which will make its misuse impossible, and which will, if possible, make usable to all the people that value increase which it receives without labor of the individual.[16]

Then followed a series of immediate demands. These were, however, by 1904, omitted from the platform.[17]

The quoted sentence from the platform was an effective public relations formula, but—as we shall see, consciously phrased to be non-committal. It enabled everyone to participate who was ready to see in the land question an especially important "part" of the social question. The statement of purpose was intentionally so couched as to make it possible "that all streams of the movement . . . could find room in it." (Damaschke[18])

At its center was placed the demand to eliminate any misuse of land; a demand to which any decent person could subscribe without considering what he thought such misuse to be and what means for its prevention he desired. In this connection, Josef Wagenbach, a follower of Damaschke and author of a small land reform book, comments: "The platform speaks of the creation of a law. . . . Through this formulation of the statement of principle, that the land be 'placed under a law,' a statement that does not say what kind of law is to be instituted . . . the Union is able . . . to cover a wide spectrum."[19]

Only after the demand to prevent future misuse of the land followed—in a typical form for Damaschke—the Georgist postulate that the land rent be made community property. Damaschke expresses this in the phrase that the land rent should be made "useful to all the people," and this "if possible."

This formulation is typical for its author because it corresponds to his principle, to "resist any programmatic commitment to detailed questions."[20] Damaschke wanted to create a large movement, and "a movement that wants to grow must consciously renounce 'self-righteous belief.' "[21]

The demand for making the land rent usable is only a weak, vague echo of the goal of strict land reformers. It is even further diluted through the added phrase, "if possible." This addition possibly provides the key to the secret of the success of Damaschke's movement after the turn of the century. It is interesting to read what Damaschke later, in his memoirs, had to say about this phrase, "if possible."

> This program has now been in force 28 years. It was changed only once. When after the great insurgences [of 1918] radical trends came to the fore everywhere, there was in this Union as well a demand to proceed more vigorously than before. When we asked the friends pressing us what changes they wished to make in our platform, they demanded the elimination of the words "if possible" in the last sentence. This was, to tell the truth, a bit childish, for that which is not possible cannot be carried through. But of course we gave in.[22]

Remarkable, and for the pure tactician typical, is the interpretation as 'nonsensical' of the phrase "if possible," as well as the final sentence about yielding in the face of a demand seen as childish.

III

Damaschke's Version of the Single Tax Limited

DAMASCHKE WAS NO DOCTRINAIRE. He gave no generally binding prescription for reaching the goal striven for. In fact, a compilation of the most important, more or less concrete demands was, initially, put at the very end of the program passed in 1898. It is indicative of the author that this catalog of demands was eliminated, as early as 1904, without any substitutions.[23] For it would have shown, despite its broad outlines, a still undesirable commitment.

The individual demands are revealing, however, as far as the movement in Germany was concerned, because they perhaps echoed the goals of the prevalent "Damaschke direction."

I. Organic transfer of real estate credit to public revenues. II. Prevention of community-damaging utilization of natural resources and prevention of monopolistic industry and corporations. III. 1. Maintenance and planned expansion of the community landownership. 2. Institution of a residence law that prevents speculative and excessive land use and that excludes residences which do not meet proper requirements in matters of either health or morals. 3. Taxation of unused urban land according to the value which is determined by self-assessment. The community's right to expropriation according to the value determined by self-assessment. 4. In all cases of value increases which occur through improvements done at public expense . . . taxation of those landowners whose property is thereby increased in value in proportion to this increase. 5. In cases of forced land sales, the community, respectively the State, is to have prior purchase right. 6. Planned internal/colonization by the State, and this in a form which excludes speculative utilization and excessive mortgaging of the newly created property. 7. Securing of the demands of the construction workers. 8. Support of such building cooperatives which uphold a policy of community property, including the leasing of public lands."[24]

There is no mention here of the abolition of taxes inhibiting production or of protective tariffs—to say nothing of the substitution of all taxes by the Single Tax. Missing also is any indication of a direct linking of land reform with the general problem of freedom. Damaschke did not want to take away by taxation all the land rent, only to tax it (III.3) and that only in the case of under developed urban sites. He placed much more weight on taxing away a part of the unearned increase of value of the land rather than on a land value tax (III.4), something in which he follows J. S. Mill. He was evidently able to make this point in his program clear with relative ease to his public, in the manner of the example of Rip Van Winkle cited by George.[25]

Another characteristic peculiar to the German land reform movement, which was probably due to the tactical instincts of Damaschke, was the Union's primary emphasis on urban problems, and its tendency to play down, generally, the difficulties of agrarian lands (*cf.* especially III.3 as well as 2, 7, and 8). Damaschke's demand for securing an increasing landownership by the community and for its option to purchase land (III.1 and 5) after a planned colonization (III.6) and after a reform of mortgage rights (I) did actually apply to rural areas as well, but evaded, in fact, really delicate controversies. Obviously, Damaschke wanted to sidestep the disputes between farmers and large landowners.

In particular, then, the Union of German Land Reformers espoused a whole catalog of more or less land reform-styled platform principles which in part derived from George's postulates, but in part contradicted them.

Yet, for Adolf Damaschke all these concrete demands were not questions of principle. The basic thought of his work was, actually, "that every German must have the ability to obtain access to and a share in German land, at a reasonable price."[26] His idea was the image of a community of the German people in which every citizen could live on his own soil, in his own home; land reform was for him "an organic rooting of the German people in German soil; German children in light and air and sun, German children, healthy in body and existence."[27]

For Damaschke, the point of chief importance was that the Union, "somewhat like a public graduate school,"[28] instill in the Germans a feeling of the urgency of the land question: "Our next great problem must be to gain the confidence, yes, even only the ear, of the masses."[29] He was filled with the assurance that merely the dim consciousness of the land problem among the German populace would, sooner or later, bring about a fair or at least a fairer solution of the land question and, with it, of the social question in general.

Any step in this direction was welcome to Damaschke, regardless of whether or not it agreed with all the land reform principles. A particular point in his memoirs, where he speaks about "all sorts of encounters," is characteristic for the attitude of this opponent of a "firm elucidation of our basic principles"[30]: "Others, again, who have taken hold of a great objective, now see nothing any longer than this objective and do not know that recognizing an objective is one thing, but clearing the path toward it is another; that it is true that a navigator should never lose sight of the port, but precisely for the sake of reaching port he may be forced, in case of contrary winds, into many tasks."[31]

IV

Damaschke and the More 'Orthodox' Georgists

THERE WOULD SEEM, at first glance, to exist an unbridgeable gap between the position of Damaschke, the German land reform leader, and that of Henry George. While the German was always ready for compromise, the American was as averse to any contradiction as he was faithful to his principles. To George, the basic tenets of an order according to natural law, an order which was valid for all people at all times and unconditionally, and which could never change, were ever in his mind.

But in regard to the differences between the two men, Damaschke never denied that he felt himself to be a successor of Henry George, whose teachings he had encountered for the first time in 1890, initially by way of Flürscheim's interpretation.[32] "For him [*i.e.* Damaschke] the encounter with Henry George's doctrine and his German herald, Mr. Flürscheim, was fateful,"[33] writes Heuss in the already cited article, and Damaschke confirms this fact in his memoirs, when he comments regarding Michael Flürscheim: "In 1890, we all learned the most through his inspiration."[34]

But while Damaschke's judgment about his immediate teacher Flürscheim was on the whole negative, there is discernible throughout his writings like a red thread the great admiration he had for the American social reformer, even and precisely where he did not follow him in details. For in general, in the broad outline of ideas, he felt himself to be entirely linked to Henry George.

He believed, however, as Wilhelm Schrameier, Damaschke's close collaborator after his retirement from civil service, reports, that George's ideas would have to be changed. He writes that Damaschke believed "that, in case that the idea fought for by Henry George should take hold in Germany too and should lead to a change in public life, it would have to be divested of its abstract form and be transformed into practical concepts."[35] But this "transformation into practical concepts" of the Georgist tenets meant, in actuality, their dilution, as exemplified by the colorless, ultimately meaningless statement of principles of the Union; and when it became a question of exerting the broadest possible influence on the German people, Damaschke resigned himself not only to emptiness of content but to internal contradictions.

Crass evidence of the latter was clearly visible in the last program composed by him, in 1893, for the then Freese-led German Union for Landownership Reform. In this platform, there was for the first time no longer any mention of the "transfer of landed property or of land rent from private hands to the community."[36] Mention was made only of the "ownership sovereignty of the community over the treasures of nature"[37]—whatever that might mean—(Sentence 1), and it was demanded that "the values which have not been produced by an individual should not be given over completely to any single person."[38] Nothing was said as to the degree of "completeness" that would have to be achieved before this "giving over" would become improper.

In the third and last sentence of the program of 1893, Damaschke then enumerates, on the other hand, the entire catalog of Georgist measures—here citing even the abolition of customs duties (which, however, was not brought up again). We read here:

"The Union is convinced that the consequences of the reform desired by us—cessation of all unearned income from mortgages, promissory notes, state debentures, etc.; substitution of all taxes and duties by a land tax or land rent—will open the way to a condition in which economic justice and personal freedom will be joined."[39]

True, Damaschke does not expressly demand the imposition of a Single Tax on land values (or even the leasing of land), but he believed these practices would be consequences of the demands made in Sentences 1 and 2. But since he puts as the ultimate goal a completely Georgist economic order, he shows that he has taken over the ultimate goal from George, and that he shares the latter's conception of the function of land rent. (One finds something similar in the book *The Land Reform,* where Damaschke, wholly in the spirit of George, writes: "This is the land reform doctrine: this land rent is to be retained for the community and, where it has become lost, it is to be gained back. To each his own! To each one the optimum return for his labor and his capital! But also that for the community which belongs to the community!"[40]

Damaschke's opinion about George did not change even when he became the leader of the German land reformers. In January of 1899, he spoke before the Economics Section of the Free German Foundation at Frankfort on the Main. The theme of his speech was "Henry George."[41] After a description of George's life and work, in which Damaschke gave appropriate credit to the success and influence of the American,[42] Damaschke talked briefly, at the end of his address, about his own Union. He said the following about its relationship to Henry George and his teachings: "The German followers of Henry George have organized themselves to form the Union of German Land Reformers. . . . They know that one cannot safely take even the smallest step without 'keeping the supreme Idea always before one's eyes.' And this supreme Idea they find in the tenets which Henry George has laid down."[43]

Damaschke's attitude toward the author of *Progress and Poverty* remained unchanged throughout the decades of his land reform activities. Much later, in 1930, in a description of a discussion with an American, which turned on the question of clarifying his positive attitude toward Henry George, he pointed to the just cited speech in 1899.[44]

In his larger writings as well, Damaschke writes in detail about the American social philosopher and prepares for him, as Schewe puts it, "a place of honor" among his books.[45] In his *History of Economics* he cites in three tightly packed pages, in which he gives a summary of the Georgist Congress of 1893 held in Chicago,[46] the "epoch-making doctrine"[47] of this "pioneer of land reform".[48] In *The Land Reform* he devotes a whole section to George.[49] In this book one finds, as well, in another place the already quoted comment about the nature of land rent, a comment which could have been taken verbatim from George.[50]

V

Damaschke's Differences With George

YET DAMASCHKE was quite conscious of the fact that, despite such occasional echoes of *Progress and Poverty* in his works, the direction taken by him did not correspond to the Georgist ideal. He did not, nonetheless, explain the differences on the basis of objections in principle against George's conceptions. That which the American proposed for the solution of social problems was entirely sensible, but it could only be valid under circumstances which were prevalent at that time in the United States. Given different circumstances, other measures were needed for the realization of the land reform goal.

Henry George was, as we have seen, convinced that there existed everywhere and at all times only one just solution of the social ills, namely one based on natural law. This natural law was historical for him only insofar as it received a particular imprint according to each historical circumstance. But in the last analysis, he saw this natural law as ahistorical, because it was after all a time-related formulation of the basic principles of eternal justice.

Damaschke, on the other hand, did not care for such eternal values. He believed that every land had to find the way which was appropriate to its historical development for the realization of land reform. In a discussion of Karl Schewe's *Land Reform and Land Reform Party in England,* the German land reform leader explained how he regarded the differences between his Union and the Anglo-Saxon movement in their relations to Henry George: "In principle, the German movement is distinct from the Anglo-Saxon one in that we in Germany give the place of decisive influence to the historical conception rather than to that of natural law, which is predominant in the movement. That which, in the hot-house atmosphere of California in which Henry George's *Progress and Poverty* was created, may well have been fully justified, is by no means so in a country with our development."[51]

But while he did not want to take over unreservedly the American's prescription for Germany, he did not see the ways in which the German land reformers were proceeding as universally valid. In a memorandum to the Chinese government in 1930, in which he rendered an opinion, Damaschke stated: "The realization of the land reform idea will depend in manner and extent on the historical development of each people . . . and so it is well possible that the doctrine of the German land reform movement cannot be applied unconditionally and in each detail to China."[52]

By the way, the same rejection of the Georgist claim to have found timeless truths and to have made proposals for valid solutions, independent of historical circumstances, is made by Marcus Hitch, a Socialist. He compared Henry George with Joseph Dietzgen, called "our philosopher"[53] by Karl Marx in 1872, a philosopher who spoke in great detail of Henry George and of his teachings in his "Letter about Logic."[54] Hitch wrote in 1908 in the *Socialist Monthly:* "George could not distinguish between justice and justice. Dietzgen could. George knew only one sort of justice: the eternal justice. Dietzgen knew of many kinds of justice, which together were valid only temporarily."[55]

But apparently, Damaschke did not oppose George's conception of natural law for dogmatic reasons. Rather it seems that tactical considerations played a decisive role here, since he did not believe that the Georgist program could be carried out in Germany.

Next to his tactics, another important factor in Damaschke's success in the German Empire was his language, the nationalistic, earth-bound diction, which met the sentimental-national needs of broad circles of the population. The rationalist George conceived of the land as an economic entity, as the one necessary production factor which was given to all and whose share in the production, the land rent, was accordingly due to all in the same way. For the German land reformer, on the other hand, something irrational and mystical adhered to the concept "land," particularly German land. Damaschke, who at the time showed definitely mystical tendencies—he was at séances, according to his own testimony, a "welcome guest, because a rather strong impulse for those strange movements [*i.e.* at dictation] flowed forth from my fingertips"[56]—described this magical force of the German earth as follows in an address at the celebration on the occasion of his 50th birthday (in 1915):

"Yes, the soil has a mystical power! Today this mystique is revealed to our people! Only for the soil that is called Germany can we demand sacrifices from our people, sacrifices unheard of in history since Germans have been called upon to live on this corner of the earth. Not money, not any merchandise or values that can be pushed back and forth—only the 'mystique of the soil' speaks: I am the fatherland, I am sacred. For my sake you must face blindness, crippling, death; for only on this soil can the German spirit grow and unfold as a blessing to all!"[57]

In contrast to Damaschke's renunciation of an internally integral and non-contradictory program, this phraseology thoroughly accorded with his conviction. His inner feelings emerge clearly there where he compares himself to his first teacher, Michael Flürscheim: At the outset, he reports about the latter's extended travels to foreign countries, in the course of which the factory owner spent lengthy periods in England, Australia, New Zealand and the U.S.A., in order to propagandize for his ideas.

Flürscheim was, indeed, as he confessed himself, convinced that it was in the final analysis of no importance where in the world the battle for land reform was fought, since a victory for social justice anywhere would eventually benefit all parts of the earth.[58] (It should be mentioned here that Flürscheim could not understand why for Damaschke the land was, as the Union's program of 1898 had stated, "the basis of all national existence," "as if," he objected, "it is not the basis of all existence."[59]) All his senses, Damaschke said, revolted against such a view,[60] and he took Flürscheim for this reason to be a man "full of strange disquiet," a "nomad who is indifferent as to where he pitches his tent."[61]

At this point in his memoirs, Damaschke describes himself thus in contrast to Flürscheim: "With all the fibers of my being I feel that in death and life the German fatherland alone can be my work and combat arena, and that for me all my destiny can only be decided in Germany."[62]

In these comments one can see perhaps most clearly the divergence of the German land reform leader from Henry George, who was as a matter of course a citizen of the world and who espoused justice—equal justice—everywhere.

Finally, another special characteristic in Damaschke's style, tone, and way of thinking should be pointed out. It is the sentimental component in his work already strongly noticeable in the quotations just cited, a sentimental strain which is illustrated by the following excerpt, one especially typical for Damaschke, from the second volume of his autobiography.

Damaschke notes the resolution of the Town of Salzuflen to call two cross streets Pohlmann and Damaschke Streets. There the leader so honored sees in his mind "the German father, who relaxes from his day's work, in the circle of happy children, healthy in body and soul, rooted firmly in German soil and—perhaps he just now answers the question of his eldest: "You want to know why our street carries this name? . . . When the need became ever greater, men stood up and said: You cannot treat air and light and soil and water like merchandise! The German fatherland is much too sacred for that. It is given to us to gain with it secure homesteads for living and for trade! And finally the people followed these men, and so we have won these homesteads! And among the men who first preached this message to our people there were two friends, Pohlmann and Damaschke—and these streets are named in their memory! And it would then be the realization of all our work and yearnings if the children would shake their heads in wonder: 'But, Father, how can one make a special point of honoring these men for that; after all, it is self-understood!' If the father knows anything about the efforts and battles and sacrifices of the German land reform movement, a quiet smile will play over his lips; but he will say nothing more than: 'Naturally, children, hold fast to that; for Germans this is really quite self-understood!' "[63]

This is a genuine quotation, by no means a malicious stylistic caricature. An interesting contrast is the following comment by Henry George. At a workers' meeting in New York, George once was introduced by the chairman of the meeting as "a friend of the workers." Thereupon George opened his speech with the following words:

"I have never claimed to be called a special friend of the workers. . . . I have never represented special interests of workingmen. I only espouse the rights of all people—an equal right for all."[64]

VI

Damaschke's Practical Results

DAMASCHKE AND HIS ADHERENTS brought about in Germany—as previously in Kiaochow—the imposition of a tax on the increase in value of urban real estate.[65] In 1903, Oetzsch in Saxony was the first town to institute the value increase tax; this was followed by several hundred other towns, among them Frankfort on the Main (in 1904), as well as Munich and Berlin (both in 1910). In 1911 a federal value increase tax law was passed, but only after long discussions and in a form which caused State Secretary Wermuth to say that "the soul has been drawn out of one part of the law."[66]

It was a law, however, so complicated, so filled with loopholes, that it turned out to be useless in practice. Already by 1913, the Reich had renounced this source of revenues and had left it again to the towns.[67]

Another outgrowth of the movement, a "favorite child of the German land reformers," as Heinrich Erman put it[68] was the hereditary building right ("Erbbaurecht") (an encumbrance upon real property consisting of a transferable and heritable right to build or develop the land above or below the surface). Such a right had been established among the ancient Romans[69] and with the acceptance of Roman law it was established in Germany.[70] To popularize it the Union agitated untiringly.

In the 19th century it was used in Germany only seldom. The German Civil Code, proclaimed in 1896, only included it because it had not been expressly eliminated. But because of the lack of actual need for it, it was referred to only in a somewhat "abstract and fragmentary" form.[71] When the hereditary right expires, the construction—that is, the improvement in or on the land, passes automatically to the landowner. But the holder of the right is entitled to compensation.

The regulation in the Code soon proved to be inadequate for a changing legal reality. Josef Ring, the editor of the section about the hereditary building right in *J. von Staudinger's Commentary about the Civil Code,* writes:[72] "After publication of the Code of Civil Law, a sudden change occurred in the conception of the significance of the hereditary building right and of its practical application as well, chiefly through the goal-directed propaganda efforts of the German land reformers. The Union was headed by Damaschke, who was supported by legal authorities (Heinrich Erman, Rudolph Sohm, Paul Oertmann) . . . [all leading members of the union.] Statesmen close to the Union, especially Miquel and Count Posadowsky, participated in these efforts."[73]

Thus, the hereditary building right now was "used, particularly due to the efforts of the land reformers, as effective means for furthering the construction of small apartments and for combatting the land and building credit speculation."[74] Already in 1919, the incomplete regulation in the Civil Code was replaced by an all-embracing *Order Regarding the Hereditary Building Right.*

It must be seen as the greatest moral success of Damaschke's direction that in 1919 a proposal of the Union was accepted by the Weimar National Assembly, with a few amendments and changes, as Article 155 of the National Constitution. This says:

> 1) The distribution and use of the land is to be supervised by the State in such a way as to prevent its misuse and to strive toward the goal of securing for every German a healthy home and for all German families (especially those with many children) a homestead for residence and for business that accords with their needs. (War veterans are to be given special consideration in the Homestead Regulation to be created.)
>
> 2) That land, the acquisition of which is necessary for satisfying the needs for a residence, for furthering the settlement and cultivation, or for aiding the agrarian economy, may be expropriated. (Estate entail is to be dissolved.)
>
> 3) The cultivation and use of the land is an obligation of the landowner toward the community. The value increase of the land, which has come about without labor or utilization of capital on that land, is to be made useful to the community.
>
> 4) (All minerals resources in the ground and all economically useful natural forces are placed under State supervision. Private royalties are to be transferred to the State by way of legislation.)[75]

Except for the amendments here put in parentheses,[76] this Constitutional Article owes its creation to the initiative of the Union of German Land Reformers, and "grew wholly from its proposals and its platform." (Erman[77]).

Article 155 rests on a proposal advanced by the Union in February of 1919.[78] The only really significant change in the formulation conceived by the Union demands utilization for the community only of the "increase in value of the land" (in paragraph 3). The proposal of the land reformers sounded strictly Georgist: "The land rent, *i.e.* the yield from the land which results without capital and labor expenditures of the owner, is to be made useful for the cultural activities of the community."[79]

But even in this weakened form, which lays claim only to the increase in value, this demand remained a mere declaration of intent in the National Constitution. As for the Homestead Right regulation, the judicial presuppositions were created in 1920 by a national Homestead Law; "however, homesteads did not find a broad acceptance in Germany."[80]

In any case, Article 155 of the Weimar Constitution has not had any further practical consequences.

In the 1920s, the movement stagnated. The world economic crisis thrust any interest in the Union into the background. Nor did the National Socialists have any deeper understanding for Damaschke's efforts, despite the fact that points of contact between the blood-and-soil mystique and the phraseology of the land reform leaders did not go unnoticed. (The system of entailed succession of agricultural estates of the Third Reich was based on earlier plans along the lines of Damaschke's thinking). Still, the land reform movement was only tolerated by the National Socialists. The periodical of the movement, *Land Reform,* was able to publish until 1939, at which time it was suspended, it was said, for the duration of the war. Max Liertz wrote in 1948 that, in National-Socialist Germany, the Union of German Land Reformers did "not dissolve, but was laid to rest."[81]

Notes

1. Theodor Heuss, "Damaschke, Adolf Wilhelm Ferdinand," *Neue Deutsche Biographie* (hereafter NDB), III, Berlin, 1951, p. 497.
2. Rudolph Schmidt, *Starting Anew in Germany* (London, 1949), p. 5. According to reports by Johannes Lubam, *Wesen und Ziel der Bodenreform* (Leipzig, 1907), p. 60, the number at that time of "organized followers" was over 560,000. These included, in addition to the immediate members, also those of such associations which, on their part, were associated members of the Union of German Land Reformers.
3. Damaschke, *Aus meinem Leben* (Leipzig, 1924), p. 266.
4. *Ibid.,* p. 269.
5. *Loc. cit.*
6. *Ibid.,* p. 268.
7. *Ibid.,* p. 269.
8. Heinrich Freese, *Die Bodenreform* (Berlin, 1918), pp. 173, 224, 251.
9. *Op. cit.,* pp. 289*ff.*
10. Wilhelm Schrameier, *Die deutsche Bodenreformbewegung* (Jena, 1912), p. 32.
11. Damaschke, *Zeitenwende* (Leipzig, 1925), pp. 369*ff.*
12. See above.
13. Flürscheim, *Not aus Überfluss* (Leipzig, 1909), p. 3.
14. "Notizen," *Jahrbuch der Bodenreform,* I, 1905, p. 240.
15. Adolf Damaschke, *Die Bodenreform: Der Weg zu sozialen Versöhnung* (Berlin, 1924), p. 24.
16. Freese, *Die Bodenreform,* pp. 260*ff.*
17. See below, p. 111.
18. Damaschke, *Zeitenwende,* p. 177.
19. Josef Wagenbach, *Deutscher Bodenreform Wille und Weg* (Gladbach, 1929), p. 11.
20. Damaschke, *Zeitenwende,* p. 293.
21. *Ibid.,* p. 261.
22. *Ibid.,* p. 178.
23. Freese, *Die Bodenreform,* p. 361fn.
24. *Ibid.,* p. 361.
25. Damaschke, *Die Bodenreform,* pp. 108*ff.*
26. Quoted from Max Liertz, *Adolf Damaschke und die deutsche Bodenreform* (Düsseldorf, 1948), p. 10.
27. Damaschke, *Die Bodenreform/Der Weg . . .*, p. 28.
28. Damaschke, *Zeitenwende,* p. 175.
29. Damaschke, *Aus meinem Leben,* p. 300.
30. Damaschke, *Zeitenwende,* p. 392.

31. Damaschke, *Aus meinem Leben,* p. 326.

32. This was disputed by only a few successors, such as Rudolph Schmidt, who wrote in 1949, *op. cit.,* p. 4: "Damaschke . . . in the 1890s began to study the slum problem and saw the importance of the land question. Independently of Henry George he arrived at conclusions similar to George's." And one of the oldest collaborators of Damaschke, Max Liertz, who knew nothing of Damaschke's fateful encounter with George's doctrine, commented about Damaschke, who supposedly knew already about the need for reform of the land law: "With a clear eye for the conditions and realities of life and for the character and spirit of the German people, he rejected Henry George's Single Tax theory as not appropriate for the German people." (*Op. cit.,* p. 6).

33. Heuss, *op. cit.,* p. 497.

34. Damaschke, *Aus meinem Leben,* p. 335.

35. Schrameier, *Die deutsche Bodenreformbewegung,* p. 11.

36. Freese, *Die Bodenreform,* p. 356*ff.*

37. *Op. cit.,* p. 360.

38. *Loc. cit.*

39. *Loc. cit.*

40. Damaschke, *Die Bodenreform,* p. 60.

41. Damaschke's speech "Henry George" is reprinted in *Berichte des Freien Deutschen Hochstiftes zu Frankfurt am Main,* N.F.XV (Frankfurt, 1899), pp. 179–199.

42. *Op. cit.,* p. 198.

43. *Op. cit.,* pp. 198*ff.*

44. Adolf Damaschke, "Eine Versuchung," *Jahrbuch der Bodenreform,* XXVI, 1930, pp. 251–256 (254); the author here describes a meeting with the American industrialist and Georgist Josef Fels (1854–1914), who supported with large sums the dissemination of George's ideas. He had offered, though unsuccessfully, to contribute 200,000 Marks annually to the Union of German Land Reformers, if it would champion the "pure teachings of George." (*Cf.* Arthur Power Dudden, *Joseph Fels and the single-tax movement,* (Philadelphia, 1971), pp. 215, 225).

45. Karl Schewe, "Angelsächsische Bodenreform und deutsche Kultur," *Jahrbuch der Bodenreform,* XXVI, 1930, pp. 235–251 (247).

46. Adolf Damaschke, *Geschichte der Nationalökonomie,* Vol. I, 13th ed. (Jena, 1922), p. 400.

47. *Op. cit.,* p. 333.

48. *Op. cit.,* Vol. II, pp. 316*ff.;* on the Georgist Congress in Chicago *cf.* C. A. Barker, *Henry George,* (New York, 1955), p. 588.

49. Damaschke, *Die Bodenreform,* pp. 304*ff.*

50. *Op. cit.,* p. 60.

51. Adolf Damaschke, "Besprechung von Karl Schewe, *Bodenreform und Bodenreformpartei in England,*" *Jahrbuch der Bodenreform,* XXI, 1925, pp. 60–62.

52. Damaschke, "Zum Bodengesetz der Republik China vom 30. Juni 1930/Ein Gutachten," *Jahrbuch der Bodenreform,* XXVII, 1931, pp. 1–9 (2).

53. Quoted from Traugott Konstantin Oesterreich, "Die deutsche Philosophie des neunzehnten Jahrhunderts und der Gegenwart," *Friedrich Ueberwegs Grundriss der Geschichte der Philosophie,* Vol. IV, 13th ed. (Tübingen, 1951), p. 397.

54. Josef Dietzgen, *Sämtliche Schriften,* II (Wiesbaden, 1911), pp. 110–175.

55. Marcus Hitch, "Josef Dietzgen und Henry George," *Sozialistische Monatshefte,* 1908, Vol. II, p. 1078.

56. Damaschke, *Zeitenwende,* p. 258.

57. *Op. cit.,* p. 467.

58. Damaschke, *Aus meinem Leben,* p. 339.
59. Flürscheim, *Not aus Überfluss,* p. 3.
60. Damaschke, *Aus meinem Leben,* p. 339.
61. *Ibid.,* p. 341.
62. *Ibid.,* p. 339.
63. Damaschke, *Zeitenwende,* pp. 374*ff.*
64. Damaschke, "Henry George" (address), p. 193.
65. Hans Köppe, *Das Zuwachssteuergesetz vom 14. Februar 1911* (Munich, 1911), p. 5.
66. *Ibid.,* p. 14.
67. Wagenbach, *op. cit.,* p. 42.
68. Heinrich Erman, *Erbbaurecht und Kleinwohnungsbau* (Münster, 1907), p. III.
69. Damaschke, *Zeitenwende,* pp. 210*ff.*
70. *Cf.* Paul Jörs, Wolfgang Kunkel, *Römisches Privatrecht,* 3rd ed. (Berlin, 1949), Par. 90 (p. 152).
71. Josef Ring, "Verordnung des Reichs-Arbeitsamts über das Erbbaurecht vom 15. Januar 1919," *J. v. Staudingers Kommentar zum Bürgerlichen Gesetzbuch mit Einführungsgesetz und Nebengesetzen,* 11th ed., Vol. III, Part 1 (Berlin, 1956), pp. 864–1004 (867).
72. Damaschke, *Zeitenwende,* p. 212.
73. Ring, *op. cit.,* pp. 867*ff.*
74. Max Degenhart, "Erbbaurecht," *Palandt, Bürgerliches Gesetzbuch,* 30th ed. (Munich, 1971), pp. 997–1013) (997).
75. Heinrich Erman, *Die Bodenreform in der Reichsverfassung,* p. 3.
76. *Ibid.,* p. 3.
77. *Ibid.,* p. 7.
78. The Land Reformers' proposal went as follows: "The land together with its forces and treasures is to be placed under a law which prevents any misuse and which opens up to every German family the possibility to gain a homestead (own home with utility garden) or, in the case of professional training, an economic homestead (gardening or smallholder property), which will be secured for its continual usage. The land rent, *i.e.* the land yield which is created without the owner's labor or capital expenditures, is to be made available for the cultural projects of the community." (*op. cit.,* p. 9).
79. See note 78 above.
80. Fritz Baur, *Lehrbuch des Sachenrechts,* 4th ed. (Munich, 1968), p. 237.
81. Max Liertz, *op. cit.,* p. 5.

11

Henry George and Europe:
Hungary Began a Promising Venture in Georgist Tax Reform But Revolutionary Turmoil and Inflation Ended It

By MICHAEL SILAGI*

Translated by SUSAN N. FAULKNER

ABSTRACT. The kingdom of *Hungary* still faced an unsolved *land question* as the 20th century dawned. More than half the land belonged to *latifundia,* large estates, archaically mismanaged with sweated labor. Unrest among the 6 million *rural poor,* a third of the population, brought forth embryonic *land reform* aspirations. The founder of the first farmers' party, Andras Achim, sought their expropriation and parcelling out. Publication of *Henry George*'s writings in Hungarian by the sociologist *Robert Braun* and especially the activities of the physician and statistician *Julius J. Pikler* made the Georgist proposals known. In 1917 and 1918, Dr. Pikler's ingenious lobbying succeeded in winning over the city councils of Budapest and eight other Hungarian towns. The leaders of the 1918 republican *revolution* included *land value taxation* in their program. But the turmoil of 1919, Horthy's *counter-revolution* and torrential currency *inflation* destroyed the Georgist advance.

I

The Plight of the Hungarian Landless

AT THE END of the 19th century, Hungary—then a Kingdom united with Austria within the Habsburg Empire—was burdened with an unsolved land problem.[1] The situation was similar to that of Ireland, although stemming from entirely different historical antecendents. In Hungary, serfdom had not been abolished until 1848, and even after that, archaic conditions of land tenure persisted in the country's agricultural sector. More than half of the arable land belonged (incidentally until after World War II, 1945) to huge estates, so-called latifundia.[2] The management of these estates was, in most instances, outdated; technology and administrative procedure were backward; mismanagement often reigned.

1848 was a year of revolution in Europe. In Hungary, the turmoil lasted until 1849. The Magyars rebelled against the Habsburgs but were defeated. The next 18 years were marked by oppression and hostility. But in 1867, an inter-state agreement, called Compromise, brought about reconciliation between Austria

* Michael Silagi, Dr. jur. et phil., is a Senior Research Fellow at the Institut für Volkerrecht, Georg-August Universität, Platz der Göttinger Sieben 5, Blauer Turm, D-37073 Göttingen, Germany.

American Journal of Economics and Sociology, Vol. 53, No. 1 (January, 1994).

and Hungary. This was followed by a decade of economic prosperity, and the condition of the poor smallholders and of the landless agricultural laborers also became more bearable. Moreover, growing industrialization created new urban jobs and many farm laborers migrated to the cities to escape from rural penury.

Yet soon, during the great European agricultural crisis of the 1880s, want and misery again engulfed the small farmers and the landless agrarian proletariat, and an enormous wave of overseas migration from Hungary developed.[3] But not only the very poor—many owners of medium sized and even of larger farms got into trouble.

The landless poor, including dependents, were estimated to number 6 million, that is, about one third of the total population of the country.[4] As the crisis worsened, there was widespread unrest among these masses.[5] In the 1890s, disquiet often erupted into open uproar. It was in these days that for the first time embryonic land reform aspirations surfaced in the Kingdom: a politically articulate tiny minority among Hungary's poor peasant millions was desparately looking for a way out, for some goal that could be communicated to the untutored masses. The first pioneers found what they needed in the program of the Social-Democratic Party of Hungary.[6]

In actual fact, the Hungarian Social Democrats did not have an elaborate plan for a land reform; but in firm adherence to Marx's teachings and unlike the 1875 Gotha program of the German Social-Democracy,[7] their program included the thesis that "landed property and all means of production should be placed under public ownership."[8] The first known spokesman for the aroused propertyless rural population, the agricultural laborer János Szánto-Kovács, adopted this item on the program as his slogan. He was arrested in 1895 and sentenced to 5 years in jail for incitement.[9] He declared himself to be a Social-Democrat and to be striving for the nationalization of the large estates. But he emphatically (and truthfully) denied having agitated for the carving up of the latifundia among those without land.

It might appear incomprehensible, if only at first glance, that the rural proletariat—in contrast to Parnell and the majority of dissatisfied tenant farmers in Ireland—did not seek farm ownership, but instead wanted to be employed at government-owned estates. But these people, like their fathers before them, had never had land of their own. They had rather always sought to find work at large estates. Moreover, the situation of the small landowners did not arouse their envy, for these small farmers did not have it much easier. They carried the additional burden of worries about over-mortgaging their property, and with it the terrible fear (one shown by statistics, not to be unjustified[9a]) of losing it. The unpropertied farmhands of Szánto-Kovács' kind had to perform their labors for starvation wages, but were glad even to find a job. Thus it is understandable that when they dreamed, it was not of owning their "own soil," but of getting fair wages and secure employment, a dream which the program of nationalization of the large estates promised to fulfill.[10]

At first, when the dissatisfaction of the small and medium-sized farmers began to take concrete form, the desire for breaking up large estates into small parcels became a political demand—as in the program written by the farmer Andras Achim,[11] who founded the first substantial Hungarian farmers' party.[12] According to Achim's program the tremendous estate entails, the vast church lands, and all other estates above 10,000 "hold" [1 "hold" = 0.57 hectares = 1.4 acres] were to be nationalized and then parcelled out into small rentable plots; later on, Achim reduced the upper limit of the properties to be left untouched to 1,000 "hold".[13]

Actually, since the end of the eighties, some owners of latifundia and medium-sized estates had been giving consideration to the elimination of the manifold social ills. Yet even while their proposals were later to be represented as, *inter alia,* a first step toward a land reform movement,[14] more likely these were proposals which, with few exceptions, could never be realized. They were proposals which were designed to improve the existing order through a far-reaching lease system[15] or through dividing up state and community property into parcels,[16] and thereby to secure the existing order against crises. Another intention, at times stated explicitly, was to arrest the "racial loss" which Hungary had sustained by the already mentioned emigrations, by establishing Magyar settlements in the territories of the national minorities.[17]

Within the conservative, Hungarian Christian-Socialist movement, the so-called progressive wing might be said to have represented most closely those ideas which could be described as land reform-styled. The most important spokesman of this wing was Ottokár Prohászka,[18] after 1905 the Bishop of Székesfehérvár (Stuhlweissenburg). Prohászka, a celebrated demagogue of his time, and a staunch anti-semite, emphasized that the unpropertied agrarians should be helped to obtain land, but that this goal was opposed, not only by economic liberalism and what he called Jewish plutocracy, but also by the latifundia system.[19] As early as 1898, he declared—a statement revolutionary not only for his time, but for Hungary as a whole until 1945—that sooner or later there would inevitably come a secularization of church lands.[20]

In 1916, the Bishop made the acquaintance of Adolf Damaschke, then visiting Budapest, and as a result became an active follower of the program of the Union of German Land Reformers.[21] At that time, he himself publicized a land reform proposal which suggested the creation of war veterans' homesteads.[22] However, his antisemitic and antiliberal position forbade a joining of forces with the Leftist land reformers, of whom we shall speak shortly, and his conservative side rejected land reform ideas, even those of Damaschke's brand.[23] As a result, the Bishop's proposals were not implemented.

Those who espoused land reform in Hungary until 1914, whether in the direction of socialization or of parcelling large estates, were Socialist politicians. Two notable groups among them were members of the Social Science Society and of the club of the reform-happy young students, the Galilei Circle. These two organizations were the spiritual pioneers of the "bourgeois" revolution in Hungary of October 1918.[24] But these efforts did not, prior to World War I, achieve any political significance, much less any movement toward land reform.

It is, therefore, not surprising that, in 1913, the largest Hungarian encyclopedia of the 20th century did not mention, under the heading "Földbirtokreform" (landownership reform), any Hungarian movement, not even any Magyar authors. Rather it cited, first, the earlier English precursors and, second, it spoke of Henry George as "initiator of landownership reform in the narrower sense." It then went on to describe in detail the German land reform movement and the relevant socialist, especially Marxist efforts. Only the last sentence of the encyclopedia article dealt with Hungary. It says: The Hungarian Social Democratic party "still could not agree on an appropriate agrarian program [*i.e.* one which also took the needs for protection of the small farmers into consideration]."[25] To be sure, behind this sentence is hidden the fact that the agrarian problem was the subject of controversial discussions within the party," notwithstanding the lack of definitive conclusions.[26]

The land reform scene came to life at last in June of 1914, when the avant-garde of the Leftist intelligentsia, active partly in the Masonic lodges, and partly in the Social Science Society, founded a radical agrarian party which was to become the bearer of the republican October revolution in 1918.[27] In its platform, radical land reform stood in foremost place.[28] Among its principles (as well of the Independence Party, founded in 1916 by the "Hungarian Kerensky," Count Michael Károlyi,[29] head of the short-lived bourgeois revolution of 1918/19) was the demand for "democratic land reform."[30]

Furthermore, the promise of "far-reaching" land reform[31] was in the foreground of the republican government's program, but now enhanced by a significant fiscal-political element. In a *History of Hungary,* published in 1967 under the aegis of the Hungarian Academy of Sciences in a second, revised edition, we read the following in connection with the land reform endeavors of the revolutionary government of 1918: "The majority of the bourgeois radicals sought to introduce, consistent with the teachings of an American economist, Henry George, a land value tax in order to solve the land problems, and wanted to use the revenues of this tax (this land value tax would have been equal to the annual land rent) for social purposes. Their ideas included the confiscation of part of the large landed estates. . . . Some of the Socialists leaned toward this conception, while other [Socialists] championed the cause of private property based on small farm holdings."[32]

II

Julius J. Pikler, Effective Publicist of Georgism

How did it happen that Georgism, which had played no role whatsoever in Hungary until 1914, moved so strongly into the foreground in 1918, if only—as we shall see—for a short time and without lasting effects? This was due to the entrance into the picture of a single individual, a physician and statistician, Julius J. Pikler[33] (1864–1952[34]). No writings exist about Pikler except for short articles in encyclopedias and a footnote in a work about the intellectual history of Hungary.[35] One of his surviving students,[36] however, portrays him rather effusively as "a personality of manifold knowledge, of superior intellectual force, and of utterly irresistible powers of persuasion."[37]

The Georgist doctrine had actually reached Hungary earlier: the *Pester Lloyd,* the German-language daily of the Hungarian intelligentsia, reported in 1886—the only significant periodical to do so—in two lead articles the efforts of the Land League just founded in Berlin.[38] But Pikler did not learn about the doctrine until shortly before the first World War. The intermediary was the sociologist Robert Braun (1879–1937),[39] who maintained a close relationship with the American world of learning. Braun, prior to World War I, had met with the American adherents of the Single Tax theory.[40] Braun started the publication of George's work in Hungarian translation. In 1909, he began by issuing a Magyar version of *Protection or Free Trade* (*Vámvédelem vagy szabadkereskedelem*), followed in 1912 by the rendering of a Georgist novel written in English in 1894,[41] and in 1914 he brought out *Progress and Poverty,* for the first time in Hungarian (*Haladás és szegénység*).[42] A review of this work may be counted as Pikler's own first Georgist publication.

Pikler had studied medicine in Vienna and, after receiving his accreditation, settled in Koröshegy as circuit doctor. Then he worked for some time in Budapest as a panel doctor. After having made a name for himself with publications in the areas of medicine and statistics, particularly mortality statistics, he entered, in 1897, the service of the Statistics Office in the capital, where, in 1906, he was named Deputy Director. Both as country doctor in the backward province and as panel doctor in Budapest—then synonymous with doctor for the poor—he obtained an insight into the misery of the masses, an insight to which he gave expression as an author.

Pikler's interests were multi-faceted; whenever he encountered problems, he tried to solve them by strictly logical and rational means. In the realm of the rational he was at one with George, but the emotional warmth of the American was alien to him. (By the way, the same reproach often leveled at George, that he operated with eternally valid natural laws and lacked a historical sense, was also directed at Pikler.)

There is no complete bibliography of Pikler's publications, but even the extant data about his works demonstrate a decided versatility. He published not only medical and statistical works;[43] in 1910, he subjected the bally-hoo about the "calculating horses of Elberfeld"[44] to a devastating critique. In 1927, he offered in *Schmoller's Year Book* (a German economic journal), a proposal for solving the problems of monetary stability.[45] Finally, in 1940, he began writing a study in which he as a Jew was also interested existentially. It was initially meant to concern itself with discovering the sources of the social phenomenon of the hostility toward Jews. But this work eventually expanded to become a far-reaching analysis and inventory not only of antisemitism, but—as Pikler put it—of "anti-ism" in general.[46]

As Deputy Director of the Public Statistics Office in Budapest, Pikler attended, together with Robert Braun, the International Congress of Georgists held in Oxford in 1923.[47] At that time he reported in a speech that, in 1913, he had occupied himself primarily with housing statistics and with the housing shortage.[48] He steeped himself in the problem and, in the process, turned to the literature of the German land reform movement. From it he learned a great deal, but he rejected "its practices which were false and which complicated things (value increase tax, land tax, estate entail-styled restitution of family-owned farms, purchase and sale of land through the community etc.)"

His own thinking and the study of Henry George's works led him to the conviction that the solution of the land question—yes, of the entire social question—could be found in the idea of the "pure, simple, and concession-less land value tax." "Thereupon I determined to institute the urban land value tax in Hungary, in the hopes of expanding it in time into a tax which would embrace all real estate in the whole country," Pikler writes.

He deliberately decided upon doing this by himself, without founding any movement, any organization, any party—for this purpose, or even without tying himself to any particular political group. He believed that he could reach his goal simply through logical argumentation, if he could just get the ear of the men in authority.

His first publication about Henry George's doctrine, as already stated, was devoted to the Hungarian edition of *Progress and Poverty*. The review article appeared in the influential scholarly journal *Huszadik Század* [*Twentieth Cen-*

tury],[49] the organ of the Social Science Society. According to its program, this Society had originally been supra-partisan, a-political, but was now dominated by the pioneers of the bourgeois revolution of 1918.[50]

The Freemason Pikler held his first speech about a land value tax in his lodge "Demokrácia." His remarks evoked a strong echo among the Hungarian Masons, although the group as a whole did not identify itself with Georgist theses.[51]

As the respected Deputy Director of a high city administration office, Pikler found many doors open to him. In addition, with the help of his Masonic brethren, he obtained entrance even there where perhaps as statistician, however much esteemed, he might not have been able to find a hearing.

As lobbyist, then, for the idea of the land value tax, he conducted what might be called a one-man campaign. To gain support, he wrote for the great liberal daily founded by the Masons, *Világ* (the word means "world" as well as "light")[52] and for the official periodical of the capital, *Városi Szemle* [*Urban Review*]. He also held speeches at the Social Science Society, in the Galilei Circle, and before any union or group whose interest he could arouse. In fact, he went so far as to use personal conversations to win over resistant city politicians.[53]

Pikler did not, however, propagandize overtly for Georgism or for the Single Tax. He merely pointed out again and again that he was proposing a new kind of taxation. This was the argument which had the strongest effect on the councillors of the City of Budapest, battling a constant deficit[54]—for it promised revenues while increasing production of homes and thus served to ameliorate the shortage of residences. Yet it was eminently fair, required little administrative cost, and could not be fraudulently evaded. It was only later that Pikler indicated that, of course, other taxes, those which were anti-social, production-inhibiting, and corruption-inciting, could (and must) be eliminated at the same rate that revenues from the new taxes, land value taxes based on generally accepted valuation, were flowing in.[55]

After the town of Arad (today Romania) had accepted the land value tax in May of 1917,[56] Pikler achieved a breakthrough in Budapest in November. Here, in 1917, he converted the Mayor, István Bárczy,[57] his deputy, Ferenc Harrer, and the head of a large center-party, Vilmos Vázsonyi,[58] who, during the last years of the war, was at times also Attorney General.

In November of 1917, the Budapest City Council also adopted, with a large majority, an "Ordinance for the city land value tax in Budapest,"[59] which was proclaimed on December 17th of the same year with the approval of the Secretaries of Finance and of Interior.

According to this ordinance, a land tax was to be instituted, based on generally accepted valuation and strictly in accord with orthodox Georgist principles.[60] There was no mention—yet—of any taking away by taxation of the whole land rent, and the annual tax rate amounted to only 0.5 percent of the assessed land value (Par. 14 of the Ordinance); at the same time, a special city tax, the so-called "rent-dime," was reduced by 50 percent (Par. 20). The tax basis was the generally accepted land value, defined as follows: "As per the paragraph below, the city land value tax is determined according to the market value of the parcel of land. The value of the improvements existing in and above the land (construction above and below ground, trees, plants, etc.) are not to be taken into consideration in the computation of the tax basis." (Par. 4) The market value was to be determined every three years (Par. 5). A special city office was created for the evaluation of the land value (Par. 6); Julius J. Pikler was named Director of the Budapest Land Valuation Office.

Pikler had no doubt that the favorable experiences with the land value tax would inevitably lead to a gradual increase by the city administrations of the 0.5 percent tax rate, along with an equal decrease of other taxes, until the rate corresponded to the entire land rent, in other words, to about 5 percent. The image he had before him as goal was something similar to the tax system of Kiautschou, China, the province he characterized as late as 1948 as the "model state."[61]

After his success in Budapest, Pikler traveled in 1917 and 1918 throughout Hungary and proceeded everywhere in the same way as in Budapest, except that in his attempts to persuade the provinces he could now point to the ordinances passed in the capital. Within twelve months, seven other cities had decided to institute the land value tax: Szeged, Debrecen, Kaposvar, Ujpest (today part of Budapest), Györ, Marosvasarhely (today Tirgu Mures, in Romania), and Sopron.[62]

In the cases of Szeged and Debrecen, Pikler's success was especially remarkable, since these towns at that time (1918) could not be called towns in West European terms, but were rather enormous agrarian settlements around an urban core, a tiny one in proportion to the expanse of the total area. So, for example, the entire precinct of Debrecen, the city which in Hungary was called the "Calvinist Rome," had a diameter of 70 kilometers—with around 80,000 inhabitants.[63] Pikler's land value tax, in accord with Georgist doctrine, placed a levy on each site without exception, on each piece of real estate, whether urban or rural, at the same percentage of the generally accepted value. Thus, in Debrecen the Georgist program was accepted—though, it is true, formally through city ordinances—in a large agricultural area; and Pikler reports that he was surprised at having been able to convince the leader of the small farmers in Debrecen more quickly of the justice and usefulness of the new tax than the upper class.[64]

During 1918, an appraisal was made in all applicable cities of the value of all real estate property—without consideration for their use, possible construction, or improvements; the imposition of the tax was to begin in Budapest on January 1, 1919 (Par. 1 of the Ordinance).

Shortly before, however, on October 31, 1918, the revolution broke out in Budapest. The comment cited above in the *Hungarian History* of the Budapest Academy illustrates how strongly even the historical writings of Marxists who clearly rejected Henry George's teachings have assessed the Georgist influences at that time. But in actuality this impact was due, in Pikler's own opinion, rather to his personal propagandistic efforts and to the example of the land value tax introduced in nine cities.

These two factors lent the Georgist program a sort of nationalistic flavor, so much so that the republican regime of Count Michael Károlyi, eager to stabilize its popularity, included in its program among other items the introduction of a land value tax throughout the country. This was alongside other demands which were deemed to be effective propaganda weapons, but which were incompatible with Georgism.[65] In fact, however, it did not come to a realization of this statement of intentions.

On March 21, 1919, the regime of Count Károlyi was replaced by the Hungarian Soviet Republic which in turn broke down on August 1. And on August 3, Romanian troops marched into Budapest and occupied the capital until the middle of November. On November 16, 1919, Admiral Nikolaus von Horthy with his national army seized power in Hungary; as a result, groups of right extremists attained control of the government.[66] This change also meant the end of the relatively liberal self-governing bodies in the cities.[67]

The Budapest Ordinance concerning the land value tax was not actually rescinded by any of these changing administrations, but to the political disorders was added the rapid decline in value of the Hungarian currency. An inflation now set in which was similar in magnitude to the Austrian one, so that by 1919 the revenues from the tax, which had been based on the land value assessments of the previous year, were reduced to insignificance.

The rightist parties, which were supported by the tenement house owners' lobby and which ruled in Budapest at the time, now organized a campaign against Pikler.[68] Their principal objection—at the time a very effective one—against the land value tax was simply that this was an invention of the (then banned) Masons and of the Jews. Pikler, though still head of the capital's Land Valuation Office, had no contact with the new city delegates; but he writes that these men still could not bring themselves to abolish without a proper substitute the Ordinance of December 1917. During the decisive City Council debate, the speakers took turns countering each other's arguments directed against this Ordinance.[69] Finally, in 1921, it was decided that, while at that time the law was not to be rescinded, the collection of the tax was to be suspended for the time being. The legal department of the city was instructed to formulate a new, more "Christian" and more truly nationalistic land value tax ordinance.[70]

Things remained at that stage. The city agencies have not returned to the matter since then.

III

Pikler's Influence Abroad

THE NEWS OF JULIUS J. PIKLER'S initial successes in Hungary reached Vienna during the first World War.[71] The Viennese Socio-Pedagogical Society, founded by the Austrian Freemasons,[72] invited him to give an address in Vienna. Pikler's arguments were persuasive in Vienna as well: the Christian Socialist mayor, Dr. Richard Weiskirchner, and his deputy, von Goldemund, received Pikler and became converted by him to the idea of the land value tax.[73] Thus, already before the dissolution of the monarchy, the preparations began here too for the passing of appropriate legislation, which were not even undercut, whether by the revolutionary upheaval, by the reform of the franchise, by Weiskirchner's defeat at the polls on May 4, 1919, or by the entry of a two-thirds Socialist majority into the City Council.[74]

The contact with Pikler had been interrupted since the beginning of 1919, but on December 18, 1919, the "law concerning a tax on the current land value (land value tax) in the metropolitan area of the City of Vienna" was passed.[75] It followed in several ways the Budapest model, and the tax rate of 0.5 percent of the market price was taken over as well. But one major difference, a fact which later drove Pikler to bitter protest, lay in the provision that the amount was to be based on the landowners' self-appraisal.[76] Pikler saw in this a direct violation of the spirit of Georgism which required the creation of a tax measure through which no one could gain an advantage by cheating the community; and for the same reason, no one should be exposed to the temptation of making false statements. In a system truly governed by natural law, there would be no tax declarations, and the evaluation of a piece of land should, as had been done in Hungary, be done through an independent assessment office. This office, if required, would have to justify its assessment in writing to the concerned taxpayer, and would have to make all values available for public inspection in order to facilitate comparisons (in Budapest, Par. 8 of the City Ordinance provided that the values be issued as a city publication); and its decisions could be appealed in court.[77]

Whether the self-appraisal actually would have had a negative effect of this sort could not be determined empirically in Vienna. The valuations were carried out in 1920, and the tax collections began in 1921; but the revenues which, with a relatively stable currency, would have been quite substantial, appeared in the whirl of the galloping inflation from a fiscal standpoint to be hardly worth the trouble.[78] The Socialist majority in the City Council showed from the outset little enthusiasm for this tax. On one hand, the little man, whose grandparents had built a meager cottage at the far-away city limits, and who still lived modestly in this tiny home while the city had grown beyond his piece of land, the value of which had grown a thousand-fold—this little man was now to be burdened with a high tax. On the other hand, the wealthy tenement house owner on the parcel next to him would not have to pay more land value tax than the modest neighbor and, as far as his rental edifice was concerned, would be as tax-exempt as the little man's cottage. This did not sit well with a Marxist Socialist.[79] The Georgist thinking was that this wealthy man was useful to the community as a residence provides by using his land for rental apartments, while the poor neighbor was withholding a costly site from the community. Therefore, objectively speaking, the latter was a land speculator, even though the ultimate, unearned super-gain might not fall to him but to his heirs. However, such a viewpoint was incomprehensible to the Viennese Socialists.

In Budapest as in Vienna, it was doubtless the inflation and the thereby diminished revenues from the land value tax which helped its enemies to achieve an easy victory. Still, it must have been a tragic experience for Pikler to be forced to witness the wrecking, not only of his project, based on Henry George's teachings, but also of the law of his Viennese followers, even though it was a law slightly divergent from his conception. In Vienna, it was the Socialists whose ideology drove them to tax, not the land but the members of the propertied class, their enemies. They officially abolished the Viennese land value tax at the end of 1923.[80] In contrast, in Budapest it was the real estate owners who, supported by the majority in the City Council, prevented for understandable reasons of self-interest the taxation of their private land monopolies.

The news of Pikler's seemingly thoroughgoing success in Budapest reached, long after the demand for a land value tax had vanished in Hungary, into far-off foreign countries. In consequence of an article in the British Georgist journal, *Land & Liberty,* in which Dr. Pikler reported about his activities,[81] he was invited at the beginning of the 1920s by land reformers in northern Germany and Denmark to make a speaking tour. Pikler was able, through financial support of the United Committee for the Taxation of Land Values in London to make this trip, which ordinarily would have been impossible for a Hungarian, in straitened circumstances as a result of the war. In addition to Copenhagen, he visited the Hansa cities of Lübeck, Hamburg, and Bremen, where he spent, respectively, two, four and eight days.[82]

True, the periodical *Land Reform* of the Union of German Land Reformers, published by Adolf Damaschke, did not take any notice of the Hungarian's trip through northern Germany. But how Pikler was received there is indicated by a letter about the visit of the chairman of Bremen's Land Reformers, Otto Erich Günther, to the editor of *Land & Liberty*. In this letter, characterized by the editor as "enthusiastic," we read:

"Dr. Pikler's presence and activity in Bremen was entirely in keeping with our method of conducting our campaign, which aims at the introduction of as clean a form of Taxation of Land Values as possible. This has been our aim during all the years we have been working for the cause, and we have always put stress on this in our negotiations with friend and foe, in public and privately. It was our former chairman, Mr. Elwert, who, being a subscriber to *Land & Liberty*, had his attention drawn to Dr. Pikler by an article in that journal describing his work in Budapest. . . . In looking back upon Dr. Pikler's visit I can but say that the high expectations we had placed in it have been far surpassed. Quite apart from his being a charming man to know, he put an enormous amount of energy and self-sacrifice into his work, that we cannot but cherish the memory of his visit and personality among the pleasantest experiences we have had for a long time."[83]

Pikler also left a deep impression with his audience by the speech, cited previously in this chapter, before the participants at the International Georgist Congress in Oxford in 1923. The correspondent of the British Georgist periodical wrote about this event:

"Dr. Percy McDougall presided, and said he was introducing one of their friends whom they were all waiting to hear because of his eminent services as chief of the Land Valuation Department of Budapest. Dr. Pikler had already taken some part in their deliberations, and in these contributions had given them an insight into the great talents he possessed. Dr. Julius J. Pikler had chosen as the title of his address, 'Theoretical and Tactical Lessons to be learned from the Land-Value Policy in Hungary.' . . . Dr. Pikler's address, which occupied more than an hour's time, marshalled in masterly fashion a whole dossier of facts and arguments. It made a profound impression on his audience, and speakers in the discussion were glad to express their hearty appreciation of his informing treatment of the subject, especially complimenting on the way in which he had dealt with questions of controversy."[84]

In the years of Admiral Horthy's regency, Pikler's influence was shattered, and his potential for effectiveness was extinguished. He did, it is true, continue to enjoy much respect in the circles of the liberal intelligentsia. But the rigid and intolerant logicality of his theories and the extreme sharpness of his polemics had the result that, in Hungary after 1920, he could assemble only a small group of compatriots who, under a conservative regime, had become as ineffective as he. He made speeches and took part in panel discussions. On those occasions he was assured, as reports his closest collaborator Aládar Sós, of complete success owing both to his arguments and to his sarcastic comments, but his sarcasm did little to gain friends among the other participants in the debates. From 1934 to 1937 he published (together with Sós) a scientific periodical, *Állam és polgár* [State and Citizen], in which he sought to deepen the theoretical basis of Henry George's system and to solve, along his own lines of thinking, some problems not touched upon by George.

Pikler held fast to the Georgist tenets, as well as to the differentiation between two kinds of property, "the land (site) and men (respectively, labor power and its products)."[85] He believed that he could divide every social system according to the ways in which it dealt with these two kinds of property, of which the first (land) belonged by right to the community and the other (labor power and its products) definitely to the individual.[86]

Pikler was asked in 1948, four years before his death, at the end of an interview granted a German-language, Viennese, Jewish periodical, "Do you have hopes for the actualization of your teachings?" He gave an answer which was typical for his thinking, so opposed to any political compromise or compromise of any sort, and so strictly rationalistic, but indicative at the same time of his presentiment that his efforts were going to fail: "We are against collectivism, against a planned economy, in fact against any unnecessary ties or any avoidable coercion. Yet, we are also just as unrelenting in our hostility toward the misusers of monopolies as are the Communists. In other words, we are thoroughly out of step with the times. But I believe I know one thing: Our propositions are equal in rank of logic to the arithmetic equations of the multiplication table. Even if today someone were to forbid, in the name of some ideals, the use of the multiplication table, and were to turn the masses against it through the appropriate educational-propagandistic measures—the equation $2 \times 2 = 4$ would still win through in the end. That I shall scarcely see this happen is my private grief and sorrow."[87]

Notes

1. On the general situation and on the land question in the Kingdom of Hungary see Gyula Szekfü, *Hóman-Szekfü, Magyar történet* ['Hungarian History'], Vol. V, 2nd ed. (Budapest, 1936), p. 537 *ff.*; Erik Molnár *et al.*, *Magyarország története* ['History of Hungary'], Vol. II, 2nd ed. (Budapest, 1967), p. 188 *ff.* Magda M. Somlyai (publ.), *Földreform 1945* ['Bodenreform, 1945'] (Budapest, 1965), p. 7 *ff.*

2. According to Aladar Mód, *400 év küzdelem az önálló Magyarországért* [The 400-year battle for an independent Hungary'], 7th ed., (Budapest, 1954), p. 357. In 1895, 1,945 large estate owners shared 13.7 million "hold" (about one-third of the agricultural land of Hungary), while

1,358,875 smallholders had to be content with 2.5 million (about 6 per cent of the agricultural land).

3. Between 1899 and 1911, more than one million Hungarian residents emigrated overseas (Mód, *op. cit.*, p. 369; *cf.* also Zoltán Horváth, *Die Jahrhundertwende in Ungarn*, Neuwied/ Budapest, 1966), p. 345).

4. Molnar, *op. cit.*, p. 189.

5. Molnar, *op. cit.*, pp. 130 *ff.*

6. *Op. cit.*, p. 136 fn.

7. Mod, *op. cit.*, p. 376 fn.

8. *Op. cit.;* also see Molnár, *op. cit.*, p. 124.

9. On Szánto-Kovács *cf.* Agnes Kenyeres (ed.), *Magyar Életrajzi Lexikon* ['Hungarian biographical lexicon'], Vol. II (Budapest, 1969), p. 705 fn.; Szekfü, *op. cit.*, p. 542; Molnár, *op. cit.*, p. 141; Somlyai, *op. cit.*, p. 13, and Tibor Süle, *Sozialdemokratie in Ungarn* (Cologne, 1967), p. 33.

9a. See Mód, *op. cit.*, pp. 360 *ff.*

10. Somlyai, *op. cit.*, p. 11.

11. On Achim see I. Reinert-Tárnoky, "Ăchim L (iker), András," *Biographisches Lexikon zur Geschichte Südosteuropas* (Munich, 1972), p. 10 fn.

12. *Op. cit.*

13. *Loc. cit.*

14. Thus János Iván, *Földbirtokreform és társadalmunk 1890–1914* ['Landownership reform and our society 1890–1914'] (Budapest, 1935), p. 4 *ff.*, 34 *ff.*, 55 *ff.*, 80 *ff.*

15. *Op. cit.*, p. 67.

16. *Op. cit.*, p. 105.

17. *Op. cit.*, p. 41 fn, 43 fn, 53.

18. *Magyar Életrajzi Léxikon*, II, p. 444; on Prohászka see also Horváth, *op. cit.*, p. 249.

19. Iván, *op. cit.*, p. 70.

20. *Loc. cit.*

21. Damaschke, *Geschichte der Nationalökonomie*, II, p. 336; Damaschke, *Zeitenwende*, p. 294.

22. Ottokár Prohászka, "Ein Antrag zur Durchführung der Kriegerheimstätten in Ungarn," *Jahrbuch der Bodenreform*, XII, 1912, pp. 129–133.

23. Damaschke, *Geschichte der Nationalökonomie*, II, p. 337.

24. Horváth, *op. cit.*, p. 120 *ff.*, 240 *ff.;* about the Galilei-Circle: *op. cit.*, p. 351 *ff.* and Paul Ignotus, *Hungary* (London, 1972), p. 141.

25. *Révai Nagy Lexikona* [Révai's great lexicon], Vol. VII, (Budapest, 1913), p. 757 fn.

26. Süle, *op. cit.*, p. 140 *ff.*

27. *Op. cit.*, p. 166.

28. Molnár, *op. cit.*, p. 255.

29. On Count Károlyi *cf.*, *Magyar Életrajzi Lexikon*, I (Budapest, 1967), p. 870.

30. Damaschke, *Geschichte der Nationalökonomie*, II, p. 336.

31. *Op. cit.*, p. 337.

32. Molnár, *op. cit.*, p. 297.

33. The Hungarian form of his first name is Gyula. In his German and English publications he himself used the international form "Julius." (The translation of Hungarian first names was customary in Hungary before 1945 in interchange with foreign countries.)

34. *Magyar Életrajzi Lexikon*, II, p. 416; Julius J. Pikler should not be confused with his cousin, legal scholar and psychologist Julius Pikler (1864–1937; *ibid.*).

35. Paul Ignotus, "Die intellektuelle Linke im Ungarn der 'Horthy-Zeit' ", *Südost-Forschungen* XXVII (Munich, 1968), pp. 148–241 (239). In the footnote, Pikler's place of work of many years is given as the National Statistics Bureau instead of, correctly, the Budapest Public Statistics Office.

36. Insofar as in the following comments no other sources are indicated, the portrayal of the person and of the influence of Pikler's is based on data supplied by his closest collaborator in the area of Georgism, the architect and urban planner, Aladar Sós (about him *cf.* Revai XXI, 1935, p. 752), in letters of May 31, 1971, and August 24, 1972, as well as oral information of a student of Pikler, economist and historian Robert Major. Secalso Silagi, "Aladar Sós," *Land & Liberty*, London, LXXXII, 1975, p. 73.

37. Ignotus speaks of Pikler's "numerous enthusiastic students, who were fascinated by his incorruptible, razor-sharp logic" ("Die intellektuelle Linke . . . ," p. 239).

38. Hans Wehberg, *A. Th. Stamm* . . . , p. 25.

39. *Magyar Életrajzi Lexikon*, I, p. 263.

40. The editor of the *Single Tax Year Book*, Joseph Dana Miller, wrote in 1917 in his contribution "Historical Addenda," p. 194: "his visit to America a few years ago is pleasantly remembered by many Single Taxers in New York and other cities."

41. *Kormányzósagom története.* The English original was entitled *The Story of my Dictatorship* and appeared initially anonymously in 1894 in England. It describes how a politician, called to be dictator of England, translates George's program into action for the welfare of all.

42. In 1921, Braun published a translation of Henry George's *Social Problems* ('Társadalmi problémák').

43. An incomplete list of Pikler's medical and statistical writings: *Magyar Életrajzi Lexikon*, II, 416. According to this article, Pikler edited "for some time" the German-language periodical *Pester Medizinisch-Chirurgische Presse* and contributed to it "numerous medical and social-hygiene articles."

44. See Karl Krall, *Denkende Tiere*, 4th ed. (Leipzig, 1912), *passim.*

45. Julius J. Pikler, "Zur Frage der Dynamik und Systematologie des Geldes," *Schmollers Jahrbuch*, LI (Munich, 1927), pp. 723–760 (reprint of an address given by the author before the Oesterreichische Politische Gesellschaft in Vienna.).

46. According to Sós the voluminous manuscript of the unfinished work is lost. Pikler also wrote a whole series of combative and controversial essays, such as for the *Wiener Medizinische Wochenschrift, inter alia* about genetics, on the definition of life, and about the psychology of lying.

47. This and the following paragraph are based on Julius J. Pikler, *A magyar városi telekértekadó elméleti és gyakorlati tanulságai* ['The theoretical and practical lessons from the Hungarian city land value tax'], ms. [Budapest] [1924], p. 46. The subtitle of the 65-page brochure reads as follows: "Expansion of the speech given at the International Conference in Oxford, August 13–20, 1923." Meant is the international conference of Georgists, which takes place at several years' intervals in diverse places throughout the world. This brochure was the "Bible" of the Hungarian Georgists between the two world wars, and was labeled the "speech of Oxford" by them. The text appears to be a transcription rich in the rhetorical elements of a speech, but in view of its size only part of it could have been read to the audience. It is impossible to determine at this point what was actually spoken and what was expansion or subsequent addition. An excerpt of the Oxford speech is recorded in the Conference report: "Land Value Policy in Hungary - Theoretical and Practical Lessons," *International Conference on the Taxation of Land Values, Oxford, 1923, Official report of proceedings* (London, 1923), pp. 45–50. This excerpt was reprinted on 1960 as "A Land Values Classic" in *Land & Liberty*, LXVII, pp. 165–168; 185 fn, and a separate

reprint of the article in the journal was distributed as a pamphlet by the British Georgists. (In my text the Hungarian brochure is cited as "Oxford speech.")

Following Pikler, Robert Braun spoke on the theme "Social Conditions in Hungary." An excerpt of his speech is reprinted in the *Official Report,* p. 50 fn.

48. On the housing scarcity *cf.* György Kiss, *A budapesti várospolitika* ['The communal policy of Budapest'], 2nd ed. (Budapest, 1958), p. 95 *ff.*

49. On *Huszadik század* see Ignotus, *Hungary,* p. 112 fn and Horvath, *op. cit.,* p. 121, 129 fn.

50. Horvath, *op. cit.,* p. 121, 240 fn.

51. Information by letter from A. Sós.

52. Adolf Szabó, *Az Eötvös-Paholy hetveneves története* ['The 70-year history of the Lodge Eötvös'], (Budapest, 1947), p. 17 *ff.*

53. Information by letter from A. Sós.

54. Kiss, *op. cit.,* p. 143.

55. *Oxford Speech,* p. 46 fn.

56. Damaschke, *Geschichte der Nationalökonomie,* II, p. 337.

57. *Magyar Életrajzi Lexikon,* I, p. 115.

58. *Op. cit.,* II, p. 977.

59. The German translation of the regulation is reprinted in the *Jahrbuch der Bodenreform,* XVIII, 1918, pp. 174–179; the most important sections, together with a commentary by Pikler, are contained in the excerpt from the Hungarian's speech published by the English Georgists (see Note 592).

60. Pikler, *Oxford Speech,* p. 43.

61. Julius J. Pikler, "Der Weg zum Musterstaat," *Neue Welt und Judenstaat,* II, 14 (Vienna, 1949), p. 8.

62. Pikler, *Oxford Speech,* p. 48 fn.

63. *Op. cit.,* p. 49.

64. *Loc. cit.*

65. *Op. cit.,* p. 50.

66. Ignotus, *Hungary,* p. 141 *ff.*

67. Ignotus, "Die intellektuelle Linke . . . ," p. 156.

68. Pikler, *Oxford Speech,* p. 50.

69. *Op. cit.,* p. 51.

70. *Op. cit.,* p. 52.

71. *Op. cit.,* p. 53.

72. As King of Hungary the monarch permitted legal, open activities of the Freemasons; as Emperor of Austria, however, he upheld to the last the ban on the Lodges issued there at the end of the 18th century. This was the case through 1918, the end of the dual monarchy. As a result, when the Austrian Freemasons desired to take part in Lodge activities, they travelled to Hungary; at home they functioned under camouflage, through humanitarian and reform associations such as the "Social-Pedagogical Society." [Gustav] Kuéss, [Bernhard] Scheichelbauer, *200 Jahre Freimaurerei in Osterreich* (Vienna, 1959), p. 117 fn, 161 fn.)

73. Pikler, *Oxford Speech,* p. 53.

74. Rudolf Till, *Geschichte von Wien in Daten* (Vienna, 1948), p. 151; Karl Ziak, ed., *Unvergängliches Wien* (Vienna, 1964), p. 404.

75. *Entwurf für ein 'Wirtschaftsbefreiungsgesetz,'* 6th document of the Bundes österreichischer Bodenreformer, 2nd ed. (Vienna, 1933), p. 3.

76. *Op. cit.,* p. 4.

77. Pikler, *Oxford Speech,* p. 20 *ff.*

78. Philipp Knab, *Bodenwertbesteuerung in Österreich* (London, 1959), p. 2.

79. Josef Schwarzl, *Franz, Camillo und Siegfried Sitte* (Vienna, 1949), p. 4.

80. Till, *op. cit.,* p. 153. A home building tax was substituted for the previous realty tax to finance the municipal housing projects which later became world famous. But the new tax, however much it may have served a useful purpose, was by Georgist standards inhibiting to production and therefore inimical to the economy.

81. Julius J. Pikler, "The Valuation and Taxation of Land Value in Budapest," *Land & Liberty,* XXVII, 1920, p. 549 fn, and Pikler, "Hungary," *op. cit.,* XXIX, 1922, p. 276.

82. Pikler, *Oxford Speech,* p. 53; "Notes and News," *Land & Liberty,* XXX, 1923, p. 59.

83. "Notes and News," *Land & Liberty,* XXX, 1923, p. 59.

84. "Land Value Policy in Hungary," *Land & Liberty,* XXX, 1923, p. 175.

85. D. Sabbatai, "Ein humanistischer Sozialismus - Gespräch mit dem Sozialphilosophen Dr. Julius J. Pikler," *Neue Welt und Judenstaat,* I, 2, 1948, p. 8.

86. See also "A helyes társadalmi rendszer problémája" ['The problem of the correct social order], *Állam és polgár,* 1934, No. 1, pp. 2–12 (10 ff.)

87. Sabbatai, *loc. cit.*

12

Henry George and Europe:

In Denmark the Big Landowners Scuttled the Age-old Land Tax But the Smallholders, Moved by George, Restored It

By MICHAEL SILAGI*

Translated by SUSAN N. FAULKNER

ABSTRACT. The basic ideas of *Henry George,* 19th century American economist and social philosopher, were not novel in *Denmark,* which had a tradition of *land value taxation* and *free trade.* But they had special appeal for its small-holder farmers. They demanded that George's principles be applied more fully, getting all *tax revenues* from *the land*'s unimproved value, so that taxes on buildings, personal property and wages could be abolished. *Viggo Ullman*'s Danish-Norwegian translation of *Progress and Poverty* won the commitment of folk school movement leaders and the intelligentsia. In 1903 large landowners gained control of the Liberal Party and proceeded to abolish the traditional land tax, producer of up to 50 percent of State revenues. The Radical Liberals split and took over, to some extent carrying out George's taxation principles. In 1919 a Georgist party, the "*Retsforbundet*" was founded; it won the balance of power in 1957. But lack of finances and organizing ability and growing voter apathy ended its progress.

I

Danish Anticipations of George's Ideas

IN DENMARK, the reception of Henry George's thoughts took a different course than in England, Ireland, Germany, Hungary and Austria. Here, the taxation of land was not proposed—prior to the appearance of George's classic *Progress and Poverty,* by only a few scarcely noticed writers, as was the case, for example, in England. Free trade had been introduced in Denmark by the government as early as 1797, half a century earlier than in Great Britain, together with the abolition of all duties and import taxes.[1] Similarly, the land value tax was here, as we shall see, a traditional instrument of tax practice, so much so that the Copenhagen Member of Parliament and Secretary of State, Viggo Starcke, could say in 1957: "The ideas of land value taxation and free trade are old in Denmark.

* [Michael Silagi, Dr. jur. et phil., is a Senior Research Fellow at the Institut für Volkerrecht, Georg-August Universität, Platz der Göttinger Sieben 5, Blauer Turm, D-37073 Göttingen, Germany.]

American Journal of Economics and Sociology, Vol. 53, No. 4 (October, 1994).

Therefore, the philosophy of Henry George is popular in Denmark. It is blood of our blood."[2]

In other words, Henry George did not bring to Denmark a new discovery, the possibility and practicality of taxing the land; rather, he delivered, at the turn of the century, to the advocates of a long-existing domestic tax mode, new arguments for its imposition.

The impact of Georgism in Denmark is peculiar insofar as here the theses of the American social philosopher evoked the strongest echoes in rural areas, among the broad class of smallholders and not, as in other continental countries (as well as in the United States), in the cities. On November 8, 1902, the delegates of about a hundred agricultural cooperatives, at a meeting in the coastal town of Köge, passed the following Georgist-styled resolution:

> The Smallholders Association does not ask to be favored by the abolition of established real estate taxes and tithes which already exist at the time the property is taken over, and which are already taken into consideration by being deducted from the purchase price. The abolition of such burdens would, in effect, because of the resulting diminution of society's assets and at a loss to the unpropertied classes, accrue unjustly to the advantage of a single generation, and for the most part only to the large landowners.
>
> The Smallholders Association does demand, however, the earliest possible abolition of all duties and taxes which are imposed directly or indirectly on consumer products, as for example food stuffs, clothing, buildings, livestock, tools, machinery, raw materials, and labor-produced earnings, because such taxes place an unfair burden on labor and on the little man.
>
> In their place, the Smallholders Association asks that, to cover public expenditures, that value of the land be taxed which is not derived from individual labor, but which is due, rather, to the growth and development of society. This value reaches, especially in the large cities, tremendous proportions and enriches, undeservedly, private speculators, instead of being collected by the State or the community. Such taxes will not inhibit labor, but will make the land cheaper and will enable everyone to establish his own home.[3]

How did the delegates, belonging chiefly to the class of small farmers, arrive at these tax law concepts? What prompted them to entertain such argumentation based on natural law, not on class interest? The answer to these questions no doubt lies in the uniqueness of the historical development of the Danish farm classes. We will discuss these matters first, before taking up briefly the presuppositions of Danish tax history.

Until far into the 18th century, social conditions existed in rural Denmark similar to those in the rest of Europe: The farming population largely owned no land and was, since 1733, generally in bondage.[4] During the last third of the 18th century, a change, brought about by the spirit of the Enlightenment, took place which led within a few decades to the emancipation of the Danish rural population.[5] Initially hesitant attempts at reform were made under the aegis of the Court physician and Cabinet Minister of the ailing King Christian VII, Johann Friedrich Struensee.[6]

The coup d'état of Crown Prince Frederic (1784) signaled the beginning of thorough and systematic reforms of the legal and economic situations of the farmers. In 1786, a Land Cultivation Commission was appointed, consisting of landowners and royal officials, whose Secretary was the Norwegian jurist Christian Colbjornsen (1749–1814).[7] He was an advocate of the Enlightenment's doctrine of natural law and was, therefore, opposed to all class differences. He was able to win through in the Commission with his views, and in agreement with his conceptions, the decisive step was taken in 1788 toward the goal sought by him of a free farmers' class. A gradual elimination of land servitude was decided upon, and at the same time, regulations were laid down which re-ordered the relationship between landowners and tenants in favor of the latter. In addition, legislative changes were made which facilitated, and even promoted, the transfer of land to ownership by the farmers. Together with the legislative measures, steps for the modernization of agricultural methods were undertaken which resulted in "an increased production and a greater feeling of self-esteem" (Carlsson[8,9]).

Thus, within a few decades a class of independent owners of small farms was created, numbering in the hundred thousands.[10] While the Danish farmers had, until 1788, hardly owned any land, an 1873 census counted 70,959 small farms and 131,162 small plots.[11]

In the final decades of the 19th century, in Denmark as everywhere in Europe, the competition from overseas grain and meat producers became increasingly severe. The overseas producers not only worked on larger acreages and more efficiently; but with the advent of the steam engine they were able to transport their products at relatively low cost and now put pressure on the European markets. But Danish agriculture succeeded in changing over, within a few years, from grain and cattle production to the dairy industry and product processing.[12]

This "goal-oriented and successful"[13] changeover of agriculture was carried out so smoothly and rapidly only because the Danish rural population had developed an extraordinary readiness to adapt to changing circumstances. This was the result of a broadly based and highly effective educational undertaking, the adult education provided by the celebrated Danish folk schools. This movement, stimulated and led in the 1840s by the theologian, poet and historian Bishop Severin Gruntvig (1783–1872),[14] effected a breakthrough in the years following 1864.

Under the impact of the defeat by Prussia and Austria and the loss of the duchies of Schleswig, Holstein, and Lauenburg, Gruntvig circulated the slogan that that which had been lost externally must be rewon internally.[15] The folk schools promoted internal colonization and founded numerous "agricultural schools," schools of vocational education which provided the farmers with the mechanical and mental tools needed to win the sharpened battle of international competition.[16]

These men of the folk school movement also were the first ones in Scandinavia to have come upon Henry George.[17] In 1886, seven years after its first American edition, a Danish-Norwegian translation appeared of *Progress and Poverty,* the work of the Norwegian folk school principal and later President of Parliament, Viggo Ullman. A short time later, editions followed of *Social Problems* and *Protection or Free Trade.*[18] In Norway, as in Sweden, Henry George's ideas remained by and large without effect,[19] but in Denmark they fell on fertile soil.

As already stated, land value taxation here was a long-time tradition, reaching back into the Middle Ages.[20] One of the leading men in the circle of the enlightened reformers surrounding Crown Prince Frederic, estate-owner and Minister Count Christian Detlev Reventlow (1748–1827),[21] submitted a study which followed up older models. In it he pointed out that land should be taxed, not according to its size but "according to its value," since this value "shows most clearly how much money can be obtained form this parcel of land, and on the basis of this value of the potential yield . . . the taxes could be paid rightly by all."[22]

This proposal was realized in 1844 when a so-called "hartkorn tax" was introduced, the amount of which was determined by the natural fertility and the potential yield of the piece of land to be taxed. In Danish, "hartkorn" was originally the designation for barley and rye, but with time took on the meaning of a unit of measurement of the value as well of all other kinds of crops, which were converted, in accordance with a fixed scale,[23] into "tons of hartkorn" (land-tax tons). Since 1688, the "hartkorn ton" had also served as both measure of area and bounty.[24] In a farmland book prepared in the middle of the 19th century, about 2.83 hectares of the best land corresponded to one hartkorn ton. On the average, however, the land-value ton corresponded to a land area of 9.6 hectares.[25]

The "hartkorn tax," which at times constituted more than 50 percent of the state revenues,[26] and which at times contributed to the state treasury more than half the land rent,[27] was abolished in 1903 by the governing Liberals. The place of this levy—till then the only direct tax—was to be taken, on a step-by-step basis, by a combination of progressive income taxes and property taxes. In regard to land taxation this meant that the land rent would no longer be the assessment base, but rather that the sales value of the land, improvements, and buildings together would be taxed at a uniform rate.[28]

The Liberal Party, which in the 1870s had represented the progressive part of Denmark as the "united Left," had become through the years increasingly a party of the Center, yes even of the Right.[29] It lost its impetus toward reform and came to represent the interests of the large landowners. Their lobby successfully fought against the old hartkorn tax and forced the introduction of tax legislation favorable to them.

This tax reform of 1903 discriminated greatly against the small farmer. On their intensively managed, small holdings stood valuable agro-technical constructions and buildings; and among them, on whom the tax system of the Liberals placed additional, heavy burdens,[30] there was much resistance.

The Irish tenant-farmers saw in land ownership the remedy for their suffering, while in Hungary the agricultural workers, seeking an articulation of their needs, encountered the program of the Socialists. But the rebellious Danish smallholders found in the Georgist program, about which they learned in the agricultural schools of the folk school program, that which appeared to them to point to a way out.

II

The Georgist Struggle for Land and Tax Reform

THE MEN OF THE FOLK SCHOOLS had become acquainted with the ideas of Henry George through a young colleague, agricultural teacher and later Director of the Smallholders' School of the Füne Foundation in Odense, Jakob E. Lange. In 1886, while he was studying botany in Kew in England, he had become acquainted with the American's teachings,[31] and in the ensuing years he propagandized for Henry George's ideas in the high school organ, *Höjskolebladet.*

Lange's articles met with strong encouragement among many readers: "Many high schoolmen," writes the chronicler of the Danish folk school movement, Fridlev Skrubbeltrang, "saw in George's social concepts, which demanded—along with personal freedom—the equal rights to the goods of nature, a timely continuation of the reform ideas of the 18th century."[32]

In 1889, Jakob E. Lange, together with Viggo Ullman, succeeded in winning over a few colleagues for the founding of the Union for Social Reform, the first Georgist association in Scandinavia.[33] But until 1901, Georgism in Denmark remained a matter for a handful of pedagogues active in adult education. Among the broad public, the Union was hardly noticed, and when after some time Ullman ceased publication of the Union journal edited by him, the movement appeared to have come to a complete end.

In 1902, however, one of the Danish Georgists had the idea to invite, by means of a newspaper advertisement, the followers of the American land reformers to a meeting in Copenhagen. Twenty men heeded the call and, on March 2, 1902, founded the Henry George League. This League, of which Jakob E. Lange became Chairman, issued the following statement of principles, whose content has remained until today the program of the Danish League:

> It is our purpose to work for the solution of the social problems through the economic liberation of the people with those means which Henry George has shown us, namely: The realization of full taxation of the land value and of free trade, as well as the abolition of all taxes on values and earned income produced by human labor. For the attainment of this goal we seek fellow combatants from all social classes and all political parties.[34]

Although initially only twenty people responded to this organizing appeal, the Danish Georgists and the adult educators were able, in a very short time, to win over the small farmers to the ideas of the land value tax and free trade. This second founding of a land reform association occurred at the precise time when the smallholders were beginning to fight the tax plans of the Liberal Party, and the theses of Georgism and natural law supplied the beleaguered group with welcome arguments. Within only eight months, on November 2, 1902, the Georgist line of thinking was admitted into the above mentioned declaration of the delegates of the Cooperatives in Köge.

As we have seen, the smallholders advocated retaining and improving the old tax on land value, because on their intensively cultivated farms the value of the improvements was disproportionately large compared to that of the land. In the Köge declaration, the "elimination of all duties" was called for—this too a peculiarity in the catalogue of demands of a farmers' movement. In Belgium, and especially in Great Britain, it was the powerful industrial and trade interests who had compelled the adoption of free trade—over the protests of the domestic farming class, which, without protectionist measures, could not withstand overseas competition. In Denmark, in contrast, agriculture had a profound interest in the abolition of obstructive trade barriers, since with its processed products which were superbly competitive internationally, it depended on foreign markets.[35]

As early as 1902, the delegates of other cooperatives, meeting in Odense on Fünen and in Roskilde on Seeland, made the Köge declaration their own,[36] and within a short time it became the foundation of the tax program of all smallholders in the Kingdom.[37] The small Danish Georgist League had found among the smallholders a mass base; these smallholders obtained entrance for the idea of land value taxation within the platform of the young radical Left.

This new movement split off in 1903 from the now only nominally "Liberal" Party and adopted the designation of "Radical Left." In foreign policy matters, the new group took a pacifist stand and found its most powerful support in the country among the freethinking, urban intelligentsia and the smallholders.[38]

The hour for the secessionists—and with it, for the smallholders—came at the end of 1909, when the Radicals, though the smallest fraction in Parliament, were charged, following a government crisis, with forming a new cabinet.

The newly appointed Minister of the Interior, Peter Munch, failed in his attempt to hold up the effectuation of the step-by-step plan to convert the old land-value tax into a tax on all unmovable property (land plus buildings plus improvements). But his proposal, to carry out—on an experimental basis—an appraisal on one hand of the land alone, on the other hand of buildings, carried despite the vigorous resistance by the Conservatives and old Liberals.[39] Although the Radicals remained in power less than a year, initial, tentative land appraisals took place in 1911 in a few provinces.

In the years after 1910, the Georgist movement received a new lift through generous financial grants of Joseph Fels, American manufacturer and adherent of Henry George's doctrine. It was he who had unsuccessfully offered the German land reformers an enormous annual contribution if they would adopt principles based exclusively on George's teachings.[40] Thanks to Fels' aid, the Danish Single-Tax supporters were able to found an institute for the propagation of Henry George's ideas, thereby vastly strengthening their recruitment efforts. As a result, their membership rose to about 3,000.[41]

When the Radicals regained power after the General Election in 1913, they tried to push through a law which provided for a general reappraisal of all land with separate valuation of land and of improvements. While this law was unanimously adopted by the Lower House, it was, however, defeated by a veto of the Upper House. But the Radicals did not give up, and at the second try they achieved success; at the end of 1915 their law was passed. In the following year, a valuation of unmovable property was undertaken in which land values were considered apart,[42] and this was repeated in 1920.

In 1922, the great breakthrough took place: The principle of separate appraisal of land without improvements and buildings was anchored in a land tax law which had strongly Georgist features. The national land tax, the amount of which until then had been based on the total value of land and improvements, was separated into two taxes, one on the value of the land alone in the amount of 1.5 parts per mill, and one on buildings and improvements, the rate of which was one-quarter lower.[43] A short time later, a differentiation for the communal land tax at the corresponding rates was adopted as well, at a ratio of 4 to 3.[44]

Dan Björner, a Danish Georgist, has commented about these fiscal measures taken by the Radicals at the beginning of the 1920s: "We are indebted to the political party *det radikale Venstre* (the Radical Liberals) for the enactment of this law which, although from the revenue point it was an extremely small installment, did after all establish a principle in our legislation."[45]

As a matter of fact, the principal presupposition, aside from considerations of morality and natural law, for the imposition of a land value tax was an understanding of the feasibility of a separate appraisal of land values. That there might at times be borderline cases where it could not be determined whether value increase factors were nature-given and, therefore, to be collected by society, or were brought about by individual labor, did not disturb the Danish legislator. When in doubt, he decided—wholly in the spirit of Henry George[46]—in favor of the community. Improvements at the expense of the owner, which are connected with the land in such a way as to have become part of its value, could be deducted from the taxed land value for only 30 years, but in the case of forests for 60 years.[47]

After this ground-breaking success, the Danish Georgists were unable, however, to effectuate further substantial tax law reforms along their lines of thinking. But with the principle of a separate taxation of land and improvements, and at different rates, a basic Georgist tenet became an established part of the Danish tax system; it was not touched even by succeeding governments.[48]

So in Denmark, too, there was an end, by the onset of the 1920s, of the great impact of Henry George's ideas. But it is worth noting that in this country a political party was founded in 1919 whose program was based on the Single-Tax doctrine—a unique event in the history of Georgism. Its name was the "Party of Justice" ('Retsforbundet').

Among its founders was the pioneer of sociology in Scandinavia, the Copenhagen university professor Carl Nicolai Starcke (1858–1926),[49] who had, since the turn of the century, contributed through numerous scientific writings to the dissemination of George's teachings.[50] In his last, extensive work—which did not appear until 1932, 6 years after his death—*Laws of Social Evolution and Social Ideals,* he commented on George's "panacea" for the solution of the social and economic problems, the land-value tax:

> "It is only natural that those who possess the privilege of the possession of land make every effort in their power to preserve it, and, on one side, use their actual power to destroy those who might threaten to take it from them, on the other side, spread various Duk-Duk myths of their capable administration of the riches of the earth, of their clever financial administration, etc. One of the most generally used of these Duk-Duk myths is to call Henry George a quack doctor who deludes people with the idea that society may be cured through the application of a panacea. It is overlooked that it has been proved that the cause of the principal disease in society is the fact that the enormous rape of land has been allowed to subsist. Just as simple as is the disease, must be the remedy: through ground-duty to put a stop to this robbery."[51]

The Party of Justice has been represented in the Danish Parliament since 1926. It achieved notable successes after World War II, when Henry George's ideas experienced a renaissance, though short-lived. In 1947 the party increased its seats from two to six. Its leadership was assumed by the physician Viggo Starcke,[52] son of the party's co-founder C. N. Starcke.

With Viggo Starcke, a man came to be leader of the party whose statesmanlike qualities were recognized even by political opponents.[53] In 1950, he led the Danish Georgists to their greatest electoral success: 8.2 percent of the votes gave the party twelve delegate seats. Yet, between 1957 and 1960, the Party of Justice reached the acme of its political influence: With its nine (out of 179) delegates it became the "pointer on the scale" in the parliamentary power struggle, and in a coalition with Socialists and Radicals, it was able to have three Cabinet ministers appointed (the Minister of the Interior, the Minister of Fisheries, and—in Viggo Starcke—one Minister without Portfolio).[54]

The work of this coalition government was extraordinarily successful. The "realistic, relatively tight course of its social and financial policies" prompted the *Neue Zürcher Zeitung* to speak, in October 1960, of a "Danish 'economic miracle' "[55]; and W. Glyn Jones, in 1970, in his book *Denmark,* called the years of 1957 to 1960 "a time of hitherto unknown prosperity in Denmark."[56]

Still, only the Socialists were able to improve their membership even slightly in the 1960 election. The Radicals suffered heavy losses, and the Georgists ruinous ones[57] of which they have been unable to recover.

The decline in membership of the Party of Justice is generally attributed to the small number of habitual, convinced voters.[58] Its success in the 1950s, in fact, is to be credited in large measure to the great political and rhetorical abilities of its leader, Viggo Starcke, who was able from time to time to win many dissatisfied protest votes for the Single-Tax party.[59]

Viggo Starcke himself sees the limitations in finances and in people to carry on publicizing and lobbying efforts of his party as the chief cause of its demise: "Most people understand that if you put taxes on land the selling price falls—but if you put taxes on production, consumers' goods, housing and trade the prices rise. . . . But if you can exclude these arguments from the newspapers, the Parliament, or the radio, most people are victims of the well organized teachings of monopolism. . . . The social and political background for our policy was sound. What was wrong was our lack of money, press and organization."[60]

As to the significance of his oratorical talents for the appeal of the Danish Georgists during the 1950s, Starcke says: "My oratorical abilities were not greater than those of most political orators, but what made me dreaded by the other parties was what I said. When oratorical abilities are added to common sense the effect is formidable."[61]

Notes

1. Viggo Starcke, *The History of Land-Taxation in Denmark* (London, 1949), p. 3.
2. Starcke, *The Danish Government* (London, 1959), p. 1.
3. Damaschke, *Geschichte der Nationalökonomie,* II, p. 322.
4. Sten Carlsson, "Der Norden 1720–1815," *Historia Mundi* IX, ed. Fritz Valjavec (Bern, 1960), pp. 172–196 (179 fn).

5. Roar Skovmand, "Emancipation of the Peasant," *Scandinavia—Past and Present,* II, ed. Jörgen Burkdahl *et alia* (Odense, 1959), pp. 643–646, *passim.*

6. Carlsson, *op. cit.*, p. 194; on Struensee *cf.* K. Wittich, "Struensee: Johann Friedrich," *Allgemeine Deutsche Biographie,* XXXVI (Leipzig, 1893), pp. 647–661.

7. On Colbjörnsen *cf.* Francis Bull, "Colbjörnsen, Christian," *Norsk Biografisk Leksikon,* III (Oslo, 1926), pp. 58–67.

8. Carlsson, *op. cit.*, p. 181.

9. Skovmand, *op. cit.*, p. 643*ff.*

10. Carlsson, *op. cit.*, p. 181.

11. Per *Meyers Konversations-Lexikon,* 4th ed. (Leipzig, 1890), Vol. IV, p. 503.

12. Hans Lund, "Danish Agriculture," *Scandinavia—Past and Present,* III, ed. Aage Heinberg *et alia* (Odense, 1959), pp. 503–514 (505).

13. Palle Lauring, *Geschichte Dänemarks* (Neumünster, 1964), p. 209.

14. Fridlev Skrubbeltrang, *Die Volkshochschule* (Copenhagen, 1952), p. 14*ff.*

15. *Op. cit.*, p. 45 ff. and A. Victor Murray, "Education," *The New Cambridge Modern History,* XI (Cambridge, 1962), p. 200.

16. Lauring, *op. cit.*, p. 209.

17. Dan Björner, *The Henry George Movement in Denmark; Efforts and Achievements over Fifty Years* (London, 1952), p. 4.

18. P. Larsen, "Denmark" and S. Wielgolaski, "Norway," *Single Tax Year Book* (New York, 1917), pp. 164–170 and 174 fn.

19. George Raymond Geiger, *The Philosophy of Henry George* (New York: Macmillan, 1930), p. 447 n fn.

20. Starcke, *History,* p. 3*ff.*

21. Zu Reventlow *cf.* Hans Jensen, "Reventlow, Christian Ditlev Frederik," *Dansk Biografisk Leksikon,* XIX (Copenhagen, 1940), pp. 429–435.

22. Starcke, *History,* p. 1.

23. *Cf.* the section "Valuation and Hartkorn Assessment" in the English "Summary" by C. Rise Hansen and Axel Steensberg, *Jordfordeling og Udskifting* (Copenhagen, 1951), p. 434*ff.*

24. Axel Nielsen, *Dänische Wirtschaftsgeschichte* (Jena, 1933), p. 15, 172.

25. *Meyers Konversations-Lexikon, loc. cit.*

26. Starcke, *History,* p. 2.

27. K. J. Kristensen, *Land Valuation and Land-Value Taxation in Denmark* (London, 1964), p. 11.

28. *Loc. cit.*

29. Kenneth E. Miller, *Government and Politics in Denmark* (Boston, 1968), p. 57 fn.

30. Kristensen, *op. cit.*, p. 11.

31. Larsen, *op. cit.*, p. 164.

32. Skrubbeltrang, *op. cit.*, p. 89.

33. Björner, *op. cit.*, p. 5.

34. *Loc. cit.*

35. F. H. Hinsley, "Introduction," *The New Cambridge Modern History,* XI, ed., author (Cambridge, 1962), pp. 1–48 (8).

36. Damaschke, *Geschichte der Nationalökonomie,* II, p. 322.

37. Larsen, *op. cit.*, p. 167.

38. K. E. Miller, *op. cit.*, p. 60.

39. Larsen, *op. cit.*, p. 169.

40. Michael Flürscheim, *Rent, Wages and Interest* (1891; 3rd ed. rev.: London: William Reeves, 1895). Lewis Henry Berens, *Toward the Light* (London: Swan Sonnenschein & Co. 1903).

41. Larsen, *op. cit.*, p. 166*ff.*

42. *Ibid.*, p. 169*fn.*

43. Kristensen, *op. cit.*, p. 12.

44. *Loc. cit.*

45. Björner, *op. cit.*, p. 6.

46. "In the oldest country in the world no difficulty whatever can attend the separation, if all that be attempted is to separate the value of the clearly distinguishable improvements, made within a moderate period, from the value of the land, should they be destroyed. This, manifestly, is all that justice or policy requires. Absolute accuracy is impossible in any system, and to attempt to separate all that human race has done from what nature originally provided would be as absurd as impracticable." (George, *Progress and Poverty*, p. 423*ff.*

47. K. J. Kristensen, *op. cit.*, p. 12.

48. *Op. cit.*; but in fact K. J. Kristensen, in his article *The Georgeist Situation in Denmark* (London, 1964), p. 7 fn., points out that the share of the land value tax in the total Danish tax revenues sank from 8.4% in 1938/39 to 4.6% in 1963/64, and that the farmers had the land value tax payments returned to them in the form of subsidies.

49. On C. N. Starcke see S. v. Rasmussen, "Starcke, Carl Nicolai," *Dansk Biografisk Leksikon*, XXII (Copenhagen, 1942), pp. 416–19.

50. A bibliography of his works with all here pertinent titles is appended to his English-language book *Laws of Social Evolution and Social Ideals*, published posthumously (Copenhagen, 1932), on p. 408*ff.*

51. *Op. cit.*, p. 355 fn.

52. On Viggo Starcke (b. 1895) see Poul Hansen, *Contemporary Danish Politicians* (Copenhagen, 1949), pp. 165*ff.*

53. As by the prominent Danish Social-Democrat Poul Hansen in the book cited above about contemporary Danish politicians of 1949.

54. Viggo Starcke, *Government*, p. 1 fn.

55. "Das dänische 'Wirtschaftswunder,'" *Neue Zürcher Zeitung*, 1960, issue 285.

56. W. Glyn Jones, *Denmark* (New York, 1970), p. 196.

57. *Op. cit.*, p. 201.

58. *Op. cit.* and K. E. Miller, *op. cit.*, p. 93.

59. K. E. Miller, *op. cit.*, p. 93; Poul Hansen wrote about Starcke's political magnetism: "Crowds flock to his public meetings." *Op. cit.*, p. 169.

60. Information in letter of Viggo Starcke of November 2, 1972.

61. *Loc. cit.*

13
Appendix
Henry George and Pope Leo XIII's Encyclical, Rerum novarum

SINCE 1882 the Roman Curia had shown an interest in Henry George's land reform theses. Its attention had been attracted by a speech given by the Catholic priest, the Rev. Edward McGlynn (1837-1900)[1] at a meeting of the Friends of the Irish Land League. Father McGlynn had been pastor of St. Stephen's, one of the largest Catholic parishes in New York, since 1866. McGlynn had endorsed without reservation the remedy proposed by George for eliminating mass poverty in the United States and in Ireland.[2] After a report about the speaker's views had been sent to Rome, the Prefect of the Congregation for the Propagation of the Faith — which had supervision over the churches in the United States, then still regarded as a missionary country — Cardinal Giovanni Simeoni,[3] asked McGlynn's superior, the New York Archbishop, Cardinal John McCloskey,[4] to reprimand and, if necessary, suspend the priest for his espousal of the Georgist 'heresy.'[5]

Thereupon, McGlynn promised the Archbishop not to campaign publicly in the future for George's teachings. But after McCloskey's death in 1885, McGlynn no longer felt himself bound by his promise. With the successor, Archbishop Michael Augustine Corrigan,[6] a stiff-necked opponent of Henry George, the conflict became exacerbated,[7] and reached its climax in 1887 with McGlynn's excommunication.[8]

Corrigan was not only concerned, however, with reprimanding the refractory priest, he wanted to attack the Georgist movement as a whole. Therefore, he tried to obtain a ban on George's classic, *Progress and Poverty,* from Rome. His endeavors found strong echoes in certain circles of the Curia,[9] and the congregation of the Inquisition (the Holy Office) began to subject George's book to critical study.

Two Anglo-Saxon churchmen, the Archbishop of Baltimore, Cardinal James Gibbons,[10] and Cardinal Henry Edward Manning[11] of London, were able to prevent a public condemnation of Henry George's teachings. In fact, Gibbons had already been active as peacemaker, though unsuccessfully, in the case of McGlynn.[12] Like the majority of the American episcopacy, he opposed a ban on *Progress and Poverty,* but not because he himself was in any way a follower of the Single-Tax doctrine. He believed that such a step would hurt the Church, since George's cause would thereby merely gain unwanted publicity. In his correspondence with the Holy See, he therefore advised repeatedly against a ban, and he expressed this view as well in several audiences with Pope Leo XIII.[13]

Gibbons found his most powerful ally in his friend, the Archbishop of Westminster and member of the Congregation of the Index. Cardinal Manning, the latter in 1884, had made the personal acquaintance of the American social philosopher.[14] Aside from the question whether the expropriated landowners were to be compensated, he advocated views quite similar to George's.[15] George, in his open letter of 1891 to Leo XIII, *The Condition of Labor,* placed at its head as motto a quotation from the English churchman about the land problem.[16] In 1885, Manning, as member of the Royal Commission on the Housing of the Working Classes, had voted in favor of the final report.[17] Gibbons turned to him with the request that he should use his influence as member of the Congregation of the Index[18] and was assured by Manning that *Progress and Poverty* would not be placed on the list of books to be banned.[19] (The congregation was dissolved in 1917.)

In effect, there was no public condemnation of Henry George on the part of the Vatican. True, the Holy Office declared in 1889 that the American's works were deserving of disapproval. But Cardinal Simeoni, in informing Cardinal Gibbons on behalf of the Congregation of the sentence of the Cardinals of the Inquisition, stated:

> The books published by Henry George have been examined by the Holy Office on Wednesday, February 6, 1889, and they have been found worthy of condemnation. The members of the Congregation were, however, aware of the special circumstances of time and place and of the zeal and passion with which all bishops of the Republic care for the protection of the believers entrusted to them from proclaimed heresies. Therefore, they have decided to abstain from making known publicly their disapproval. But they are confident that all local bishops, as far as land is concerned, will stick to the perpetual Catholic doctrine on private property, as defined repeatedly and as stressed most recently in the encyclical letters *Qui pluribus* of Pope Pius IX, and *Quod Apostolici muneris* of Pope Leo XIII. They are confident, too, that the local bishops will beware of the wrong theories which Henry George tries to sell thereon.[20]

What connection there may have been between this condemnation of Henry George's teachings and the publication of *Rerum novarum,* "the first encyclical which systematically defined the Catholic social doctrine" (H. Sorgenfrei[21]), by Pope Leo XIII two years later, will probably never be completely clear. But it is a fact that Cardinal Gibbons, since early 1888, had urged the Pope several times that he, instead of banning *Progress and Poverty,* oppose in an encyclical Henry George's doctrine with an authoritative statement by the Catholic Church regarding the question of property.[22] Cardinal Gibbons saw in the encyclical the fulfillment of a long-harbored wish.[23]

In fact, it is noticeable in *Rerum novarum* what a predominant role is played in the discussion of private property rights by the defense of landownership (Nos. 4-8 of the edition arranged by Gustav Gundlach).[24] Leo XIII's effort to justify private property in land begins with paragraph 4. In his open reply to the Pope, *The Condition of Labor,* Henry George condensed this paragraph to the "quite correct formula" (Sorgenfrei)[25] that everything that was bought with lawful property in turn became lawful property.[26] The only property for which this is expressly proven by the Pope is land; when a worker invests his savings in a piece of land, such a parcel of land is "nothing else than wages, only in a new form."[27]

At the end of the next paragraph we read the following: "Now, since man is among all animal creatures a being of intellect, it is his due that he may not only use the earth's goods like the other creatures, but have them as his inalienable and permanent property; this applies not only to the things of direct use, but also to durables."[28] That the term "durable" goods — not what is now called consumer durables — meant chiefly land is made clear in the next paragraph, No. 6: "Since it is given to man that he can choose the objects of his needs not only for the moment, but also for the future, man has the power to dispose not only of the fruits of the earth, but of the land itself. For the land alone guarantees by its inexhaustible wealth the constant supply of human needs."[29]

The following comments regarding the property rights are likewise concerned almost exclusively with the land. Leo XIII explains at the beginning of the next paragraph why the dogma, that God had given the earth to mankind as a whole, did not contradict the right of private landownership,[30] and he then continues:

> Although the land is special property of individuals, one should not forget that it always remains for the use of the community; for there is no mortal who in some way does not live by the land's products. Who does not own land, substitutes with his labor for that. Therefore one can say rightly that all means to take care of the necessities of life are provided through labor, namely, through labor on one's own land or in another area of the production of goods. Thereby, however, the earnings are due again, in the final analysis, to the manifold yields of the land and represent its equivalent.
>
> These facts prompt anew the conclusion that private property is definitely a requirement of nature. For the earth, it is true, spends with great generosity the requisites for the maintenance and improvement of the living standard. Yet it does so in no way by itself but only through the efforts and care of men. But

> whenever man uses his mental powers and physical force to obtain nature's goods, he thereby orders that part of the material world in which he participates in the direction of his own person; at the same time, he adds something personal so that one can assert rightfully that this part is his untouchable property.[31]

The emphasis with which Leo XIII repeatedly stresses the moral justification, especially, of landownership, could only lead Henry George to the conclusion that "the most strikingly pronounced condemnations of *Rerum novarum* were directed against the ideas of *Progress and Poverty* (Barker).[32] He was reinforced in this view by Cardinal Manning's comment to Henry George Jr., the social philosopher's son then living in London, that the papal encyclical was directed against his father's teachings.[33] Adolf Damaschke also saw in the encyclical a criticism of the American and his theories: "For it turns predominantly against George's doctrine and thereby proves what significance the land reform movement must have attained in the last ten years."[34]

Leo does introduce his remarks about private property with an account of the Socialist attempts at solving the ills of the existing system.[35] But one can hardly see in the comments to follow an attempt at refuting Marxist Socialism. For Socialists, as we have seen, land played essentially no special role comparable to that of capital. Perhaps Leo XIII viewed the land reformers as Socialists — more precisely, agrarian Socialists — and their doctrine as a variety, one most difficult to refute, of Socialism; surely, most of the Pope's arguments against Marxism fell wide of the mark. Hence, Barker says justly: "The Henry George evidence does seem to indicate that not Karl Marx, the materialist, but a disturbing American idealist has been the great enemy in ideas, at whom Pope Leo was striking."[36]

Leo unequivocally turns against Henry George and the land reformers in the 8th paragraph, which immediately follows the above citation, and in which the Pope summarizes his earlier reasons for justifying private landownership:

> This is so evident and demonstrable that the contradiction by a few revivers on long-rejected opinions is surprising. These people do concede, in fact, to man the use of land and the utilization of its manifold yield, but they deny him the right to own the real estate on which he is building or the parcel of land which he is farming. They overlook, in actuality, that they are thereby depriving man of the fruit of his labors. For an acre is [...] completely changed [...] by the hand of the cultivator. The means used for improvements now have become so bound up with the land and have become so much a part of it that they are almost totally inseparable from it. [...] It is in the order of things that the fruit of work efforts belongs to him who does the labor, in the same way that the things which are produced are to be classed with the cause which created them.[37]

In his study about "The Ideological Background of the Social Encyclical *Rerum novarum"*, Helmut Sorgenfrei, too, is of the opinion that some passages of the papal work are directed against Henry George.[38] But when he assumes their initiator to be the editor of the encyclical, Cardinal Camillo Mazzella, S. J.,[39] "for he lived for years in America and certainly became acquainted there with agrarian Socialists,"[40] he is in error: Mazzella came from Italy to the U.S.A. in 1867 in order to teach theology at Woodstock College, but he followed a call of the Gregoriana to Rome, in other words, before the publication of *Progress and Poverty* in 1878. Thus he could not have become personally acquainted with the "agrarian Socialists," as Sorgenfrei calls Henry George's followers. Much more likely, the pertinent remarks in the encyclical *Rerum novarum* appear to have originated with Cardinal Gibbons.[41]

Notes

1. On McGlynn *cf.* John A. Ryan, "McGlynn, Edward," Dictionary of American Biography, XII (London, 1933), pp. 53 *ff.*

2. John Tracy Ellis, *The Life of James Cardinal Gibbons,* I (Milwaukee, 1952), p. 550.

3. On Simeoni (1816-1892) *cf.* A. Randall, "Simeoni, Giovanni," *New Catholic Encyclopdia,* XIII (New York, 1967), p. 219.

4. On McCloskey (1810-1885) *cf.* Brendan A. Finn, *Twenty-Four American Cardinals* (boston, 1947), pp. 19-43.

5. Ellis, *op. cit.* p. 550.

6. On Corrigan (1839-1902) *cf.* Richard J. Purcell, "Corrigan, Michael Augustine," *Dictionary of American Biography,* IV (London, 1930), pp. 450-452.

7. In connection with Corrigan's attitude toward McGlynn and George, Shane Leslie *(Henry Edward Manning/His Life and Labors,* London, 1921, p. 352) gives the following portrayal of the New York Archbishop: "Dr. Corrigan appeared too humble and sensitive to rule as an Archbishop. But gentle as a woman to all whom he met in the ordinary course of life, when confronted with a vital issue he could become a lion in defence of faith."

8. Ellis, *op. cit.* p. 570; George Jr., *op. cit.* pp. 493 *ff.*

9. Ellis, *op. cit.*, p. 555.

10. On Gibbons (1834-1921) *cf.* Ellis, *op. cit.* I and II, *passim,* as well as Finn, *op. cit.*, pp. 45-74.

11. On Manning (1808-1892) see Vincent Allan McClelland, *Cardinal Manning* (London, 1962), *passim,* and J. M. Rigg, "Manning, Henry Edward." *The Dictionary of National Biography,* XXXVI (London, 1893), pp. 62-68.

12. See "The Case of Henry George and Dr. McGlynn," Ellis, *op. cit.* Chapter XIII, pp. 547-574.

13. *Op. cit.*, pp. 555-584.

14. George Jr., *op. cit.*, p. 438.

15. "He had met and liked the great advocate of the single land tax, Henry George, and supported his advocacy of land reform." McClelland, *op. cit.*, p. 191.

16. The quotation from Manning's letter to Lord Grey about Ireland (McClelland, *op. cit.*, p. 150) reads as follows: "The land question means hunger, thist, nakedness, notice to quit, labour spent in vain, the toil of years seized upon, the breaking up of hoomes, the miseries, sicknesses, deaths of parents, children, wives; the despair and wildness which spring up in the hearts of the poor when legal force, like a sharp arrow, goes over the most sensitive and vital right of mankind. All this is contained in the land question."

17. *Cf.* McClelland, *op. cit.*, pp. 137 *ff.*

18. Leslie *op. cit.*, p. 364 *ff.*

19. *Op. cit.*, p. 365; McClelland, *op. cit.*, pp. 152 *ff.*

20. The Latin original is quoted by Ellis, *op. cit.*, p. 584. It reads:

"Libri in vulgis editi ab Henrico Georgio examini Supremae Congregationis S.R. et Universalis Inquisitionis fer. IV die 6 Februarii 1889 subiecti fuerunt, mihique demandatum, ut significarem Eminentiae Tuae eosdem damnatione dignos inventos fuisse. Attentis tamen peculiaribus temporum et locorum circumstantiis, et habita praesertim ratione zeli ac sollicitudinis, qua omnes sacrorum Antistites istius Republicae vigilant, ut fideles eorum curae concrediti, ab erroribus qui circumferuntur, serventur immunes; Emi. Patres Generales Inquisitores a condemnatione evulganda supersedendum censuerunt. Omnio enim confidunt, istarum regionum Episcopos una tecum industriam ac diligentiam esse adhibituros, ut quae Catolica Ecclesia de privatae proprietatis iure, vel si id terram respiciat, perpetuo docuit et pluries definivit, ac movissimis etian temporibus per Summos Pontifices Pium IX, Litteris Encyclicis *Qui pluribus,* et Ssmum. D. N. Leonem XIII, Litteris pariter Encyclicis *Quod Apostolici muneris,* inculcavit, fideles ac potissimum ecclesiastici viri, nulla eorum admixtione, retineant, atque a falsis theoriis, quas ea super re Henricus Georgius venditat, sibi caveant."

21. Helmut Sorgenfrei, *Die geistesgeschichtlichen Hintergrunde der Sozialenzyklika "Rerum Novarum"* (Heidelberg/Lowen, 1970), p. 9.

22. Ellis, *op. cit.*, pp. 578 *ff.*

23. He wrote to the Pope: "My desire has been realized, my hopes have been satisfied." Ellis, *op. cit.*, p. 590.

24. Gustav Gundlach, *Die sozialen Rundschreiben Leos XIII. und Pius' XI.*, 2nd ed. (Paderborn, 1933), pp. 5-22; Nos. 4-8 of the Gundlach edition correspond to Nos. 5-10 in the English translation of *Rerum novarum* reprinted by Henry George in his *The Condition of Labor.*

25. Sorgenfrei, *op. cit.*, p. 140.

26. George, *The Condition of Labor,* p. 24.

27. Gundlach, *op. cit.*, p. 7 (Latin text on oppostite page).

28. *Loc. cit.*

29. *Op. cit.*, p. 9.

30. *Loc. cit.*

31. *Op. cit.*, pp. 9-11.

32. Barker, *Henry George,* p. 573.

33. George Jr., *op. cit.*, p. 565.

34. Damaschke, "Henry George," *op. cit.*, p. 190.

35. Par. 3, Gundlach, *op. cit.*, p. 190.

36. Barker, *Henry George,* p. 573.

37. Gundlach, *op. cit.*, p. 11.

38. Sorgenfrei, *op. cit.*, pp. 147 *ff.*

39. On Mazzella (1833-1900) *cf.* Finn, *op. cit.*, pp. 381-391.

40. Sorgenfrei, *op. cit.*, p. 147.

41. Finn, *op. cit.*, p. 388.

Afterword

The serious reader can read more about Henry George's analysis of the world-wide problem of landlessness and wage slavery, and his solution, a free economy in a free society governed by ethical democracy, in his books, *Progress and Poverty, Social Problems, Protection or Free Trade, The Land Question,* and *The Science of Political Economy.* These may be found in your local library or bookstore. They may be purchased from the publisher, the Robert Schalkenbach Foundation, 149 Madison Ave., Suite 601, New York NY 10016. For a free catalogue, write the foundation.

George has been fortunate to have several brilliant biographers. Two you may especially enjoy are *Henry George: An Essay* by Albert Jay Nock (and Dr. Nock's tabloid biography entitled *Henry George: Unorthodox American),* as well as *Henry George* by the historian Charles Albro Barker, which many consider the definitive biography. The official biography, *The Life of Henry George* by Henry George Jr., is unsurpassed as a reference source.

On George's system of ideas, Professor George Raymond Geiger's work, *The Philosophy of Henry George,* is an outstanding exposition. Other excellent works include Dr. Geiger's *The Theory of the Land Question;* Professor Steven Cord's *Henry George: Dreamer or Realist?;* the collective work, *Critics of Henry George,* edited by Professor Robert Andelson; *The Power in the Land* by Fred Harrison and *Alternative America* by Professor John L. Thomas. For specialists in economics there are the works of the committee on Taxation, Resources and Economic Development (TRED), particularly *Land and Building Taxes,* edited by Professor Arthur W. Becker, and *Property Taxation USA,* edited by Professor Richard W. Lindolm.

Three earlier books in this series, also published by Schalkenbach, may be helpful: *George and the Scholars, George and Democracy in the British Isles,* and *George and Ohio's Civic Revival.*

W.L.
D.B.L.

INDEX

Robert Schalkenbach Foundation

RSF is a non-governmental and non-profit organization devoted to publishing PROGRESS AND POVERTY and other works by Henry George (1839-1897), and to researching and promoting the application of his economic analysis to today's world.

We distribute books and other materials concerning land tenure and tax reform, social justice, economic freedom, and related issues.

For a complete catalog, please contact us at:

149 Madison Avenue, Suite 601
New York, NY 10016-6713

Phone: 212-683-6424
Toll-free: 800-269-9555
Fax: 212-683-6454

E-mail: schalkenba@aol.com
Website: www.schalkenbach.org
On-line catalog: www.progress.org/books

RSF